T0192308

# Bootstrap

If you want to build websites, understanding Bootstrap will save you a lot of time and effort. Bootstrap is a user-friendly CSS framework that allows developers to create mobile-friendly and responsive websites.

Bootstrap is the most widely used framework for creating mobile-first, responsive websites. It fixes a number of issues that we experienced previously, including cross-browser compatibility. Today, webpages are optimized for all browsers (Internet Explorer, Firefox, and Chrome, to name but a few) and screen sizes (desktop, tablets, phablets, and phones).

Regardless of project size, Bootstrap provides a solid foundation for any website. It includes Reboot, which is based on Normalize.css and aids with the smoothing out of browser disparities for various page elements. Bootstrap also has fantastic typography. Checkboxes, radio buttons, choose choices, and other basic HTML form elements have been restyled to give them a more modern look.

Bootstrap's scope extends beyond online app design to include devices, allowing for a more seamless user experience. CSS, reusable segments, and JavaScript portions are some of its key characteristics. It has a much clearer design, JavaScript tools, and CSS, among many other capabilities that front-end developers employ. In short, when it comes to UI, the scope is enormous.

Key Features:

- A step-by-step approach to problem-solving and skill development

- A quick run-through of the basic concepts, in the form of a "Crash Course"

- An advanced, hands-on core concepts, with a focus on real-world problems

- An industry-level coding paradigm, practice-oriented explanatory approach

- A special emphasis on writing clean and optimized code, with additional chapters focused on coding methodology

# Bootstrap

## The Ultimate Guide

Sufyan bin Uzayr

CRC Press
Taylor & Francis Group
Boca Raton London New York

CRC Press is an imprint of the
Taylor & Francis Group, an **informa** business

First edition published 2023
by CRC Press
6000 Broken Sound Parkway NW, Suite 300, Boca Raton, FL 33487-2742

and by CRC Press
4 Park Square, Milton Park, Abingdon, Oxon, OX14 4RN

*CRC Press is an imprint of Taylor & Francis Group, LLC*

**Library of Congress Cataloging-in-Publication Data**

Names: Bin Uzayr, Sufyan, author.
Title: Bootstrap : the ultimate guide / Sufyan bin Uzayr.
Description: First edition. | Boca Raton : CRC Press, 2023. | Includes
  bibliographical references and index.
Identifiers: LCCN 2022025679 (print) | LCCN 2022025680 (ebook) | ISBN
  9781032313627 (hardback) | ISBN 9781032313610 (paperback) | ISBN
  9781003309383 (ebook)
Subjects: LCSH: Bootstrap (Computer program) | Web site
  development--Computer programs.
Classification: LCC TK5105.8885.B66 B56 2023  (print) | LCC TK5105.8885.B66
  (ebook) | DDC 006.7/6--dc23/eng/20221011
LC record available at https://lccn.loc.gov/2022025679
LC ebook record available at https://lccn.loc.gov/2022025680

ISBN: 9781032313627 (hbk)
ISBN: 9781032313610 (pbk)
ISBN: 9781003309383 (ebk)

DOI: 10.1201/9781003309383

Typeset in Minion
by Deanta Global Publishing Services, Chennai, India

# Contents

Acknowledgments, xvii

About the Author, xix

CHAPTER 1 ▪ Crash Course in Bootstrap                    1

  INTRODUCTION TO BOOTSTRAP                    1

  HISTORY OF BOOTSTRAP                          2

  VERSIONS OF BOOTSTRAP                         3

    Bootstrap 1                               3

    Bootstrap 2                               3

    Bootstrap 3                               3

    Bootstrap 4                               4

    Bootstrap 5                               7

  WHAT CAN YOU DO WITH BOOTSTRAP?               8

  ADVANTAGES OF BOOTSTRAP                       8

  DISADVANTAGES OF BOOTSTRAP                    8

    Basic Concepts                            9

      *Containers*                          9

      *Sizing*                              9

    Code Example                             10

  COLORS IN BOOTSTRAP                          10

  ADDING BACKGROUND COLOR AND BORDERS         10

    Code Example                             11

  ADDING PADDING AND MARGIN                    11

    Property                                 11

Sides                                                                11

Size                                                                 11

Code Example                                                         12

GRID SYSTEM                                                          12

Code Example                                                         13

Code Example                                                         13

Code Example                                                         14

GETTING STARTED WITH BOOTSTRAP                                       14

SETTING UP                                                           14

HOW TO DOWNLOAD BOOTSTRAP USING A PACKAGE
MANAGER                                                              15

Downloading Bootstrap Using npm                                      16

Downloading Bootstrap Using Yarn                                     16

Downloading Bootstrap Using Composer                                 16

HOW TO DOWNLOAD BOOTSTRAP USING A CDN                                17

CHAPTER SUMMARY                                                      18

CHAPTER 2 ■ The Bootstrap Framework                                  19

GETTING STARTED WITH BOOTSTRAP                                       19

HOW TO DOWNLOAD BOOTSTRAP USING PACKAGE
MANAGER                                                              20

DOWNLOADING BOOTSTRAP USING NPM                                      20

Downloading Bootstrap Using a Cable                                  21

Download Bootstrap Using Composer                                    21

HOW TO DOWNLOAD BOOTSTRAP USING CDN                                  21

WHAT IS CDN?                                                         21

BOOTSTRAP CDN LINK AND SCRIPTS                                       22

For CSS                                                              22

For JavaScript                                                       22

For Jquery Library                                                   22

For Popper.js                                                        22

How to Use Bootstrap CDN                                             22

BOOTSTRAP TEMPLATE                                                   23

IS POPPER.JS REQUIRED FOR BOOTSTRAP 4?                               24

RESPONSIVE META TAG                                          24

HISTORY                                                      24

    Bootstrap 2                         25

    Bootstrap 3                         25

    Bootstrap 4                         25

    Bootstrap 5                         25

FEATURES                                                     26

CREATE A HOME PAGE WITH BOOTSTRAP                            27

    1.   Add HTML5 Document Type          27

    2.   Bootstrap 3 Is Advanced          27

BASIC BOOTSTRAP PAGES                                        28

BOOTSTRAP CONTAINERS                                         28

BOOTSTRAP GRID SYSTEM                                        30

GRID CLASSES                                                 31

BASIC STRUCTURE OF A BOOTSTRAP GRID                          31

    Explanation                         32

    Code Example                        33

    Code Example (Extra-small Grid)     34

    Code Example (Small Grid)           34

        *Code Example (Medium Grid)*              35

        *Code Example (Small and Medium Grid Combined)*   35

    Code Example (Large Grid)           36

    Code Example (Extra-large Grid)     37

HOW THE GRID WORKS                                           38

THREE EQUAL COLUMNS                                          39

TWO UNEQUAL COLUMNS                                          39

FLEXBOX                                                      42

FLEXBOX PROPERTIES IN CSS                                    43

    Display                             43

        *Syntax*                            43

FLEXBOX PROPERTIES IN BOOTSTRAP                              44

    Flex-direction in CSS               45

    Syntax                              45

FLEX-DIRECTION IN BOOTSTRAP 45

Flexbox Features 46

FLEX-WRAP IN CSS 47

*Syntax* 47

FLEX-WRAP IN BOOTSTRAP 47

FLEX-FLOW 48

Syntax 48

JUSTIFY-CONTENT IN CSS 49

Syntax 49

Positional Alignment 50

ORDER 51

JUSTIFY-CONTENT IN BOOTSTRAP 54

ALIGN SELF 55

ALIGN ITEMS 56

GROW AND SHRINK 57

FILL 58

RESPONSIVE BREAKPOINTS 58

Z-index 59

COMPONENTS IN BOOTSTRAP 59

Bootstrap Alerts 59

Alert Links 60

BOOTSTRAP BADGES 61

BOOTSTRAP JUMBOTRON 62

FULL-WIDTH JUMBOTRON 62

BOOTSTRAP BUTTONS 63

BUTTON SIZES 64

BLOCK-LEVEL BUTTONS 64

ACTIVE/DISABLED BUTTONS 64

SPINNER BUTTONS 64

COLORED SPINNERS 64

BUTTON TAGS 64

OUTLINE BUTTONS 65

DROPDOWNS 66

| | |
|---|---|
| NAVBAR | 67 |
| How It Works | 67 |
| SUPPORTED CONTENT | 68 |
| UTILITIES | 69 |
| Border | 69 |
| CHAPTER SUMMARY | 69 |

## Chapter 3 ■ Designing Templates — 71

| | |
|---|---|
| CREATING A BLOG TEMPLATE | 71 |
| Code | 72 |
| Navbar | 73 |
| Code | 73 |
| Code | 74 |
| Code | 75 |
| Code | 75 |
| Code | 75 |
| Code | 75 |
| Code | 76 |
| Code | 76 |
| Code | 77 |
| Code | 77 |
| Home Page | 78 |
| Code | 78 |
| Code | 78 |
| Code | 78 |
| Code | 79 |
| Code | 79 |
| Code | 80 |
| Code | 80 |
| Newsletter | 81 |
| Code | 81 |
| Code | 81 |
| Code | 81 |
| Code | 82 |

| | |
|---|---|
| *Code* | 82 |
| *Code* | 82 |
| *Code* | 83 |
| *Code* | 83 |
| Blog Section | 83 |
| *Code* | 83 |
| *Code* | 84 |
| *Code* | 85 |
| *Code* | 86 |
| *Code* | 87 |
| *Code* | 88 |
| *Code* | 88 |
| *Code* | 90 |
| Blog Post 1 | 90 |
| *Code* | 90 |
| Blog Post 2 | 91 |
| *Code* | 91 |
| Blog Post 3 | 91 |
| *Code* | 91 |
| *Code* | 93 |
| Some Content | 93 |
| *Code* | 93 |
| *Code* | 93 |
| *Code* | 94 |
| About Section | 94 |
| *Code* | 94 |
| *Code* | 95 |
| *Code* | 95 |
| *Code* | 95 |
| *Code* | 96 |
| Contact Section | 96 |
| *Code* | 96 |
| *Code* | 97 |

| | |
|---|---|
| *Code* | 97 |
| *Code* | 98 |
| Footer | 98 |
| *Code* | 99 |
| CREATING A PORTFOLIO TEMPLATE | 99 |
| *Code* | 99 |
| *Code* | 100 |
| Navbar | 100 |
| *Code* | 100 |
| Home Section | 101 |
| *Code* | 101 |
| About Section | 102 |
| *Code* | 102 |
| Portfolio Section | 104 |
| *Code* | 105 |
| Contact Section | 106 |
| *Code* | 106 |
| Footer Section | 108 |
| *Code* | 109 |
| MOBILE-FRIENDLY DESIGN | 109 |
| TYPES OF MOBILE-FRIENDLY DESIGN | 110 |
| Responsive Design | 110 |
| *Advantages* | 110 |
| *Disadvantages* | 111 |
| Adaptive Design | 111 |
| *Advantages* | 111 |
| *Disadvantages* | 112 |
| CHAPTER SUMMARY | 112 |
| CHAPTER 4 ▪ Creating Admin Panels | 113 |
| CREATING AN ADMIN PANEL IN BOOTSTRAP | 113 |
| Code | 114 |
| Code | 114 |

| | |
|---|---|
| Navbar | 115 |
| *Horizontal Navbar* | 115 |
| Code | 115 |
| *Vertical Navbar* | 116 |
| Code | 116 |
| Code | 118 |
| Code | 119 |
| Main Section | 119 |
| Code | 119 |
| Code | 122 |
| Code | 123 |
| WHAT WE LEARNED | 124 |
| BACKEND UI | 125 |
| Popular Front-end Frameworks and Libraries | 127 |
| Popular Back-end Programming Languages | 129 |
| Popular Back-end Frameworks | 130 |
| CREATING A BACKEND UI IN BOOTSTRAP | 131 |
| Code | 131 |
| Code | 132 |
| Code | 132 |
| Navbar | 132 |
| Code | 132 |
| Sidebar | 133 |
| Code | 134 |
| Code | 134 |
| Code | 136 |
| Breadcrumb | 137 |
| Code | 137 |
| Main Content | 138 |
| Code | 138 |
| Code | 138 |
| Code | 139 |

Code                                                                141

Code                                                                142

Code                                                                143

Code                                                                143

Code                                                                143

Code                                                                143

Footer                                                              145

Code                                                                145

What We Learned                                                     146

ADDITIONAL CONSIDERATIONS AND UX                                    151

Qualitative versus Quantitative Research                            153

Attitudinal versus Behavioral Research                              154

Generative versus Evaluation Research                               155

CHAPTER SUMMARY                                                     155

CHAPTER 5 ■ Bootstrap and JavaScript                                157

INTRODUCTION TO JAVASCRIPT                                          157

WHAT IS JAVASCRIPT USED FOR?                                        159

HOW DOES JAVASCRIPT WORK?                                           167

ATTRIBUTES                                                          169

Syntax                                                              169

Global Attributes                                                   169

Syntax                                                              169

Global Event Attributes                                             170

All Attributes in Bootstrap                                         171

*For modals*                                                        171

*For dropdowns*                                                     171

*ScrollSpy*                                                         171

*Toggleable tabs*                                                   171

*Tooltip*                                                           171

*Popovers*                                                          172

*Alert messages*                                                    172

      *Buttons*                              172

      *Collapse*                            172

      *Carousel*                           173

      *Affix*                                 173

   ALERTS                              173

   CAROUSEL                        175

   CHAPTER SUMMARY             182

Chapter 6 ■ Code Optimization          183

   WHAT IS CODE OPTIMIZATION?       183

   GOALS OF CODE OPTIMIZATION       185

   CATEGORIES OF OPTIMIZATION       186

   CODE OPTIMIZATION TECHNIQUES     186

   CHAPTER SUMMARY             187

Chapter 7 ■ Integrations and API       189

   CREATING AN HTTP CLIENT         189

   WORKING WITH APIS IN BOOTSTRAP    191

   UTILITY API IN BOOTSTRAP         192

   INTEGRATING BOOTSTRAP WITH JEKYLL   198

   INTEGRATING WITH ASP.NET        200

   CHAPTER SUMMARY             201

Chapter 8 ■ Cheat Sheet 1            203

   WHAT IS BOOTSTRAP?              203

   WHY CHOOSE BOOTSTRAP?         204

   FEATURES OF BOOTSTRAP           204

   BOOTSTRAP CHEAT SHEET          204

   INITIAL SETUP (USING CDN)         204

     CSS                              204

     Popper                        204

     JavaScript                     205

Bundle (Popper + JavaScript) 205
Bootstrap Icons 205
INITIAL SETUP (USING NPM) 205
Bootstrap 205
Bootstrap Icons 205
BOOTSTRAP SCREEN SIZING 205
BOOTSTRAP GRID SYSTEM 206
TYPOGRAPHY 211
UTILITY CLASSES 213
Utility: Colors 213
Utility: Borders 215
Utility: Flex 216
Utility: Display 225
Utility: Misc 229
Utility: Position 232
Utility: Spacing 234
Utility: Text 241

CHAPTER 9 ▪ Cheat Sheet 2 245
UTILITY: OPACITY 245
BOOTSTRAP KEY COMPONENTS 246
Alerts 246
Badges 248
Breadcrumb 250
Button 251
Button Plugin 253
Button Group 254
Cards 257
Carousel 273
Collapse 280
Accordion 282
Dropdowns 286

Chapter 10 ■ Cheat Sheet 3                291

   CODE SNIPPETS                      291

   IMAGES                             294

   FIGURES                            294

   TABLES                             294

   INPUT GROUP                        305

   FORMS                              308

   FLOATING LABELS                    311

   FORM LAYOUT                        312

   FORM VALIDATION                    315

   LIST GROUP                         319

   MODAL                              326

   NAVBAR                             330

   NAVS, TABS, PILLS                  339

   OFFCANVAS START                    345

   PLACEHOLDERS                       347

   PAGINATION                         348

   SCROLLSPY                          351

Chapter 11 ■ Cheat Sheet 4                353

   PROGRESS                           361

   POPOVERS                           363

   TOASTS                             365

   SPINNERS                           367

   TOOLTIPS                           368

   HELPERS                            370

   CHAPTER SUMMARY                    372

BIBLIOGRAPHY, 373

INDEX, 383

# Acknowledgments

There are many people who deserve to be on this page, for this book would not have come into existence without their support. That said, some names deserve a special mention, and I am genuinely grateful to:

- My parents, for everything they have done for me.

- My siblings, for helping with things back home.

- The Parakozm team, especially Divya Sachdeva, Jaskiran Kaur, and Vartika, for offering great amounts of help and assistance during the book-writing process.

- The CRC team, especially Sean Connelly and Danielle Zarfati, for ensuring that the book's content, layout, formatting, and everything else remain perfect throughout.

- Reviewers of this book, for going through the manuscript and providing their insight and feedback.

- Typesetters, cover designers, printers, and everyone else, for their part in the development of this book.

- All the folks associated with Zeba Academy, either directly or indirectly, for their help and support.

- The programming community in general, and the web development community in particular, for all their hard work and efforts.

**–Sufyan bin Uzayr**

# About the Author

**Sufyan bin Uzayr** is a writer, coder, and entrepreneur with more than a decade of experience in the industry. He has authored several books in the past, pertaining to a diverse range of topics, ranging from History to Computers/IT. Sufyan is the Director of Parakozm, a multinational IT company specializing in EdTech solutions. He also runs Zeba Academy, an online learning and teaching vertical with a focus on STEM fields. Sufyan specializes in a wide variety of technologies, such as JavaScript, Dart, WordPress, Drupal, Linux, and Python. He holds multiple degrees, including ones in Management, IT, Literature, and Political Science. Sufyan is a digital nomad, dividing his time between four countries. He has lived and taught in universities and educational institutions around the globe. Sufyan takes a keen interest in technology, politics, literature, history, and sports, and in his spare time, he enjoys teaching coding and English to young students.

Learn more at sufyanism.com.

## CHAPTER 1

# Crash Course in Bootstrap

## IN THIS CHAPTER

➤ Introduction to Bootstrap

➤ History & Versions of Bootstrap

➤ What can you do with Bootstrap

➤ Getting started with Bootstrap

In this chapter, we will learn about Bootstrap and its basic concepts. We will also know how Bootstrap came into being, its different versions available, and their features. We will also discuss all you can do with Bootstrap and its advantages and disadvantages.

## INTRODUCTION TO BOOTSTRAP

Every website that exists on the web uses HTML, CSS, and JavaScript at its core. Numerous frameworks are available these days that increase the functionality or the looks on any web page. However, the journey of every web developer starts with HTML, CSS, and JavaScript. The full form of HTML is Hypertext Markup Language, and it provides the basic structure of any web page. The full form of CSS is Cascading Style Sheets, and it is used to style web pages. CSS adds beauty to a bland-looking HTML page. And JavaScript is used to add functionality to any web page. Now, this is

DOI: 10.1201/9781003309383-1

where Bootstrap comes into play. Building a fully functional website from scratch from these three can be a tedious job. It is also immensely time-consuming. Bootstrap not just solves this problem but simplifies the whole process as well. So, what exactly is Bootstrap then? Bootstrap is a CSS framework that helps us create user-friendly and mobile-responsive web pages without any added hassle. A framework can be any software that provides a generic functionality and further add-ons and features that allow the users to modify and customize according to their own needs.

Basic knowledge of HTML and CSS is necessary to learn Bootstrap and to eventually master it. Bootstrap is a framework that contains HTML and CSS at its core, so understanding those two becomes essential. It has self-explanatory components that anyone can quickly learn and implement. Bootstrap is also completely free and open-source, which means the source code is openly and readily available on the internet to access and modify if you wish to do so. Making any software open-source allows for open collaboration, enabling users to contribute to software development.

Bootstrap essentially focuses on mobile-first development. Mobile-first development means that while creating any web page using Bootstrap, the primary focus is on how it is rendered on mobile devices. From there on, the user interface is scaled according to more giant screens. This approach is helpful as most users across the globe access internet using their mobile phones. Putting their needs first and ensuring that a website is working smoothly on any mobile device would increase traffic on any website.

## HISTORY OF BOOTSTRAP

Mark Otto and Jacob Thornton initially created Bootstrap. It was released for the first time more than ten years ago, in August 2011. Since then, many changes have been made, and improved versions have been released. The latest stable version was released in October 2021, and it is called Bootstrap 5. It is now one of the most popular open-source project and front-end frameworks globally.

It was initially called Twitter Blueprint as both Mark and Jacob used to work at Twitter and wanted to create a framework that would help them maintain consistency across the platform. However, utilizing multiple different libraries to make the user interface resulted in inconsistencies and differences across the platform. It was also proving difficult to maintain the code. This duo of a developer and a designer then came up with Bootstrap. After a few months of initial development and realizing the innate potential, many developers started contributing to it during Twitter's hack week.

It was then renamed Bootstrap and released as an open-source project for further use. Mark and Jacob, the original creators, continue to maintain it along with a team of developers and the contribution made by its large community of users. Also, it is still used as a style guide at Twitter for internal tools development, which was initially intended.

## VERSIONS OF BOOTSTRAP

### Bootstrap 1

Bootstrap 1 is the original version that was released in August 2011. After its creation, developers used it internally at Twitter, and then, later on, it was released in the public domain as free and open-source software.

### Bootstrap 2

The second version of Bootstrap or Bootstrap 2 was first released for public usage in January 2012. Bootstrap made several notable changes in this version. The team also added lots of new components and features to this version. One of the most notable ones amongst them was the responsive web design. Responsive web design means the styling or the layout of the page will adjust itself on its own across multiple devices like mobile phones, tablets, and desktops, depending upon the device being used. The team added Glyph icons and built-in support in this version. Glyph icons are monochromatic icons that help in visually identifying features. There are different icons available for use, both free and paid.

### Bootstrap 3

The third version of Bootstrap or Bootstrap 3 was first released for public usage in August 2013. This version was the one that introduced the shift in approach concerning mobile devices. Bootstrap started focusing more on mobile devices and adequately rendering websites on them from here onwards. Shifting its approach to mobile devices first ensured their increased user base as most internet users worldwide are concentrated on mobile devices. This version also gave increased attention to "Flat Design." Flat Design is essentially a design trend that is increasingly popular for its minimalistic themes and outlook. The usage of Flat Design has significantly increased, and it can be seen being used in graphical user interfaces, also known as GUIs. It is also used in posters, guides, art documents, etc.

Another notable feature added was the new plugin system with namespaced events. Bootstrap 3 uses jQuery to add functionality onto any page, and one of the prominent features of jQuery is namespaced events. So, what exactly are namespaced events? We need to first learn about events and event listeners to know about that. Events are any action performed on a web page that triggers the response of another HTML element. Anything could be an event like clicking on a button to submit user information in a form. There are different events like click, mouse hover, focus, and blur. There are various keyboard events as well that are triggered when a specific button is clicked on the keyboard. An event listener is an object that handles any event. It controls the response to an event in case an event is triggered.

Namespaced events are applicable when multiple event listeners are added to a single function. On performing a single event, numerous events are happening. Depending on user requirements and usage, if we wish to activate only one of the event listeners out of the many few, then namespaced events come in handy. You can turn on or off the event listeners according to the user's activity and further customize them for a better user experience.

Bootstrap 3 also removed added support for specific browser versions like Internet Explorer 7 and Firefox 3.6.

Bootstrap 4

Bootstrap 4 was one of the significant versions of Bootstrap, and it completely changed its face. The team made several substantial changes to this version. To begin with, Bootstrap 4 was first announced by Mark Otto, one of its original creators, in October 2014. However, the first alpha version was released next year in August 2015. And then, the company rolled out the beta version in August 2017. Mark, the original creator, completely stopped working on the previous version, that is Bootstrap 3, and entirely focused on Bootstrap 4. After four years of being announced to the public, it was finalized and put out in the public domain in January 2018.

The duo made significant changes in this version that somehow justified the major time gap it took to come out. The developers at Bootstrap rewrote a massive chunk of the code to make it smoother, faster, and increasingly responsive. In turn, it also reduced memory usage.

Initial versions of Bootstrap were styled using Less CSS. Less CSS is a preprocessor-based style sheet language that is dynamic in its approach. The general explanation behind its work is that it is compiled into Cascading Style Sheets, also known as CSS, and it runs on the client-side, which is the front-end part that the user has access to and visibility. It can also be run on the server-side, providing styling that could be part of the internal tools and specifications the user cannot access. Less CSS is designed by Alexis Sellier.

Bootstrap 4 completely replaced Less CSS and replaced it with Sass. Sass stands for syntactically awesome style sheets. It is also a preprocessor-based scripting language, and just like Less, it is also compiled or interpreted in Cascading Style Sheets. One of the add-ons is that Sass has its scripting language called the Sass Script. Hampton Catlin designed it. Sass consists of two different types of syntax, and the original syntax is called the indented syntax.

Sass has the upper hand over Less in multiple different ways. One of the most important things is that Sass enables you to write clean, easy, and comparatively less code in CSS compared to Less. It's quick and contains less code making it the easier and the faster option out of the two. Not just that, it is stable and provides elegant style featurettes because it is an extension of CSS. It facilitates and helps the designers efficiently create beautiful style templates within a small amount of time.

Bootstrap 4 saw the addition of another feature named "Reboot." Reboot was based on Normalize.css. Normalize.css is a small CSS file that helps render all HTML elements consistently throughout. This consistency helps maintain a single preview across all kinds of devices, browsers, and browser versions. This cross-browser consistency is essential to retain the default styling intended by the designer and the developer. Normalize uses HTML 5, the latest and widely accepted version of HTML.

Reboot was inspired by Normalize, which means it replicated one of the main features of Normalize in Reboot. In Reboot, the developers decided to put all element-specific changes into a single file. This change gave Bootstrap its widely recognized look and feel. Using Reboot helped create an elegant yet straightforward codebase to build upon by the users.

**Example**
All heading elements from <h1> to <h6> and the paragraph tag <p> don't have a value for margin-top. It is removed. All headings have a fixed margin-bottom of 0.5 rem, and all paragraphs have an in-built margin-bottom of 1 rem that allows for easy spacing and increased readability. In a similar fashion, all the list tags, namely, <ul>, <ol>, and <dl>, don't have a value for margin-top. It is removed from their inherent styling. The margin-bottom has been fixed to 1 rem. Similarly, you would not find a margin-bottom if you use nested lists.

Additional support provided for specific browsers was dropped for the outdated versions. Bootstrap 4 removed Internet Explorer Version 8, Internet Explorer Version 9, and iOS 6.

Bootstrap also decided to support CSS Flexible Box, popularly known as CSS FlexBox. CSS FlexBox is a Layout Module that helps position the content and place it concerning the preferred layout. It allows us to divide our content and identify it as per the space available. It builds an interface and aligns the items for a richer look and feel. Specific properties are used in a flexbox like flex-direction, flex-wrap, flex-basis, flex-grow, etc. We will discuss them in detail further as CSS FlexBox is an essential component in Bootstrap.

Another feature was added that helped customize the navigation across the web pages. Increased support for navigation across pages made it easier to switch between pages. Time taken to go back and forth simultaneously was reduced as a result.

This version of Bootstrap also brought about an essential feature regarding the elements' spacing and sizing. Bootstrap 4 added responsiveness to the spacing and sizing. Further notation was introduced about the sizing in classes.

Sizing notation is as follows:

- Xs – extra small

- Sm – small

- Md – medium

- Lg – large

- Xl – extra large

These keywords describe the screen sizes. If a particular feature can only be rendered on specific screen size, the user can use the given notation.

Similarly, a notation for different properties helps us space the web page accordingly.

- M – margin

- P – padding

Also, Bootstrap 4 abandoned pixels (px) as a unit in CSS and switched to rem or root ems.

The global font size across all platforms was increased to 16px from the previous 14px to improve the readability.

Specific components like panel, thumbnail, pager, and well were removed.

Similarly, the glyph icons font was also removed.

Lots of new utility classes were introduced.

In addition, the styling was also significantly improved for buttons, dropdown menus, media objects, and image classes.

Bootstrap 4 also extended support toward all the latest versions of the majorly used browsers like Google Chrome, Firefox, Internet Explorer, Opera, and Safari.

## Bootstrap 5

Bootstrap 5 is the latest version of Bootstrap that is currently available. It was officially released in May 2021.

The Bootstrap team made many significant changes in this version, just like its previous version.

One of the most significant changes was completely stripping off its dependence on jQuery and entirely switching to vanilla JavaScript. Specific new menu components were also added, like offcanvas. Offcanvas is a hidden sidebar that the user can add to a website for increased navigation capabilities. It requires a JavaScript plugin for added functionality. A sidebar component usually stays hidden until triggered by an event. Then JavaScript is used with its event listeners, and the sidebar pops up.

The existing code for adding CSS grid was rewritten to achieve more comprehensive and responsive CSS gutters.

The documentation was migrated from Jekyll to Hugo. Both Jekyll and Hugo are static site generators. Jekyll is written in Ruby while Hugo is written in Go language. The company preferred Hugo over Jekyll as it promises an increase in performance and higher stability compared to Jekyll.

Similarly, Bootstrap moved all the testing infrastructure from QUnit to Jasmine. Both of these are the open-source testing framework for JavaScript. QUnit was developed initially for testing jQuery but later moved to test JavaScript code.

A custom set of SVG icons were also added. Multiple custom CSS properties were also added. The API was significantly improved, and the forms were updated. The grid system was enhanced while also customizing the available docs.

## WHAT CAN YOU DO WITH BOOTSTRAP?

- Create full-fledged responsive websites in a short time

- Create mobile-friendly websites

- Quick and automated optimization according to different websites

- Create dynamic web pages

- Manage a large amount of content

- Create tooltips and popovers to show hint text

- Create carousel and image slider

- Create different types of forms and alert boxes

## ADVANTAGES OF BOOTSTRAP

1. **Easy to use:** Anyone with even a basic knowledge of HTML and CSS can create a full-fledged website using Bootstrap. It is that easy.

2. **Lightweight and customizable:** As a framework, CSS is incredibly light and can be customized according to one's needs.

3. **Mobile-first approach:** Putting mobile devices first leads to an increased reach among the user base.

4. **Browser compatibility:** A consistent framework that supports all major browsers and their latest versions.

5. **Plugins:** There are several JavaScript plugins available to increase functionality that can be added according to one's requirement.

## DISADVANTAGES OF BOOTSTRAP

1. **Lack of uniqueness:** Most Bootstrap websites tend to look the same, and even if you wish to change the inherent style, you need to rewrite many files and override the available styles, which can be time-consuming.

2. **Limited design options:** You need to put in extra effort and time to create a design unique to you.

3. **Verbosity:** Styles created in Bootstrap tend to be verbose and generate a lot of output in HTML, which is usually deemed unnecessary.

*Note:* We will be using Bootstrap 5 as it is the latest version of Bootstrap available at the time of writing. All the examples from here on are in Bootstrap 5.

## Basic Concepts

Now we will take a look at some of the basic concepts of Bootstrap that we need to know in order to get started.

### Containers

Containers are one of the most used elements in Bootstrap. They are mainly used to create a layout. Containers are also an essential part of the grid system. As the name suggests, containers contain the content while keeping some padding. Containers are also used to center the content and align it on the page horizontally. If the layout of a page is of a fixed width, then containers can be incredibly useful in providing a structure to the web page.

There are essentially three different types of containers available in Bootstrap:

1. .container: max-width at a responsive breakpoint

2. .container-fluid: 100% width at all breakpoints

3. .container-{breakpoint}: 100% width until it reaches the specified breakpoint

### Sizing

The width of the container changes, depending upon the screen size. You can use the notation to render a container concerning the size of the screen. For example, using class .container-sm will render a container of 960px on a large screen, whereas on a medium screen, it will be 720px.

To change the size of the container, use the following notation:

| | |
|---|---|
| .container | general size relative to screen |
| .container-sm | Small container |
| .container-md | Medium container |
| .container-lg | Large container |
| .container-xl | X-large container |
| .container-xxl | XX-large container |
| .container-fluid | 100% width irrespective to screen |

*Note:* Container is a class, and in CSS class is represented with a dot(.).

You can simply create a responsive, fixed-width container using the class container in an HTML element. The container will change according to the screen size and breakpoints, as represented in the table above.

### Code Example

```
<div class="container">
   <h1> This is a heading </h1>
   <p> This is a paragraph </p>
</div>
```

## COLORS IN BOOTSTRAP

Several predefined color utility classes help in adding colors to a Bootstrap element. Using these classes simplifies the task and makes adding colors quicker and easier. To use these color utility classes, simply use a dash (-) symbol followed by the name of the color class.

| | |
|---|---|
| -primary | Blue |
| -success | Green |
| -info | Light blue |
| -warning | Yellow |
| -danger | Red |
| -secondary | Grey |
| -dark | Black |
| -light | Light gray |

*Note:* If you wish to add 50% opacity for the black and white text class, write a dash followed by a 50 after the color class.

**Example**

.text-black-50 – this will show black text on white background with 50% opacity.

## ADDING BACKGROUND COLOR AND BORDERS

To add a background color, simply use the class bg followed by a dash symbol and then the default color code for Bootstrap classes.

To add a border, simply write the border in the class field of an HTML element. Remember, you can add multiple classes to an element. To add different classes to an element, write the name of all the classes in the field, separating each with a space.

Code Example

```
<div class="container bg-dark border">
  <h1> This is a heading </h1>
  <p> this is a paragraph of a container with a dark
background </p>
</div>
```

## ADDING PADDING AND MARGIN

Most of the CSS elements inherent to Bootstrap have a default padding or margin to provide consistency across all platforms and browsers. To apply extra padding and margin, use the following notation.

Property

- **Margin** – use m in classes to set margin

- **Padding** – use p in classes to set the padding

Sides

- **Top** – use t for padding-top or margin-top in class

- **Bottom** – use b for padding-bottom or margin-bottom in class

- **Left** – use l for padding-left or margin-left in classes

- **Right** – use r for padding-right or margin-right in classes

- **Both left and right** – use x for padding-left and padding-right or margin-left and margin-right in classes

- **Both top and bottom** – use y for padding-top and padding-bottom or margin-top and margin-bottom in classes

Size

- **0** – completely remove the margin and padding by setting it to 0

- **1** – set margin or padding to size 1 relative to the size of the root element

- **2** – set margin or padding to size 2 relative to the size of the root element

- **3** – set margin or padding to size 3 relative to the size of the root element

- **4** – set margin or padding to size 4 relative to the size of the root element

- **5** – set margin or padding to size 5 relative to the size of the root element

- **Auto** – set margin or padding to size auto relative to the size of the root element

## Code Example

```
<div class= "container py-3 my-3">
  <p> This is a paragraph within a container with
padding 3 on the y-axis and margin 3 on the y-axis
</p>
</div>
```

## GRID SYSTEM

Bootstrap's grid system is an easy way to build customized and responsive layouts for all types of content. The grid system is built using CSS flexbox. Like every other element available on Bootstrap, the grid system is also mobile-responsive. It is a 12-column system and has six responsive breakpoints.

The breakpoints are as follows:

- Extra small – xs

- Small – sm

- Medium – md

- Large – lg

- Extra-large – xl

- Extra extra-large – xxl

Twelve-column system essentially means that each row can be divided into 12 columns. You can use all the available 12 columns or combine them by grouping them and making bigger columns. For example, you can group three columns to make one single column. In this way, you will end up with four columns, each encompassing three column width. You can follow the same approach and create two columns of six. It is not required to create columns of equal width at all times. You can also create columns of four and eight and vice versa. Simply mix and match and customize according to your needs; Bootstrap will take care of the rest. No matter the number of columns you choose, the grid will rearrange itself according to the screen size.

*Note*: It is not necessary to use all 12 columns at once. However, keep in mind that the sum of columns cannot be higher than 12.

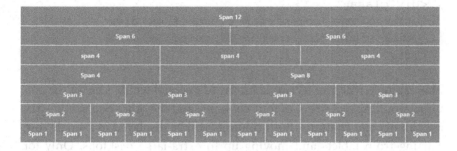

**Bootstrap Grid System**

Code Example

```
<div class="row">
  <div class="col"></div>
  <div class="col"></div>
  <div class="col"></div>
</div>
```

The above piece of code will create three columns of equal width. As the number of columns is not specified for each, the columns will be of equal width.

Code Example

```
<div class="row">
  <div class="col-sm-3">Column of 3</div>
  <div class="col-sm-3">Column of 3</div>
  <div class="col-sm-3">Column of 3</div>
  <div class="col-sm-3">Column of 3</div>
</div>
```

This example will create four columns of equal width. Each column comprises three columns. All the columns will be displayed in one row starting from tablets to extra-large desktops. However, for mobile devices or any screen that is smaller than 576px wide, Bootstrap will arrange them on top of one another forming a stack.

Code Example

```
<div class="row">
  <div class="col-sm-4">Column of 4</div>
  <div class="col-sm-8">Column of 8</div>
</div>
```

This example will give us two columns of unequal width. One of the columns would span a width of four columns, and the other one would span a width of eight columns. Both columns will be displayed in a single row, starting from tablets and moving up to extra-large desktops. Only for smaller screens, screens with a width of less than 576px, will the columns get stacked on top of one another.

## GETTING STARTED WITH BOOTSTRAP

Before getting started with Bootstrap, we need to first set up our code editor.

## SETTING UP

- First and foremost, you will need a code editor to get started with Bootstrap. There are tons of code editors available online that are free and open-source. You can choose any one of them that suits your needs. Popular code editors are VS Code, Atom, Brackets, etc. You can use any one of these code editors.

- In this tutorial, we will be using VS Code. VS Code is one of the most popular and powerful source code editors and it is created by Microsoft. It has lots of amazing tools like syntax highlighting, intellisense, etc. Intellisense helps in intelligent code completion that helps us in writing cleaner code. It also has thousands of extensions that help you customize your code editor according to your needs. VS Code supports all kinds of web technologies. including Bootstrap and works perfectly for web development. If you wish to download VS Code, you can download it from https://code.visualstudio.com/download.

- Atom is also a very powerful source code editor that works well for web technologies. It is free and open-source code editor for macOS, Linux, and Microsoft Windows. There is additional plugin support.

It is developed by GitHub. Here's the link to download Atom: https://atom.io/

- You can also download any other code editor of your choice and set it up according to the instructions provided on the official website.

- After setting up your code editor, open up a folder and create a file with the extension of .html. Bootstrap essentially provides us with a template of code written in HTML and CSS, and all you need to do is copy those templates from their official website.

- Open up your browser and go to the official website of Bootstrap: https://getbootstrap.com/

- There are two ways to get Bootstrap. Either you can include a link to Bootstrap 5 using a CDN, or you simply download Bootstrap 5 from the website straight onto your device using a package manager. You might be wondering which one is better. Both options are good in their respect, but it is better to use CDN as a beginner.

**Get Started with Bootstrap**

## HOW TO DOWNLOAD BOOTSTRAP USING A PACKAGE MANAGER

- You can download Bootstrap using different package managers like npm, yarn, and Composer. Upon downloading Bootstrap, you will get access to the source Sass and JavaScript files.

- Downloading Bootstrap using package manager requires you to have some additional tools available. First, you will need a Sass compiler in order to compile all the Sass source files into CSS files. You will also need to have a Autoprefixer for CSS vendor prefixing.

## Downloading Bootstrap Using npm

1. Assuming Node.js is already configured on your device, install Bootstrap using the npm package. Use the following command to install Bootstrap:

   $ npm install bootstrap

2. npm install downloads a package and its dependencies and can be run with or without arguments. If you run the package manager without arguments, npm install downloads all of the dependencies defined in the package.json file and would generate a node_modules folder with the install folder.

3. To load all the plugins of Bootstrap onto a Bootstrap object, use const bootstrap = require('bootstrap') or import bootstrap from 'bootstrap'. The Bootstrap module will itself export all of the plugins. In order to manually load all of Bootstrap's plugins individually, load /js/dist/*.js files under the top-level directory of the package.

4. Additional metadata in Bootstrap's package.json file is available under the following keys:

   a) sass – path to the main source file of Bootstrap

   b) style – path to the non-minified CSS precompiled using the default settings in Bootstrap. There is no added customization.

## Downloading Bootstrap Using Yarn

1. Use the following command to install Bootstrap using the yarn package:

   $ yarn add bootstrap

## Downloading Bootstrap Using Composer

1. Use the following command to install and manage Sass and JavaScript files of Bootstrap using Composer:

   $ composer require twbs/bootstrap:5.0.2

## HOW TO DOWNLOAD BOOTSTRAP USING A CDN

- If you directly install Bootstrap straight onto your device, you will also access the Sass and JavaScript files available within. You can download the same using package managers like npm, Composer, or yarn as shown above.

- If you choose to use CDN, you can copy the link https://www.jsdelivr.com/or the starter template and paste it in your code editor. CDN stands for Content Delivery Network. Bootstrap uses jsDelivr as its Content Delivery Network. jsDelivr is one of the most popular content delivery networks for open-source projects. A content delivery network helps in serving web files directly from the npm registry and GitHub repository without any added configuration on the user's part.

## Starter template

Be sure to have your pages set up with the latest design and development standards. That means using an HTML5 doctype and including a viewport meta tag for proper responsive behaviors. Put it all together and your pages should look like this:

```
Copy

<!doctype html>
<html lang="en">
  <head>
    <!-- Required meta tags -->
    <meta charset="utf-8">
    <meta name="viewport" content="width=device-width, initial-scale=1">

    <!-- Bootstrap CSS -->
    <link href="https://cdn.jsdelivr.net/npm/bootstrap@5.1.3/dist/css/bootstrap.min.css" rel="styl

    <title>Hello, world!</title>
  </head>
  <body>
    <h1>Hello, world!</h1>

    <!-- Optional JavaScript; choose one of the two! -->

    <!-- Option 1: Bootstrap Bundle with Popper -->
    <script src="https://cdn.jsdelivr.net/npm/bootstrap@5.1.3/dist/js/bootstrap.bundle.min.js" int

    <!-- Option 2: Separate Popper and Bootstrap JS -->
    <!--
    <script src="https://cdn.jsdelivr.net/npm/@popperjs/core@2.10.2/dist/umd/popper.min.js" integr
```

**Starter Template in Bootstrap**

- jsDelivr is the official CDN for Bootstrap and helps to transfer Bootstrap's CSS and JavaScript. One of the advantages of using a CDN is that it leads to a faster loading time. As Bootstrap is a reasonably popular framework, there are many websites available on the internet that are made using Bootstrap. As a result, many users already have Bootstrap 5 from jsDelivr downloaded. When they visit your site, it will get loaded straight from the cache memory resulting in a faster loading time. Also, most content delivery networks ensure that whenever a user requests a file, the file gets served from the server closest to the user, which again leads to faster loading time.

## CHAPTER SUMMARY

In this chapter, we learned about Bootstrap and its history, all the different versions available on the internet, and all we can do with it. We also learned about the advantages and disadvantages of using Bootstrap and some basic concepts to understand further how Bootstrap works. In the end, we learned how to set up a code editor, how to get Bootstrap. In the next chapter, we will dive deeper and learn grid system, flexbox, media object, and some other elements.

## CHAPTER 2

# The Bootstrap Framework

## IN THIS CHAPTER

➤ Introduction

➤ Versions of Bootstrap

➤ Bootstrap installation

➤ Usage of Bootstrap

In the previous chapter, we covered CSS concepts in detail. Now let's move into the CSS framework named Bootstrap.

## GETTING STARTED WITH BOOTSTRAP

Before we can start with Bootstrap, we need to first configure our code editor. First and foremost, you will need a code editor to get started with Bootstrap. There are tons of free code editors available online and open-source. You can choose any of these that suit your needs. Popular code editors are VS Code, Atom, Brackets, etc. You can use any of these code editors.

- Here, we will be using the VS Code. VS Code is one of the most popular and powerful source code creators and was created by Microsoft. It has many amazing tools like syntax highlighting, intellisense, etc.

DOI: 10.1201/9781003309383-2

Intellisense helps to complete intelligent code that helps to write pure code. It also has thousands of extensions that help you customize your code editor according to your needs. VS Code supports all types of web technologies, including Bootstrap, and is fully functional in web development. If you wish to download VS Code, you can download it from https://code.visualstudio.com/download.

- Atom is also the most powerful source code editor that works well in web technology. It is a free and open-source code editor for macOS, Linux, and Microsoft Windows. There is additional plugin support. It is developed by GitHub. Here is the link to download the Atom: https://atom.io/. You can also download any other code editor of your choice and configure it according to the instructions provided on the official website.

- After setting your code editor, open the folder and create a file with the .html extension. Bootstrap actually provides us with an HTML and CSS coded code template, and all you have to do is copy those templates into their official website. Open your browser and go to the official Bootstrap website: https://getbootstrap.com/.

- There are two ways to get Bootstrap. You can include the Bootstrap 5 link using the CDN, or simply download the Bootstrap 5 website directly to your device using the package manager. You may be wondering which is better. Both options are good for their dignity, but it is best to use a CDN as a starting point.

## HOW TO DOWNLOAD BOOTSTRAP USING PACKAGE MANAGER

You can download Bootstrap using different package managers like npm, thread, and Composer. When you download Bootstrap, you will gain access to Sass source and JavaScript files. Downloading Bootstrap using package manager requires you to have additional tools available. First, you will need a Sass compiler to merge all Sass source files into CSS files. You will also need to have an Autoprefixer for CSS vendor prefixing.

## DOWNLOADING BOOTSTRAP USING NPM

If you think Node.js is already installed on your device, install Bootstrap using the npm package. Use the following command to install Bootstrap:

```
$ npm install bootstrap
```

Npm install downloads package and its dependencies and can be processed with or without conflict. If you are using the package manager without conflicts, install npm to download all the dependencies specified in the package. json will also generate a node_modules folder with the installation folder.

To download all Bootstrap plugins in the Bootstrap item, use const bootstrap = search ('bootstrap') or import Bootstrap from 'bootstrap'. The Bootstrap module will automatically export all plugins. To download Bootstrap plugins individually, upload /js/dist/*.js files under the package directory.

### Downloading Bootstrap Using a Cable

Use the following command to install Bootstrap using the cable package:

```
$ yarn add bootstrap
```

### Download Bootstrap Using Composer

Use the following command to import and manage Sass and JavaScript files in Bootstrap using Composer.

$ composer require twbs/bootstrap:5.0.2

## HOW TO DOWNLOAD BOOTSTRAP USING CDN

If you install Bootstrap directly on your device, you will also have access to Sass and JavaScript files found inside. You can download the same using package managers like npm and Composer.

If you choose to use a CDN, you can copy the link https://www.jsdelivr .com/ or template first and paste it into your code editor. CDN stands for Content Delivery Network. Bootstrap uses jsDelivr as its content delivery network. JsDelivr is one of the most popular content delivery networks for open-source projects. The content delivery network helps to deliver web files directly from the npm registry and GitHub repository without any additional configuration on the user side.

## WHAT IS CDN?

CDN stands for Content Delivery Network and Content Distribution Network. It helps to improve the time and website performance. Bootstrap CDN is a free of cost content delivery network that helps us to quickly load Bootstrap CSS, JavaScript, and jQuery libraries on projects to make projects responsive, mobile friendly, and attractive.

## BOOTSTRAP CDN LINK AND SCRIPTS

For CSS

You just need to copy-paste the below link to the <head> section of your code:

```
<link href = "https://maxcdn.bootstrapcdn.com/
bootstrap/3.3.5/css/bootstrap.min.css" rel =
"stylesheet" />
```

For JavaScript

```
<script src = "http://maxcdn.bootstrapcdn.com/
bootstrap/3.3.6/js/bootstrap.min.js"></script>
```

For Jquery Library

```
<script src = "http://ajax.googleapis.com/ajax/
libs/jquery/1.12.0/jquery.min.js"></script>
```

For Popper.js

```
<script src="https://cdn.jsdelivr.net/npm/popper.js
@1.14.7/dist/umd/popper.min.js" ></script>
```

How to Use Bootstrap CDN

The below example shows that how we can use Bootstrap CDN on our code:

```
<!DOCTYPE html>
<html lang = "en">
<head>
  <title>This is a Bootstrap example of CDN </title >
  <meta initial-scale=1" name = "viewport" content =
"width = device-width">
  <link href = "https://maxcdn.bootstrapcdn.com/
bootstrap/3.3.6/css/bootstrap.min.css" rel =
"stylesheet">
</head>
<body>
<div class = "container">
  <h1 align = "center"> Bootstrap CDN </h1>
  <p>Write your text here..</p>
</div>
```

```
  <script src = "http://ajax.googleapis.com/ajax/
libs/jquery/1.11.0/jquery.min.js"></script>
  <script src = "https://maxcdn.bootstrapcdn.com/
bootstrap/3.2.6/js/bootstrap.min.js"></script>
</body>
</html>
```

JsDelivr is the official Bootstrap CDN and it helps to transfer Bootstrap CSS and JavaScript. One of the benefits of using a CDN is that it leads to faster loading time. As Bootstrap is a popular platform, many websites available online are created using Bootstrap. As a result, many users already have Bootstrap 5 from downloaded jsDelivr. When they visit your site, it will be loaded directly from the cache memory resulting in a faster upload time. Also, many content delivery networks ensure that whenever a user requests a file, the file is delivered from a server close to the user, which also results in faster upload time.

## BOOTSTRAP TEMPLATE

Make sure you have your pages set with the latest design and development standards. That means using the HTML5 doctype and inserting a meta tag for viewing proper responsive behavior. It is all over and your pages should look like this:

```
<!doctype html>
<html lang="en">
  <head>
    <!-- Required meta tags -->
    <meta charset="utf-8">
    <meta content="width=device-width, initial-
scale=1, shrink-to-fit=no" name="viewport" >
    <!-- Bootstrap CSS -->
    <link rel="stylesheet" href="https://cdn
.jsdelivr.net/npm/bootstrap@4.3.1/dist/css/bootstrap
.min.css" integrity="sha384-ggOyR0iXCbMQv3Xipma34M
D+dH/1fQ784/j6cY/iJTQUOhcWr7x9JvoRxT2MZw1T"
crossorigin="anonymous">
    <title>Hello, world!</title>
  </head>
  <body>
    <h1>Hello, world!</h1>
    <!-- Optional JavaScript -->
```

```
    <!-- jQuery first, then Popper.js, then
Bootstrap JS -->
    <script src="https://code.jquery.com/jquery-3.3
.1.slim.min.js" integrity="sha384-q8i/X+965Dz00rT7a
bK41JStQIAqVgRVzpbzo5smXKp4YfRvH+8abtTE1Pi6jizo"
crossorigin="anonymous"></script>
    <script src="https://cdn.jsdelivr.net/npm/popper
.js@1.14.7/dist/umd/popper.min.js" integrity="sha3
84-UO2eT0CpHqdSJQ6hJty5KVphtPhzWj9WOlclHTMGa3JDZwr
nQq4sF86dIHNDz0W1" crossorigin="anonymous"></script>
    <script src="https://cdn.jsdelivr.net/npm/bootstrap
@4.3.1/dist/js/bootstrap.min.js" integrity="sha384-Jj
SmVgyd0p3pXB1rRibZUAYoIIy6OrQ6VrjIEaFf/nJGzIxFDsf4
x0xIM+B07jRM" crossorigin="anonymous"></script>
  </body>
</html>
```

## IS POPPER.JS REQUIRED FOR BOOTSTRAP 4?

Tooltips rely on Popper.js for positioning. Popovers rely on Popper.js for positioning. Dropdowns are based on a third party library called Popper.js that can provide dynamic positioning and viewport detection.

So these are the Bootstrap 4 features that require Popper.js:

- dropdowns

- popovers

- tooltips

## RESPONSIVE META TAG

Bootstrap is developed for mobile first, a strategy in which we expand the code on mobile devices first and then expand sections as needed using CSS media queries. To ensure proper rendering and zoom touch on all devices, add a meta viewing meta tag to your <head>.

```
<meta name="viewport", content="width=device-width,
initial-scale=1, shrink-to-fit=no">
```

## HISTORY

Bootstrap, nicknamed the Twitter Blueprint, was developed by Mark Otto and Jacob Thornton on Twitter as a framework to promote consistency across all internal tools. Prior to Bootstrap, various libraries were used for visual enhancement, which resulted in significant overload and overhaul.

After a few months of small group development, many developers on Twitter began to contribute to the project as part of Hack Week, a hackathon style week for the Twitter development team. It was renamed from Blueprint to Bootstrap and released as a free open-source project on August 19, 2011. It continued to be kept by Mark Otto, Jacob Thornton, a small group of key developers, and a large community of participants.

## Bootstrap 2

On January 31, 2012, Bootstrap 2 was released, adding built-in support for Glyphicons, a few new features, and a wide range of existing features. This version supports responsive web-design, that means that the design of web pages is dynamically interchangeable, taking into account the features of the device used whether it is desktop, tablet, mobile.

## Bootstrap 3

On August 19, 2013, Bootstrap 3 was released. Redesign the parts to use a flat structure and the original portable method. Bootstrap 3 installs a new plugin system with events with word spaces. Bootstrap 3 has reduced support for Internet Explorer 7 and Firefox 3.6, but there is a polyfill supplement for these browsers.

## Bootstrap 4

Mark Otto announced Bootstrap 4 on October 29, 2014. The first alpha version of Bootstrap 4 was released on August 19, 2015. The first beta version was released on August 10, 2017. Mark stopped working on Bootstrap 3 on September 6, 2016, to work on Bootstrap 4. Bootstrap 4 was completed on January 18, 2018.

## Bootstrap 5

Our latest release, Bootstrap 5, focuses on upgrading the v4 codebase with as few major crash changes as possible. We have improved existing features and components, removed the support of older browsers, reduced jQuery to standard JavaScript, and adopted future-use technologies such as custom CSS architectures as part of our tools.

Major changes include:

- A new part of the offcanvas menu

- Removes jQuery dependence in favor of vanilla JavaScript

- Rewrite the grid to support responsive gaps and columns placed outside the lines

- Moves documents from Jekyll to Hugo

- Discard Internet Explorer support

- Moving testing infrastructure from QUnit to Jasmine

- Add a custom set of SVG icons

- Add custom CSS layouts

- Improved API

- Improved grid system

- Customizing advanced documents

- Forms updated

- RTL support

## FEATURES

Bootstrap is an HTML, CSS, and JS Library focused on simplifying the development of knowledgeable web pages (unlike web applications). The main purpose of adding to a web project is to use Bootstrap options for color, size, font, and layout for that project. Thus, the key is whether the leading engineers get those options the way they want. Once added to a project, Bootstrap provides simple way to style definitions for all HTML features. The result is the same look of prose, tables, and form elements in all web browsers. Additionally, developers can use the CSS classes defined in Bootstrap to further customize the look and feel of their content. For example, Bootstrap provided brightly colored and black tables, page titles, high-quality drag quotes, and highlighted text.

Bootstrap also comes with a few JavaScript features in the form of jQuery plugins. They offer additional user interaction features such as chat boxes, tips, and carousels. Each component of Bootstrap contains HTML format, CSS declarations, and in some cases JavaScript-compliant code. It also enhances the functionality of other existing interaction features, including the autocomplete function of input fields.

The most prominent features of Bootstrap are its structural components, as they affect the entire web page. The part of the basic structure is called the "Container," as everything else on the page is placed on it.

Engineers can choose between a wide-open container and a wide-open container. While the latter always complements the width of the webpage, the first one uses the same width of the five previously defined, depending on the screen size showing the page:

- Smaller than 576px

- 576–768px

- 768–992px

- 992–1200px

- Larger than 1,200px

## CREATE A HOME PAGE WITH BOOTSTRAP

### 1.  Add HTML5 Document Type

Bootstrap uses HTML elements and CSS formats that require HTML5 document type. Always include an HTML5 doctype at the beginning of the page, as well as a language identifier and a set of appropriate characters:

```
<! DOCTYPE html>
<html lang = "zu">
  <head>
    <meta charset = "utf-8">
  </head>
</html>
```

### 2.  Bootstrap 3 Is Advanced

Bootstrap 3 is designed to respond to mobile devices. Mobile-first styles are part of the basic framework.

To ensure proper rendering and zoom touch, add the following <meta> tag within the <head> feature:

```
<meta content = "width = device-width, initial-
scale = 1"

name = "viewport">
```

Width = part of the device width determines the width of the page to follow the screen width of the device (which will vary depending on the device). Initial scale section = 1 sets the first zoom level when the page is loaded in the browser.

## BASIC BOOTSTRAP PAGES

There are two classes we can use to get two Bootstrap pages that use class container and container liquid.

**Example**

```
<! DOCTYPE html>
<html lang = "en">
<head>
  <title> Bootstrap example </title>
  <meta charset = "utf8">
  <meta content = "width = device-width, initial-
scale = 1" name = "viewport">
  <link href = "https://maxcdn.bootstrapcdn.com/
bootstrap/3.4.1/css/bootstrap.min.css" rel =
"stylesheet" >
  <script src = "http://ajax.googleapis.com/ajax/
libs/jquery/3.6.0/jquery.min.js"> </script>
  <script src = "http://maxcdn.bootstrapcdn.com/
bootstrap/3.4.1/js/bootstrap.min.js"> </script>
</head>
<body>
<div class = "container">
  <h1> Container page </h1>
  <p> You can add any data. </p>
</div>
</body>
</html>
```

## BOOTSTRAP CONTAINERS

Bootstrap also requires something that encapsulates site content. There are two content classes to choose from:

1. The .container section provides a comprehensive wide-responsive container.

```
<! DOCTYPE html>
<html lang = "en">
<head>
  <title> example -- Bootstrap </title>
  <meta charset = "utf-8">
  <meta initial-scale = 1" , content = "width =
device-width name = "viewport">
```

```
<link href = "htts://maxcdn.bootstrapcdn.com/boo
tstrap/3.4.1/css/bootstrap.min.css" rel =
"stylesheet" >
  <script src = "http://ajax.googleapis.com/ajax/
libs/jquery/3.6.0/jquery.min.js"> </script>
  <script src = "http://maxcdn.bootstrapcdn.com/
bootstrap/3.4.1/js/bootstrap.min.js"> </script>
  <style>
    body{
      background-color: rgb(187, 186, 186);
    }
    .container{
      background-color: whitesmoke;
      height: 400px;
    }
  </style>
</head>
<body>
<div class = "container">
  <h1> Container page </h1>
  <p>Lorem ipsum, or lipsum as it is sometimes
known, is rough text used in laying out print,
graphic or web designs.
The passage is attributed to an unknown type setter
in the 15th century who is though to have scrambled
parts of Cicero's De Finibus
    Bonorum et Malorum for the use in a type
specimen book. It usually begins with:
  </p>
</div>
<p>Rest content is out of container.</p>
</body>
</html>
```

2. The .container-fluid section provides a comprehensive full container, covering the entire width of the viewing hole.

```
<! DOCTYPE html>
<html lang = "en">
<head>
  <title> Bootstrap example </title>
  <meta charset = "utf-8">
  <meta initial-scale = 1" , name = "viewport"
content = "width = device-width>
```

```
<link rel = "stylesheet" href = "https://maxcdn
.bootstrapcdn.com/bootstrap/3.4.1/css/bootstrap.min
.css">
<script src = "http://ajax.googleapis.com/ajax/
libs/jquery/3.6.0/jquery.min.js"> </script>
<script src = "http://maxcdn.bootstrapcdn.com/
bootstrap/3.4.1/js/bootstrap.min.js"> </script>
<style>
  body{
    background-color: rgb(187, 186, 186);
  }
  .container{
    background-color: whitesmoke;
    height: 400px;
  }
</style>
</head>
<body>
<div class = "container-fluid">
  <h1> Container page </h1>
  <p>Lorem ipsum, or lipsum as it is sometimes
known, is demo text used in laying out print,
graphic or web designs.
The passage is attribute is to an unknown typesetter
in the 15th century who is thought to have scrambled
parts of Cicero's De Finibus
    Bonorum et Malorum is for use in a type
specimen book. It usually begins with:
  </p>
</div>
</body>
</html>
```

## BOOTSTRAP GRID SYSTEM

The Bootstrap grid system is a simple and powerful way to build all structures and sizes. You can then customize it based on its system of 12 columns (12 columns are found in each row). It also has six responsive breakpoints available as default. You can even create your own breakpoint according to your needs. The Bootstrap grid system is totally based on the CSS Flexbox model. The grid system is built using CSS flexbox. The Bootstrap grid program is an easy way to create custom and responsive structures for all types of content. Like all other Bootstrap features, the grid system is advanced and fully responsive.

The Bootstrap grid system uses rows, columns, and containers to build the structure of any web page and align content accordingly. Creating a design using the grid system is one of the fastest and easiest ways to create a responsive web structure. You can use the predefined grid classes provided by Bootstrap to create faster designs.

Grid System is built using Flexbox, and will allow you to create a limit of 12 columns throughout the page or the entire screen width. You can use each of the 12 columns separately or combine columns to create a wider column. You can use six columns each and create two wide columns. Similarly, you can build three wide columns by combining four columns together. You can combine two columns to create six wide columns.

## GRID CLASSES

The grid system in Bootstrap 5 has six available classes that we can use to customize our grids as per our convenience. In order to create more dynamic and flexible layouts, we can combine these classes together to achieve our desired layout.

| | |
|---|---|
| .col- | extra small devices – screen width <576px |
| .col-sm- | small devices – screen width ≥576px |
| .col-md- | medium devices – screen width ≥768px |
| .col-lg- | large devices – screen width ≥992px |
| .col-xl- | extra-large devices – screen width ≥1,200px |
| .col-xxl- | extra extra-large devices – screen width ≥1,400px |

## BASIC STRUCTURE OF A BOOTSTRAP GRID

The following is a simple structure of a Bootstrap grid:

```
<div class="row">
  <div class="col-*-*"></div>
  <div class="col-*-*"></div>
</div>
```

**Example**

```
<! DOCTYPE html>
<html lang = "en">
<head>
  <title> Bootstrap example </title>
  <meta charset = "utf-8">
  <meta initial-scale = 1" name = "viewport"
content = "width = device-width,>
```

```
 <link href = "https://maxcdn.bootstrapcdn.com/
bootstrap/3.4.1/css/bootstrap.min.css" rel =
"stylesheet">
 <script src = "https://ajax.googleapis.com/ajax/
libs/jquery/3.6.0/jquery.min.js"> </script>
 <script src = "https://maxcdn.bootstrapcdn.com/
bootstrap/3.4.1/js/bootstrap.min.js"> </script>
 <style>
  body{
    background-color: rgb(187, 186, 186);
  }
  .container{
    background-color: whitesmoke;
    height: 400px;
  }
  .col-md-4{
    border:1px dodgerblue solid;
    height: 100px;
  }
 </style>
</head>
<body>
<div class = "container">
<h1> Bootstrap Grid</h1>
 <div class="row" >
   <div class="col-md-4">Col 1</div>
   <div class="col-md-4">Col 2</div>
   <div class="col-md-4">Col 3</div>
</div>
</body>
</html>
```

Explanation

The first line of the code row is a wrapper class, which means that the class row would wrap around all the columns. It is necessary to add a wrapper class to initiate the grid system in Bootstrap. Add as many classes after adding a wrapper class, keeping in mind that the sum of columns should not exceed 12.

In the above example, Bootstrap will create the layout by creating three columns of equal width. Each column will contain four grid columns. The columns made will be responsive and align according to the screen size.

## Code Example

```
<! DOCTYPE html>
<html lang = "en">
<head>
  <title> Bootstrap example </title>
  <meta charset = "utf-8">
  <meta name = "viewport" content = "width = device-
width, initial-scale = 1">
  <link rel = "stylesheet" href = "https://maxcdn.
bootstrapcdn.com/bootstrap/3.4.1/css/bootstrap.min.css">
  <script src = "https://ajax.googleapis.com/ajax/
libs/jquery/3.6.0/jquery.min.js"> </script>
  <script src = "https://maxcdn.bootstrapcdn.com/
bootstrap/3.4.1/js/bootstrap.min.js"> </script>
  <style>
    body{
      background-color: rgb(187, 186, 186);
    }
    .container{
      background-color: whitesmoke;
      height: 400px;
    }
    .col-md-6{
      border:1px dodgerblue solid;
      height: 100px;
    }
  </style>
</head>
<body>
<div class = "container">
<h1> Bootstrap Grid</h1>
  <div class="row" >
    <div class="col-md-6">Col 1</div>
    <div class="col-md-6">Col 2</div>
</div>
</body>
</html>
```

The first value after class col shows the responsiveness. Use default grid classes available in Bootstrap. The second value represents a number that must add up to 12 for each row.

The above example will output two columns, and each column will contain six grid column widths. In smaller screens, the columns will automatically get stacked one on the other.

## Code Example (Extra-small Grid)

```
<div class="col-6">Column 1</div>
<div class="col-3">Column 2</div>
```

The above example will create a grid where one column will span six column grids, and the other will span three. It is not always necessary that the sum of columns is 12. It can also be less than 12. In this example, only nine-column grids are used. The remaining three-column will remain unused and left empty.

## Code Example (Small Grid)

```
<! DOCTYPE html>
<html lang = "en">
<head>
  <title> Bootstrap example </title>
  <meta charset = "utf-8">
  <meta name = "viewport" content = "width = device-
width, initial-scale = 1">
  <link rel = "stylesheet" href = "https://maxcdn.
bootstrapcdn.com/bootstrap/3.4.1/css/bootstrap.min.css">
  <script src = "https://ajax.googleapis.com/ajax/
libs/jquery/3.6.0/jquery.min.js"> </script>
  <script src = "https://maxcdn.bootstrapcdn.com/
bootstrap/3.4.1/js/bootstrap.min.js"> </script>
  <style>
    body{
      background-color: rgb(187, 186, 186);
    }
    .container{
      background-color: whitesmoke;
      height: 400px;
    }
    .col-sm-7{
      background-color: blue;
      height: 100px;
    }
```

```
   .col-sm-5{
     background-color: yellow;
     height: 100px;
   }
  </style>
 </head>
 <body>
 <div class = "container">
 <h1> Bootstrap Grid</h1>
   <div class="row" >
     <div class="col-sm-7">Col 1</div>
     <div class="col-sm-5">Col 2</div>
 </div>
 </body>
 </html>
```

Small devices have a screen width between 576px and 767px. In the above example, four columns of equal width will be created because we have not specified the number of grids we would like to use for each. In case the number of col elements is not determined, Bootstrap simply divides them equally, spanning the entire width of the screen. As this example is for small devices, the columns will be horizontal up until 576px, and then they will stack on top of one another in extra small devices.

*Code Example (Medium Grid)*

```
<div class="col-md-6">Column 1</div>
<div class="col-md-6">Column 2</div>
```

Small devices have a screen width between 768px and 991px. For medium devices, we will use the ".col-md" class. In the above example, two columns of equal width will be created, and for screen sizes less than 768px, the columns will get stacked vertically on top of one another. So, for small devices and extra-small devices, the columns will be vertically stacked.

*Code Example (Small and Medium Grid Combined)*

```
<div class="col-sm-3 col-md-6">Column 1</div>
<div class="col-sm-9 col-md-6">Column 2</div>
```

You can combine multiple grid classes to specify how the columns should be stacked in screens of different sizes. When the website is accessed from an extra small device, the stack would be vertical, but as soon as it switches to a small device, it will shift to two columns of nine- and three-column width. And when the screen is scaled even higher to a medium device, it will split in half as we have divided it in an equal ratio.

Code Example (Large Grid)

```
<! DOCTYPE html>
<html lang = "en">
<head>
  <title> Bootstrap example </title>
  <meta charset = "utf-8">
  <meta name = "viewport" content = "width = device-
width, initial-scale = 1">
  <link rel = "stylesheet" href = "https://maxcdn
.bootstrapcdn.com/bootstrap/3.4.1/css/bootstrap.min
.css">
  <script src = "https://ajax.googleapis.com/ajax/
libs/jquery/3.6.0/jquery.min.js"> </script>
  <script src = "https://maxcdn.bootstrapcdn.com/
bootstrap/3.4.1/js/bootstrap.min.js"> </script>
  <style>
    body{
      background-color: rgb(187, 186, 186);
    }
    .container{
      background-color: whitesmoke;
      height: 400px;
    }
    .col-lg-7{
      background-color: blue;
      height: 100px;
    }
    .col-lg-5{
      background-color: yellow;
      height: 100px;
    }
</style>
</head>
<body>
<div class = "container">
<h1> Bootstrap Grid</h1>
```

```
<!-- Large -->
  <div class="row" >
    <div class="col-lg-7">Col 1</div>
    <div class="col-lg-5">Col 2</div>
</div>
</body>
</html>
```

Large devices are those devices that have screen widths of 992–1,199px. For large devices, we will use the ".col-lg-" class. The devices with a width greater than 1,199px will have four columns of equal width, and the rest of the devices smaller than that will have 100% width.

Code Example (Extra-large Grid)

```
<! DOCTYPE html>
<html lang = "en">
<head>
  <title> Bootstrap example </title>
  <meta charset = "utf-8">
  <meta name = "viewport" content = "width = device-
width, initial-scale = 1">
<link rel = "stylesheet" href = "http s://maxcdn
.bootstrapcdn.com/bootstrap/3.4.1/css/bootstrap.min
.css">
  <script src = "https://ajax.googleapis.com/ajax/
libs/jquery/3.6.0/jquery.min.js"> </script>
  <script src = "https://maxcdn.bootstrapcdn.com/
bootstrap/3.4.1/js/bootstrap.min.js"> </script>
  <style>
    body{
      background-color: rgb(187, 186, 186);
    }
    .container{
      background-color: whitesmoke;
      height: 400px;
    }
    .col-xl-7{
      background-color: blue;
      height: 100px;
    }
    .col-xl-5{
```

```
        background-color: yellow;
        height: 100px;
      }
</style>
</head>
<body>
<div class = "container">
<h1> Bootstrap Grid</h1>
<!-- Large -->
  <div class="row" >
    <div class="col-xl-7">Col 1</div>
    <div class="col-xl-5">Col 2</div>
  </div>
</body>
</html>
```

Extra-large devices have a screen width of 1,200px and above. In the above example, we will see two columns in large devices. One will have a grid column width of eight, and the other will have a grid column width of four.

*Note:* The sum should always be 12 or less than 12.

```
Code Example (Extra Large Grid)
<div class="col-xxl-6">Column 1</div>
<div class="col-xxl-3">Column 2</div>
```

Extra extra-large devices have a screen width of 1,400px and above. The above example will produce a column of six and a column of three, and the rest of the space comprising three columns would be left empty.

## HOW THE GRID WORKS

- Our grid supports six responsive breakpoints. Breakpoints are based on small-scale media queries, which means they affect that area and all over it (e.g., .col-sm-4 works in sm, md, lg, xl, and xxl). This means you can control the container and column size and behavior for each partition.

- Containers are in the middle and browse your content horizontally. Use .container with response pixel width, .container-fluid width: 100% for all viewing ports and devices, or responsive container (e.g., .container-md) with a combination of liquid width and pixel width.

- The rows are the folds of the columns. Each column has horizontal padding (called gutter) to control the space between them. This finish is then counteracted in the lines with the negative margins to ensure that the content in your columns is visually aligned at the bottom left. Lines also support editing classes to parallel use column balancing classes and trash classes to transform your content space.

- The columns are surprisingly flexible. There are 12 template columns available in each row, which allows you to create different combinations of elements that include any number of columns. Most of the column classes indicate the number of template columns that must be passed (e.g., col-4 extends four). The width is set as a percentage to maintain the same relative size.

- Gutters are also responsive and customized. Gutter classes are available at all breakpoints, with all the same sizes as our margin and padding space. Replace horizontal gutters with .gx- * sections, straight gutters with .gy- *, or all gutters with .g- * sections. .G-0 is also available for gutters removal.

- Sass variables, maps, and combinations enable grid. If you do not want to use the predefined grid classes in Bootstrap, you can use our Sass grid source to create your own with a sentence made with more sentences. We also added some custom CSS layouts to use these Sass variables for greater flexibility.

## THREE EQUAL COLUMNS

For small three equal column, we "use col-sm-4." If you want it, you need to add first row and then need .col-sm-4.

```
<div class="row">
  <div class="col-sm-4">.col-sm-4</div>
    <div class="col-sm-4">.col-sm-4</div>
    <div class="col-sm-4">.col-sm-4</div>
</div>
```

## TWO UNEQUAL COLUMNS

For unequal column, you can use col-sm-4 with col-md-8. You can also write col-sm-2 with col-sm-10.

```
<div class="row">
  <div class="col-sm-4">.col-sm-4</div>
```

```
    <div class="col-sm-8">.col-sm-8</div>
  </div>
```

Here you can have complete example of al the col-* used in Bootstrap
Grid System.

```
<! DOCTYPE html>
<html lang = "en">
<head>
  <title> Bootstrap example </title>
  <meta charset = "utf-8">
  <meta name = "viewport" content = "width = device-
width, initial-scale = 1">
  <link rel = "stylesheet" href = "https://maxcdn
.bootstrapcdn.com/bootstrap/3.4.1/css/bootstrap.min
.css">
  <script src = "https://ajax.googleapis.com/ajax/
libs/jquery/3.6.0/jquery.min.js"> </script>
  <script src = "https://maxcdn.bootstrapcdn.com/
bootstrap/3.4.1/js/bootstrap.min.js"> </script>
  <style>
    body{
      background-color: rgb(187, 186, 186);
    }
    .container{
      background-color: whitesmoke;
      height: 400px;
    }
    .col-xxl-7{
      background-color: yellowgreen;
      height: 100px;
    }
    .col-xxl-5{
      background-color:palevioletred;
      height: 100px;
    }
    .col-xl-7{
      background-color: brown;
      height: 100px;
    }
    .col-xl-5{
      background-color:wheat;
      height: 100px;
```

```
      }
    .col-lg-7{
      background-color: red;
      height: 100px;
    }
    .col-lg-5{
      background-color: green;
      height: 100px;
    }
    .col-md-7{
      background-color: orange;
      height: 100px;
    }
    .col-md-5{
      background-color: purple;
      height: 100px;
    }
    .col-sm-7{
      background-color: indianred;
      height: 100px;
    }
    .col-sm-5{
      background-color: pink;
      height: 100px;
    }
    .col-7{
      background-color:seagreen;
      height: 100px;
    }
    .col-5{
      background-color: orchid;
      height: 100px;
      }
</style>
</head>
<body>
<div class = "container">
<h1> Bootstrap Grid</h1>
<div class="row" >
  <div class="col-xxl-7"><h1>XXL </h1></div>
  <div class="col-xxl-5"><h1>XXL </h1></div>
</div>
```

```
<!-- Large -->
  <div class="row" >
    <div class="col-xl-7"><h1>XL </h1></div>
    <div class="col-xl-5"><h1>XL </h1></div>
</div>
<div class="row" >
  <div class="col-lg-7"><h1>LG </h1></div>
  <div class="col-lg-5"><h1>LG </h1></div>
</div>
<div class="row" >
  <div class="col-md-7"><h1>MD </h1></div>
  <div class="col-md-5"><h1>MD </h1></div>
</div>
<div class="row" >
  <div class="col-sm-7"><h1>SM </h1></div>
  <div class="col-sm-5"><h1>SM </h1></div>
</div>
<div class="row" >
  <div class="col-7"><h1> </h1></div>
  <div class="col-5"><h1></h1></div>
</div>
</body>
</html>
```

## FLEXBOX

A flex in Bootstrap allows us to manage the layout and helps us in aligning the components accordingly. Using Flexbox, we can manage the sizing of the columns in any grid and easily navigate the page. To fully grasp all the display utilities provided through flex in Bootstrap, it is essential to know about CSS Flexbox.

The flexible layout model, also called the Flexbox in CSS, is a way to provide efficient mapping out and distribution of space among all the items in a container. It helps us align and layout the items to get positioned dynamically concerning the available space. If a container becomes a flex, it can easily alter its height or width to fill the open space appropriately. This is done to accommodate all devices with different display and screen widths. The main idea is that any flex container should expand or shrink and fill the available space to prevent overflow. In CSS, the flexbox layout is generally considered more appropriate for small-scale designs, while grid layouts serve better on a large scale.

Each flex container is seen as a parent element, and each item contained within the parent element or container is referred to as the child/children element.

## FLEXBOX PROPERTIES IN CSS

Display

This property is used to define a flex container. The flex could be inline or block, depending on its value. This property makes the display container the parent. Therefore, all the elements contained within would become the direct children of this parent element.

*Syntax*

- display: block;

    - **Block:** This value will create a block-level element box which will make line breaks both before and after itself whenever it is placed in the normal flow of the page.

- display: inline;

    - **Inline:** This value will create one or more inline element boxes that will stick to each other and be in the same line if space is available. It will not generate line breaks before or after itself.

- display: inline-block;

    - **Inline-block:** This display property value would create a block-level element box that will flow with the surrounding content as if it is a single inline box.

- display: flex;

    - **Flex:** This value will make the parent container behave like a block element and layout the content inside itself according to the flexbox model. Line break would be generated before and after the container in normal flow.

- display: inline-flex;

    - **Inline-flex:** This property value makes the element behave like an inline element. However, the content within the component gets placed according to the flexbox model.

- display: grid;

  It is a 2D system that makes it easier to align and arrange elements on a web page. You can work with rows and columns together, determining how many rows and columns we want our parent element to have.

- display: inline-grid;

- Display: none

  If we set to 0% opacity, it still takes space on the page. But if we set that the thing to display: none, it is completely removed from the document flow.

- display: flow-root;

*Note:* For those browsers that support the two-value syntax, the inner value of display: flex would be enough to set the outer value to block on its own as that is the expected and default value. For specific changes, you need to define it as inline-flex explicitly.

## FLEXBOX PROPERTIES IN BOOTSTRAP

The Bootstrap properties are similar to CSS but difference is that we can use Bootstrap as the inline CSS. Responsive variations also exist for .d-flex and .d-inline-flex.

- .d-flex

- .d-inline-flex

- .d-sm-flex

- .d-sm-inline-flex

- .d-md-flex

- .d-md-inline-flex

- .d-lg-flex

- .d-lg-inline-flex

- .d-xl-flex

- .d-xl-inline-flex

Flex-direction in CSS

The flex-direction property defines the direction in which the flex items would get placed within a flex container. Flexbox essentially works by laying out all the elements in a single order. So, the elements would either get placed horizontally in rows or vertically in columns.

Syntax

- flex-direction: row;
  - **Row:** This is the default value of the flex-direction property. It goes from left to right. The main axis of the parent element is said to be the same as the direction of the text. The order of the content would be from the main start point of the container to the main endpoint of the container.
- flex-direction: row-reverse;
  - **Row-reverse:** The core behavior is the same as that of the row, the only difference being the direction in which the content goes, that is, from the container's primary endpoint to the parent container's main start point.
- flex-direction: column;
  - **Row:** This is the default value of the flex-direction property. It goes from right to left. The main axis of the parent element is said to be the same as the direction of the text. The order of the content would be from the main start point of the container to the main endpoint of the container.
- flex-direction: column-reverse;
  - **Column-reverse:** The core behavior is the same as that of the row, the only difference being the direction in which the content goes, that is, from the container's primary endpoint to the parent container's main start point.

## FLEX-DIRECTION IN BOOTSTRAP

Responsive variations also exist for flex-direction:

- .flex-row
- .flex-row-reverse
- .flex-column

- .flex-column-reverse

- .flex-sm-row

- .flex-sm-row-reverse

- .flex-sm-column

- .flex-sm-column-reverse

- .flex-md-row

- .flex-md-row-reverse

- .flex-md-column

- .flex-md-column-reverse

- .flex-lg-row

- .flex-lg-row-reverse

- .flex-lg-column

- .flex-lg-column-reverse

- .flex-xl-row

- .flex-xl-row-reverse

- .flex-xl-column

- .flex-xl-column-reverse

Set the variable direction in the flexible container with the control resources. In most cases you can leave a horizontal section here as the default browser is in line. However, you may encounter situations where you need to explicitly set this value (such as responsive properties).

Use the .flex-row to set the horizontal (browser default) or .flex-row-reverse to start the horizontal direction from the other side.

Flexbox Features

The following are some of the features of the Flexbox architecture:

- **Direction:** You can organize items on a web page in any way like left to right, right to left, top to bottom, and bottom to top.

- **Wrap:** Using Flexbox, you can rearrange the layout of web page content.

- **Fold:** In the case of static web page content (in one row), you can fold them in multiple rows (both horizontal) and vertically.

- **Align:** Using Flexbox, you can align web page content with respect to your container.

- **Resize:** By using Flexbox, you can increase or decrease the size of the objects on the page to fit in the available space.

## FLEX-WRAP IN CSS

The default behavior of any child element of a flex container is to fit into one single line. To wrap the child items according to your needs, you can use the flex-wrap property. This property would set the direction in which elements are stacked if the wrapping is permitted. The items have to be flexible to work for this property. If the items are not flexible, this property has no effect whatsoever.

*Syntax*

- flex-wrap: nowrap;

  - **nowrap:** This is the default value of the flex-wrap property. Setting the flex-wrap value to no-wrap will ensure that all the flex items are in one line. Laying out all the items in one line might cause the parent container to overflow.

- flex-wrap: wrap;

  - **wrap:** If you put the value of the flex-wrap property as a wrap, then all the child items within the parent container will wrap onto multiple lines. This wrapping could go on from top to bottom.

- flex-wrap: wrap-reverse;

  - **wrap-reverse:** This works in a similar way to the wrap property. The only difference is that the direction the child items will wrap would get reversed. All the flex items will wrap onto multiple lines in that reverse order.

## FLEX-WRAP IN BOOTSTRAP

You can change flex items wrap in a flex container and also choose from no wrapping at all with .flex-nowrap, wrapping with .flex-wrap, or reverse wrapping with .flex-wrap-reverse.

Responsive variations also exist for flex-wrap:

- .flex-nowrap
- .flex-wrap
- .flex-wrap-reverse
- .flex-sm-nowrap
- .flex-sm-wrap
- .flex-sm-wrap-reverse
- .flex-md-nowrap
- .flex-md-wrap
- .flex-md-wrap-reverse
- .flex-lg-nowrap
- .flex-lg-wrap
- .flex-lg-wrap-reverse
- .flex-xl-nowrap
- .flex-xl-wrap
- .flex-xl-wrap-reverse

## FLEX-FLOW

It is a shorthand property, and it combines two properties, namely, flex-direction and flex-wrap, which we have discussed above. The flex-flow in its entirety and the properties contained within it depend on whether the parent element is a flexible item or not. If that is not the case, then the flex-flow property in itself has no effect. Both the properties flex-direction and flex-wrap, when combined, form the two main axes of the flex container. Flex-direction property defines the main axis, while the flex-wrap property defines the cross axis. The default value of the flex-flow property is row no-wrap.

Syntax

- /* flex-flow: <'flex-direction'> and <'flex-wrap'> */
- flex-flow: row nowrap/wrap/wrap-reverse;

- flex-flow: row-reverse nowrap/wrap/wrap-reverse;

- flex-flow: column nowrap/wrap/wrap-reverse;

- flex-flow: column-reverse nowrap/wrap/wrap-reverse;

## JUSTIFY-CONTENT IN CSS

This property helps us align the items of the flexible container when the items do not use all the space available within the main axis. The main axis is usually horizontal, but it can also be changed using the flex-direction property. The need to define the alignment across the main axis arises because sometimes all the items available on a line are not flexible or have reached their maximum size. This property also helps control if there is some kind of overflow of the items. Justify-content property helps us align all the flex items at the center of the container. The default value of the property is flex-start.

Syntax

- justify-content: center;

  - **Center:** The items are positioned and packed toward each other of the main container or the parent element. The items are centered along the main axis.

- justify-content: start;

  - **Start:** The items are positioned toward the starting edge of the parent container. The positioning will be along the main axis. The items will stick to each other toward the start with no spacing.

- justify-content: end;

  - **End:** The items are positioned toward the ending edge of the parent container. The positioning will be along the main axis. The items will stick to each other toward the end with no spacing.

- justify-content: flex-start;

  - **Flex-start:** It is the default value of the justify-content property. Using this property would ensure that the items are positioned toward the start of the container. Using flex-start as the value of the property, justify-content would ensure that all the items are at the edge of the container packed to each other. The start of the container depends upon the main start side of the parent container. There would be no spacing or gap available between all the flex items. However, this property only applies to flex layout items. Any items that are not direct children of any parent container will be treated equivalent to start.

- justify-content: flex-end;

  - **Flex-end:** All the flex items are positioned toward the edge of the parent container at the end side. The main end side depends upon the alignment of the flex container. There would be no spacing between the flex items. However, this property value only works for flex layout items. For any items that are not direct children of a parent container, this value will be treated equivalent to end.

- justify-content: left;

  - **Left:** All the items are positioned toward the left edge of the parent container. If the property axis is not parallel to the inline axis of the container, then this value will behave like the start.

- justify-content: right;

  - **Right:** All the items are positioned toward the right edge of the parent container in the appropriate axis. If the property axis is not parallel to the inline axis of the container, then this value will behave like the start.

Positional Alignment

- justify-content: normal;

  - All the items will be positioned in their default place. It works as if no value of justify-content is being set. The value normal behaves like the stretch in flex and grid containers.

- justify-content: space-between;

  - All the child items are evenly spaced out and distributed throughout the parent container. The alignment of items happens along the main axis. The spacing between each item in the container is the same. The gap between all the adjacent pairs of items would also be equal. The very first item of the container would be packed toward the main start edge, whereas the last item of the container would be stuck toward the main-end edge of the parent container.

- justify-content: space-around;

  - All the child items are evenly distributed throughout the container and are separated from each other with an equal amount of space. The items are distributed along the main axis of the parent container. The space between each adjacent pair of child items is the same. There is a space at the start of the container and toward the end of the container. Even though there is spacing among all the container elements, visually, the spacing is not equal. The space before the first and the last item is equal to half of the available space between each pair of adjacent items. If an item has one unit of length against the edge of the container, then it will have two units of space with the next item.

- justify-content: space-evenly;

  - As the name suggests, the items are evenly distributed throughout the parent container. The alignment occurs along the main axis. The spacing between each available item, including the first item at the main start edge and the last item at the main end edge, is the same.

- justify-content: stretch;

  - If the size of all the available items of a container after combining turns out to be less than the parent container's size, then the auto-sized items would increase in size. This change in size occurs until the child items' combined size fills in the parent container along the main axis.

*Note:* Some of these property values don't have support for specific browser and browser versions. Like space-between doesn't have permission from some versions of edge. The values that work in most browsers and are the safest are flex-start, flex-end, and center.

## ORDER

You can change the visual order of specific flex items with a handful of order utilities. You can provide options for making an item first or last, as well as reset to use the DOM order. As order takes any integer value (e.g., 5), add custom CSS for any additional values needed.

Responsive variations also exist for order:

- .order-0
- .order-1
- .order-2
- .order-3
- .order-4
- .order-5
- .order-6
- .order-7
- .order-8
- .order-9
- .order-10
- .order-11
- .order-12
- .order-sm-0
- .order-sm-1
- .order-sm-2
- .order-sm-3
- .order-sm-4
- .order-sm-5
- .order-sm-6
- .order-sm-7
- .order-sm-8
- .order-sm-9
- .order-sm-10
- .order-sm-11

- .order-sm-12
- .order-md-0
- .order-md-1
- .order-md-2
- .order-md-3
- .order-md-4
- .order-md-5
- .order-md-6
- .order-md-7
- .order-md-8
- .order-md-9
- .order-md-10
- .order-md-11
- .order-md-12
- .order-lg-0
- .order-lg-1
- .order-lg-2
- .order-lg-3
- .order-lg-4
- .order-lg-5
- .order-lg-6
- .order-lg-7
- .order-lg-8
- .order-lg-9
- .order-lg-10
- .order-lg-11

- .order-lg-12
- .order-xl-0
- .order-xl-1
- .order-xl-2
- .order-xl-3
- .order-xl-4
- .order-xl-5
- .order-xl-6
- .order-xl-7
- .order-xl-8
- .order-xl-9
- .order-xl-10
- .order-xl-11
- .order-xl-12

## JUSTIFY-CONTENT IN BOOTSTRAP

Responsive variations also exist for justify-content:

- .justify-content-start
- .justify-content-end
- .justify-content-center
- .justify-content-between
- .justify-content-around
- .justify-content-sm-start
- .justify-content-sm-end
- .justify-content-sm-center
- .justify-content-sm-between
- .justify-content-sm-around

- .justify-content-md-start
- .justify-content-md-end
- .justify-content-md-center
- .justify-content-md-between
- .justify-content-md-around
- .justify-content-lg-start
- .justify-content-lg-end
- .justify-content-lg-center
- .justify-content-lg-between
- .justify-content-lg-around
- .justify-content-xl-start
- .justify-content-xl-end
- .justify-content-xl-center
- .justify-content-xl-between
- .justify-content-xl-around

## ALIGN SELF

You can use align-self flexbox items to change their alignment on the cross axis. Choose from the same options as align-items such as start, end, center, baseline, or stretch. Responsive variations also exist for align-self:

- .align-self-start
- .align-self-end
- .align-self-center
- .align-self-baseline
- .align-self-stretch
- .align-self-sm-start
- .align-self-sm-end

- .align-self-sm-center
- .align-self-sm-baseline
- .align-self-sm-stretch
- .align-self-md-start
- .align-self-md-end
- .align-self-md-center
- .align-self-md-baseline
- .align-self-md-stretch
- .align-self-lg-start
- .align-self-lg-end
- .align-self-lg-center
- .align-self-lg-baseline
- .align-self-lg-stretch
- .align-self-xl-start
- .align-self-xl-end
- .align-self-xl-center
- .align-self-xl-baseline
- .align-self-xl-stretch

## ALIGN ITEMS

You can use align-items on flexbox containers to change the alignment of flex items on the various cross axis (the y-axis to start, x-axis if flex-direction: column). Choose from start, end, center, baseline, or stretch (browser default) . Responsive variations also exist for align-items.

- .align-items-start
- .align-items-end
- .align-items-center
- .align-items-baseline
- .align-items-stretch

- .align-items-sm-start
- .align-items-sm-end
- .align-items-sm-center
- .align-items-sm-baseline
- .align-items-sm-stretch
- .align-items-md-start
- .align-items-md-end
- .align-items-md-center
- .align-items-md-baseline
- .align-items-md-stretch
- .align-items-lg-start
- .align-items-lg-end
- .align-items-lg-center
- .align-items-lg-baseline
- .align-items-lg-stretch
- .align-items-xl-start
- .align-items-xl-end
- .align-items-xl-center
- .align-items-xl-baseline
- .align-items-xl-stretch

## GROW AND SHRINK

You can use .flex-grow-* utilities to toggle a flex item's ability to grow to fill rest space. The .flex-grow-1 elements use all available space it can, while allowing the remaining two flex items their necessary space. Responsive variations also exist for flex-grow and flex-shrink.

- .flex-{grow|shrink}-0
- .flex-{grow|shrink}-1
- .flex-sm-{grow|shrink}-0

- .flex-sm-{grow|shrink}-1

- .flex-md-{grow|shrink}-0

- .flex-md-{grow|shrink}-1

- .flex-lg-{grow|shrink}-0

- .flex-lg-{grow|shrink}-1

- .flex-xl-{grow|shrink}-0

- .flex-xl-{grow|shrink}-1

## FILL

Use the .flex-fill class on a collection of sibling elements to force them into widths equal to their content while taking up all available horizontal space. Responsive variations also exist for flex-fill.

- .flex-fill

- .flex-sm-fill

- .flex-md-fill

- .flex-lg-fill

- .flex-xl-fill

## RESPONSIVE BREAKPOINTS

As Bootstrap has been developed to be mobile-first, we use a few media queries to create realistic breakouts for our architecture and visual connectors. These high-density points are based on the small width of the viewing hole and allow us to maximize features as the viewing hole changes.

Bootstrap primarily uses the scope of the following media queries – or breakpoint – in our Sass files that are the source of our architecture, grid system, and components.

```
// Small devices (landscape phones, 576px and up)
@media (min-width: 576px) { ... }
// Medium devices (tablets, 768px and up)
@media (min-width: 768px) { ... }
// Large devices (desktops, 992px and up)
@media (min-width: 992px) { ... }
// Extra large devices (large desktops, 1200px and up)
@media (min-width: 1200px) { ... }
```

## Z-index

A few Bootstrap sections use z-index, a CSS feature that helps control the structure by providing a third-party content editor. We use the default z-index scale in Bootstrap designed to properly navigate, navigation tools and popovers, models, and more.

These high numbers start at the wrong number, high and clear enough to avoid collision. We need a common set of this for all our horizontal parts – tools, popovers, navbes, downgrades, models – so that we can be reasonably consistent in behavior. There's no reason we couldn't use 100+ or 500+.

We do not recommend customization of these individual numbers; if you change one, you probably need to replace them all.

- $zindex-dropdown

- $zindex-sticky

- $zindex-fixed

- $zindex-modal-backdrop

- $zindex-modal

- $zindex-popover

- $zindex-tooltip

To manage cross-border parameters within components (e.g., buttons and input groups), we use the minimum single-digit values of z-index: 1, 2, and 3 for default, up, and active conditions, respectively. For high/fixed/active navigation, we bring something forward with a high z-value indicator to indicate its boundary over sibling elements.

## COMPONENTS IN BOOTSTRAP

### Bootstrap Alerts

These are used to provide way to create predefined alert messages. It adds a style to your messages to make it more appealing to the users. There are four classes that are used within <div> element for alerts.

- .alert-success

- .alert-info

- .alert-warning

- .alert-danger

In Bootstrap 4, new four alerts are added in Bootstrap Alert defined in Bootstrap 3 tutorial:

- **Primary:** This alert box indicates an important action.

- **Secondary:** This alert box indicates a less important action.

- **Dark:** Dark gray alert box.

- **Light:** Light gray alert box.

It is created with the .alert class, followed by one of the contextual classes. List of all contextual classes:

- .alert-success

- .alert-info

- .alert-warning

- .alert-danger

- .alert-primary

- .alert-secondary

- .alert-light

- .alert-dark

## Alert Links

You have to add the alert-link class to any links inside the alert box to create "matching colored links": (alert-link).

```
<!DOCTYPE html>
<html lang="en">
<head>
  <title>Bootstrap Example</title>
  <meta charset="utf-8">
  <meta name="viewport" content="width=device-width,
initial-scale=1">
```

```
<link rel="stylesheet" href="https://maxcdn.
bootstrapcdn.com/bootstrap/4.0.0-beta.2/css/
bootstrap.min.css">
</head>
<body>
<div class="container">
  <h2>Bootstrap Alert Links</h2>
  <div class="alert alert-success">
    <strong>Success!</strong>
  <div class="alert alert-info">
    <strong>Info!
  <div class="alert alert-warning">
    <strong>Warning!</strong>
  <div class="alert alert-danger">
    <strong>Danger!</strong>
  <div class="alert alert-primary">
    <strong>Primary!</strong>
  <div class="alert alert-secondary">
    <strong>Secondary!</strong>
  <div class="alert alert-dark">
    <strong>Dark!</strong>
  <div class="alert alert-light">
    <strong>Light!</strong>
  </div>
</div>
</body>
</html>
```

## BOOTSTRAP BADGES

It is used to add extra information to any content and you can use the
.badge class together with a contextual class (like .badge-secondary)
within <span> elements to create rectangular badges.

**Example**

```
<!DOCTYPE html>
<html lang="en">
<head>
  <title>Bootstrap Example</title>
  <meta charset="utf-8">
  <meta name="viewport" content="width=device-width,
initial-scale=1">
  <link rel="stylesheet" href="https://cdn.jsdelivr
.net/npm/bootstrap@4.6.1/dist/css/bootstrap.min.css">
```

```
</head>
<body>
<div class="container">
  <h2>Badges</h2>
  <p>Example heading <span class="badge badge-
secondary bg-primary">1</span></p>
</div>
</body>
</html>
```

## BOOTSTRAP JUMBOTRON

A jumbotron indicates a gray box for getting extra attention to some special content or information:

```
<!DOCTYPE html>
<html lang="en">
<head>
  <title>CSS Framework - Bootstrap</title>
  <meta charset="utf-8">
  <meta name="viewport" content="width=device-width,
initial-scale=1">
  <link rel="stylesheet" href="https://cdn.jsdelivr
.net/npm/bootstrap@4.6.1/dist/css/bootstrap.min.css">
</head>
<body>
  <div class="jumbotron">
    <p>Bootstrap is the most famous HTML, CSS, JS
framework for developing rhighly esponsive, mobile-
first projects on the web.</p>
  </div>
</div>
</body>
</html>
```

## FULL-WIDTH JUMBOTRON

If you wish to use a full-width jumbotron without rounded (circular) borders, add the .jumbotron-fluid class and a .container or .container-fluid to it:

```
<!DOCTYPE html>
<html lang="en">
<head>
  <title>CSS Framework - Bootstrap</title>
  <meta charset="utf-8">
  <meta name="viewport" content="width=device-width,
initial-scale=1">
```

```
<link rel="stylesheet" href="https://cdn.jsdelivr
.net/npm/bootstrap@4.6.1/dist/css/bootstrap.min.css">
</head>
<body>
<div class="jumbotron jumbotron-fluid">
  <div class="container">
    <p>Bootstrap is the most famous HTML, CSS, and
JS framework for developing highly responsive,
mobile-first projects on the web.</p>
  </div>
</div>
</body>
</html>
```

## BOOTSTRAP BUTTONS

It includes several predefined button styles, each button serving its own semantic purpose:

```
<!DOCTYPE html>
<html lang="en">
<head>
  <title>Bootstrap Example</title>
  <meta charset="utf-8">
  <meta name="viewport" content="width=device-width,
initial-scale=1">
  <link rel="stylesheet" href="https://cdn.jsdelivr
.net/npm/bootstrap@4.6.1/dist/css/bootstrap.min.css">
<body>
<div class="container">
  <h2>Button Styles</h2>
  <button class="btn">Basic</button>
  <button class="btn btn-primary">Primary</button>
  <button class="btn btn-secondary">Secondary</
button>
  <button class="btn btn-success">Success</button>
  <button class="btn btn-info">Info</button>
  <button class="btn btn-warning">Warning</button>
  <button class="btn btn-danger">Danger</button>
  <button class="btn btn-dark">Dark</button>
  <button class="btn btn-light">Light</button>
  <button class="btn btn-link">Link</button>
</div>
</body>
</html>
```

## BUTTON SIZES

You can use the .btn-lg class for large buttons or .btn-sm class for small buttons:

```
<button type="button" class="btn btn-primary btn-
lg">Large</button>
<button type="button" class="btn btn-
primary">Default</button>
<button type="button" class="btn btn-primary btn-
sm">Small</button>
```

## BLOCK-LEVEL BUTTONS

You can add class ".btn-block" to create a block-level button that spans the entire width of the parent element:

```
<button type="button" class="btn btn-primary btn-
block">Full-Width Button</button>
```

## ACTIVE/DISABLED BUTTONS

The class .active makes a appear pressed, the disabled attribute makes a button unclickable:

```
<button class="btn btn-primary active">Active
Primary</button>
```

## SPINNER BUTTONS

If you want to create a spinner/loader, use the .spinner-border class:

```
<button class="btn btn-primary">
  <span class="spinner-border spinner-border-sm">
Wait </span>
</button>
```

## COLORED SPINNERS

You can use any text color utilities to add a color to the spinner:

**Example**

```
<div class="spinner-border text-muted"></div>
```

## BUTTON TAGS

The .btn classes are developed to be used with the <button> element. However, you can also use any of these classes on <a> or <input> elements.

When using button classes on <a> elements that are used to trigger in-page functionality (such as collapsing content), rather than linking to new pages or sections within the current page, these links should be given a role="button" to appropriately convey their purpose to assistive technologies such as screen readers.

```
<!DOCTYPE html>
<html lang="en">
<head>
  <title>Bootstrap Example</title>
  <meta charset="utf-8">
  <meta name="viewport" content="width=device-width,
initial-scale=1">
  <link rel="stylesheet" href="https://cdn.jsdelivr
.net/npm/bootstrap@4.6.1/dist/css/bootstrap.min.css">
<body>
<div class="container">
<a class="btn btn-primary" href="#"
role="button">Link</a>
<button class="btn btn-primary"
type="submit">Button</button>
<input class="btn btn-primary" type="button"
value="Input">
<input class="btn btn-primary" type="submit"
value="Submit">
<input class="btn btn-primary" type="reset"
value="Reset">
</div>
</body>
```

## OUTLINE BUTTONS

It is used to replace the default modifier classes with the .btn-outline-* ones to remove all background images and colors on any button.

**Example**

```
<!DOCTYPE html>
<html lang="en">
<head>
  <title>Bootstrap Example</title>
  <meta charset="utf-8">
  <meta name="viewport" content="width=device-width,
initial-scale=1">
```

```
  <link rel="stylesheet" href="https://cdn.jsdelivr
.net/npm/bootstrap@4.6.1/dist/css/bootstrap.min.css">
<body>
<div class="container">
<button class="btn btn-outline-primary">Primary</
button>
<button class="btn btn-outline-secondary">Seconda
ry</button>
<button class="btn btn-outline-success">Success</
button>
<button class="btn btn-outline-danger">Danger</
button>
<button class="btn btn-outline-warning">Warning</
button>
<button class="btn btn-outline-info">Info</button>
<button class="btn btn-outline-light">Light</
button>
<button class="btn btn-outline-dark">Dark</
button></div>
</body>
```

## DROPDOWNS

Dropdowns are toggleable, text overlays for displaying lists of links and more. They made interactive with the included dropdown plugin. They are toggled by clicking, not by hovering; this is an intentional design decision.

Dropdowns are built on a third-party library, Popper.js, which provides dynamic positioning and viewport detection. Always include popper.min .js before bootstrap.bundle.min.js / bootstrap.bundle.js which contains Popper.js.

**Example**

```
<!DOCTYPE html>
<html lang="en">
<head>
  <title>Bootstrap Example</title>
  <meta charset="utf-8">
  <meta name="viewport" content="width=device-width,
initial-scale=1">
  <script src="https://cdn.jsdelivr.net/npm/jquery@
3.6.0/dist/jquery.slim.min.js"></script>
  <script src="https://cdn.jsdelivr.net/npm/popper
.js@1.16.1/dist/umd/popper.min.js"></script>
```

```
<script src="https://cdn.jsdelivr.net/npm/
bootstrap@4.6.1/dist/js/bootstrap.bundle.min.js">
</script>
<link rel="stylesheet" href="https://cdn.jsdelivr
.net/npm/bootstrap@4.6.1/dist/css/bootstrap.min.css">
<body>
<div class="container">
<!-- Example single danger button -->
<div class="btn-group">
<button type="button" class="btn btn-danger
dropdown-toggle" data-toggle="dropdown" aria-
haspopup="true" aria-expanded="false">
  Action
</button>
<div class="dropdown-menu">
  <a class="dropdown-item" href="#">Action</a>
  <a class="dropdown-item" href="#">Another
action</a>
  <a class="dropdown-item" href="#">Something else
here</a>
  <div class="dropdown-divider"></div>
  <a class="dropdown-item" href="#">Separated
link</a>
  </div>
</div>
</body>
```

## NAVBAR

### How It Works

Navbars require a wrapping of .navbar with .navbar-expand{-sm|-md|-lg|-xl} for responsive collapsing and scheme classes. Navbars and their contents are fluid by default. Use optional containers to limit horizontal width. It can use spacing and flex utility classes for the controlling of spacing and alignment within navbars. These are responsive by default, but you can modify them easily to change that. Responsive behavior depends on Collapse JavaScript plugin. Navbars are hidden by default when printing. Force them to be printed by adding .d-print to the .navbar. Make sure you should use a <nav> element or, if using a more generic element such as a <div>, add a role="navigation" to every navbar to explicitly identify it as a landmark region for users of assistive technologies.

## SUPPORTED CONTENT

Navbar comes with built-in support of subcomponents. Choose from the following as needed:

- .navbar-brand is used for company, product, or project name.

- .navbar-nav is used for a full-height and lightweight navigation.

- .navbar-toggler is used with our collapse plugin for navigation toggling behaviors.

- .form-inline is used for any form of controls and actions.

- .navbar-text is used for adding vertically centered strings of text.

- .collapse.navbar-collapse is used for grouping and hiding navbar contents by a parent breakpoint.

```
<!DOCTYPE html>
<html lang="en">
<head>
  <title>Bootstrap Example</title>
  <meta charset="utf-8">
  <meta name="viewport" content="width=device-width,
initial-scale=1">
  <script src="https://cdn.jsdelivr.net/npm/jquery@
3.6.0/dist/jquery.slim.min.js"></script>
  <script src="https://cdn.jsdelivr.net/npm/popper.
js@1.16.1/dist/umd/popper.min.js"></script>
  <script src="https://cdn.jsdelivr.net/npm/
bootstrap@4.6.1/dist/js/bootstrap.bundle.min.js">
</script>
  <link rel="stylesheet" href="https://cdn.jsdelivr
.net/npm/bootstrap@4.6.1/dist/css/bootstrap.min.css">
<body>
<nav class="navbar navbar-expand-lg navbar-light
bg-light">
  <a class="navbar-brand" href="#">Navbar</a>
  <button type="button" data-toggle="collapse"
class="navbar-toggler" data-
target="#navbarNavAltMarkup" aria-
controls="navbarNavAltMarkup" aria-expanded="false"
aria-label="Toggle navigation">
```

```
    <span class="navbar-toggler-icon"></span>
  </button>
  <div class="collapse navbar-collapse" id=
"navbarNavAltMarkup">
    <div class="navbar-nav">
      <a class="nav-item nav-link active" href="#">Home
<span class="sr-only">(current)</span></a>
      <a class="nav-item nav-link" href="#">Features</a>
      <a class="nav-item nav-link" href="#">Pricing</a>
      <a class="nav-item nav-link disabled" href="#"
tabindex="-1" aria-disabled="true">Disabled</a>
    </div>
  </div>
</nav>
</body>
```

## UTILITIES

### Border

You can use border utilities to add or remove an element's borders. Here is the complete list from which you can choose all borders or one at a time.

## CHAPTER SUMMARY

The entire chapter is about Bootstrap. We have learned that Bootstrap can be used with CSS to enhance its properties. Bootstrap can make pages more attractive. It can be added just by installing or adding CDN in you html file and you can start working on it.

## CHAPTER 3

# Designing Templates

## IN THIS CHAPTER

> ➤ Designing a Blog Template

> ➤ Designing a Portfolio Template

> ➤ Mobile-Friendly Design

> ➤ Responsive and Adaptive Design

We learned about many text and table utilities in the previous chapter. Menu and navigation utilities were also covered. We started the previous chapter by learning about the grid system, flexbox, and properties in CSS and Bootstrap. We also ended up learning about layouts. In this chapter, we will apply all the theoretical knowledge we gained in the previous chapter and create a few templates of our own.

## CREATING A BLOG TEMPLATE

In Chapter 1, we talked about code editors and how to set up one. Now, we will start working on our code editor. Open up your code editor and create a folder named Blog Template. Create a file within that folder named index.html.

Now that we have created our folder and file and set everything up, we can get the starter template. To use the starter template, go to Bootstrap's official website (https://getbootstrap.com/) and click on Get started.

You can copy the CSS and JavaScript files separately and place them accordingly, or you can simply copy the starter template. The starter

DOI: 10.1201/9781003309383-3

template contains all the files and includes the essential HTML tags for our ease. You can copy the starter template from the website or copy the following code and paste it into your code editor.

Code

```
<!doctype html>
<html lang="en">
 <head>
  <!-- Required meta tags -->
  <meta charset="utf-8">
  <meta name="viewport" content="width=device-width,
initial-scale=1">
  <!-- Bootstrap CSS -->
  <link href="https://cdn.jsdelivr.net/npm/bootstrap
@5.1.3/dist/css/bootstrap.min.css" rel="stylesheet"
integrity="sha384-1BmE4kWBq78iYhFldvKuhfTAU6auU8tT
94WrHftjDbrCEXSU1oBoqyl2QvZ6jIW3"
crossorigin="anonymous">
  <title>Hello, world!</title>
 </head>
 <body>
  <h1>Hello, world!</h1>
  <!-- Optional JavaScript; choose one of the two! -->
  <!-- Option 1: Bootstrap Bundle with Popper -->
  <script src="https://cdn.jsdelivr.net/npm/
bootstrap@5.1.3/dist/js/bootstrap.bundle.min.js"
integrity="sha384-ka7Sk0Gln4gmtz2MlQnikT1wXgYsOg+O
MhuP+IlRH9sENBO0LRn5q+8nbTov4+1p"
crossorigin="anonymous"></script>
  <!-- Option 2: Separate Popper and Bootstrap JS -->
  <!--
  <script src="https://cdn.jsdelivr.net/npm/@
popperjs/core@2.10.2/dist/umd/popper.min.js" integ
rity="sha384-7+zCNj/IqJ95wo16oMtfsKbZ9ccEh31eOz1HG
yDuCQ6wgnyJNSYdrPa03rtR1zdB"
crossorigin="anonymous"></script>
  <script src="https://cdn.jsdelivr.net/npm/bootstrap
@5.1.3/dist/js/bootstrap.min.js" integrity="sha3
84-QJHtvGhmr9XOIpI6YVutG+2QOK9T+ZnN4kzFN1RtK3zEFEI
sxhlmW15/YESvpZ13" crossorigin="anonymous"></script>
  -->
 </body>
</html>
```

It looks like this after you paste the code into your code editor.

Now, if we save the file and run it, all we would see in our browser is a simple Hello, World! This is because our body tag contains only a heading tag <h1>

## Navbar

Now, we will be creating a navbar for our blog. Start by removing the <h1> tag from our body. It is of no use to us. Copy the navbar template from the link https://getbootstrap.com/docs/5.1/components/navbar/ or copy the following code and paste it in the body tag of your HTML file.

*Code*

```
<nav class="navbar navbar-expand-lg navbar-light
bg-light">
  <div class="container-fluid">
    <a class="navbar-brand" href="#">Navbar</a>
    <button class="navbar-toggler" type="button"
data-bs-toggle="collapse" data-bs-target="#navbarSup
portedContent"
      aria-controls="navbarSupportedContent" aria-
expanded="false" aria-label="Toggle navigation">
      <span class="navbar-toggler-icon"></span>
    </button>
    <div class="collapse navbar-collapse"
id="navbarSupportedContent">
      <ul class="navbar-nav me-auto mb-2 mb-lg-0">
        <li class="nav-item">
          <a class="nav-link active" aria-
current="page" href="#">Home</a>
        </li>
        <li class="nav-item">
          <a class="nav-link" href="#">Link</a>
        </li>
        <li class="nav-item dropdown">
          <a class="nav-link dropdown-toggle"
href="#" id="navbarDropdown" role="button"
            data-bs-toggle="dropdown"
aria-expanded="false">
            Dropdown
          </a>
          <ul class="dropdown-menu"
aria-labelledby="navbarDropdown">
```

```
        <li><a class="dropdown-item"
href="#">Action</a></li>
        <li><a class="dropdown-item"
href="#">Another action</a></li>
        <li>
          <hr class="dropdown-divider">
        </li>
        <li><a class="dropdown-item"
href="#">Something else here</a></li>
      </ul>
    </li>
    <li class="nav-item">
      <a class="nav-link disabled">Disabled</a>
    </li>
  </ul>
  <form class="d-flex">
    <input class="form-control me-2"
type="search" placeholder="Search"
aria-label="Search">
    <button class="btn btn-outline-success"
type="submit">Search</button>
  </form>
  </div>
  </div>
</nav>
```

After pasting the navbar code in the body tag, save your file, and this is what your website would look like in the browser.

There is a lot of excess code with Bootstrap that we do not necessarily need. To customize your Bootstrap website, it is vital to keep the components you need and remove everything else. Let us start by changing the title of your blog. Currently, the title is Hello, World!

*Code*

```
<title>Hello, World!</title>
```

And we will change it to Blog Template:

```
<title>Blog Template</title>
```

Next up, we will change the title of the navbar. For now, it simply says Navbar.

*Code*

```
<a class="navbar-brand" href="#">Navbar</a>
```

We will change the title to Blog Template.

```
<a class="navbar-brand" href="#">Blog Template</a>
```

Remove the search bar by removing the following code from your body tag.

*Code*

```
<form class="d-flex">
        <input class="form-control me-2"
type="search" placeholder="Search"
aria-label="Search">
        <button class="btn btn-outline-success"
type="submit">Search</button>
    </form>
```

Now, we will change the color of our navbar from light to dark.

*Code*

This is what it looks like with light background:

```
<nav class="navbar navbar-expand-lg navbar-light
bg-light">
```

Now, we will change it to dark by using Bootstrap's color codes that we learned in Chapter 1:

```
<nav class="navbar navbar-expand-lg navbar-dark
bg-dark">
```

All of our content is concentrated on the left side of the navbar. We will switch it up by moving the menu bar items to the right. To do that, we will replace the class me-auto in the <ul> tag and add a class called ms-auto (margin-start auto).

*Code*

```
Before: <ul class="navbar-nav me-auto mb-2 mb-lg-0">
After: <ul class="navbar-nav ms-auto mb-2 mb-lg-0">
```

All of our nav-items will move to the right.

We have a couple of extra links here that we do not need, like disabled and the dropdown-menu. We will remove items that we do not need.

Remove the extra menu items by removing the following code.

*Code*

```
<li class="nav-item dropdown">
        <a class="nav-link dropdown-toggle"
href="#" id="navbarDropdown" role="button"
        data-bs-toggle="dropdown"
aria-expanded="false">
        Dropdown
        </a>
        <ul class="dropdown-menu"
aria-labelledby="navbarDropdown">
        <li><a class="dropdown-item"
href="#">Action</a></li>
        <li><a class="dropdown-item"
href="#">Another action</a></li>
        <li>
          <hr class="dropdown-divider">
        </li>
        <li><a class="dropdown-item"
href="#">Something else here</a></li>
        </ul>
        </li>
        <li class="nav-item">
          <a class="nav-link disabled">Disabled</a>
        </li>
```

We removed two <li> tags corresponding to the dropdown-menu and the disabled menu.

We will create a blog template that has four sections: Home, Blog, About, and Contact. We will add these sections to the navbar; to do that, we will copy the link tag and modify it.

*Code*

```
<li class="nav-item">
        <a class="nav-link" href="#">Link</a>
</li>
```

We will copy this <li> tag and paste it two times right underneath it. Now, we will end up having one home menu and three link menu items on our navbar.

Change the link to the actual sections that we need. We will change the link item's name and the href attribute. The href attribute specifies the location of the link. So, we will add # and then the name of our section.

*Code*

```
Before: <li class="nav-item">
         <a class="nav-link" href="#">Link</a>
        </li>
        <li class="nav-item">
         <a class="nav-link" href="#">Link</a>
        </li>
        <li class="nav-item">
         <a class="nav-link" href="#">Link</a>
        </li>
After: <li class="nav-item">
         <a class="nav-link" href="#blog">Blog</a>
        </li>
        <li class="nav-item">
         <a class="nav-link" href="#about">About</a>
        </li>
        <li class="nav-item">
         <a class="nav-link"
href="#contact">Contact</a>
        </li>
```

Since our blog template will be a single-page website, we will remove certain classes that denote the active page within a website. Doing this will ensure that certain menu items are not highlighted over the others on the navbar.

*Code*

```
Before: <a class="nav-link active" aria-
current="page" href="#">Home</a>
After: <a class="nav-link" href="#">Home</a>
```

We will also add a little padding on both the $x$-axis and $y$-axis on our navbar to make it look a little spacious. Now, this is what our final navbar looks like.

Let us move on to our next section.

Home Page

We have finished our navbar. It is time to move on to making our home page for our blog template. Right where our <nav> tag ends, we will start another section. We will use a section tag to divide our page and add a few utilities that we learned about previously.

*Code*

```
<section class="bg-dark text-light p-5 text-center
text-sm-start">
</section>
```

We have added a few classes that are as follows:

- bg-dark – makes the background dark
- text-light – makes the text light in color so that it is visible on our dark background
- p-5 – provides padding of 5 in all directions
- text-center – makes sure the text is in the center of the page
- text-sm-start – makes sure that the text is toward the start of the screen from a smaller screen and above

We will create a <div> tag with a class container in our section tag. All of our section elements are going to be within this container.

*Code*

```
<div class="container">
</div>
```

We will create a flexbox within this container so that every element will become a flex item.

Within our container class created above, we will add the following code:

*Code*

```
<div class="d-sm-flex">
</div>
```

d-md-flex – creates a flex that would hit the breakpoint at small screens. This means that the container would no longer behave as a flexbox on the small screen or lower.

We will also add a few more flex utilities to display the content properly.

*Code*

```
<div class="d-sm-flex align-items-center
justify-content-between">
</div>
```

Now that we have created our flexbox, it is time to make our flex items. Our flexbox will have two main components: a piece of text on the left and an image on the right.

To add images, we first need to create a folder called images in which we will keep all our images and refer to them from there.

Now, we will add our flex items. For the text, we will have a heading tag <h1>, and then the rest of the text would be within a <p> tag.

*Code*

```
<div>
        <h1 class="my-5">Lorem ipsum dolor sit
amet.</h1>
        <p class="lead my-5">Lorem ipsum dolor sit
amet consectetur adipisicing elit. Fugiat fuga
vitae,
        numquam eos iure distinctio facere eum odio
obcaecati! Nesciunt dolor minima porro qui officiis.
        </p>
        <button class="btn btn-primary btn-lg">Read
More</button>
        </div>
```

- my-5 – margin of 5 in the *y*-axis

- lead – makes the text look bigger

- btn – class for a button

- btn-primary – a button of the primary color

- btn-lg – a large-sized button

After adding the text, it is time to add our image. We will be using the <img> tag.

*Code*

```
<img class="img-fluid w-50 d-sm-block d-none"
src="/images/home.svg" alt="a girl on her
computer">
```

- img-fluid – makes the image responsive

- w-50 – reduces the width to 50% of what it was before

- d-sm-block – changes the display to block for screens bigger than the sm breakpoint

- d-none – changes the display to none

*Note:* Adding d-sm-block and d-none would ensure that the image is not displayed on smaller screens or lower than that.

- src – the source of our image. As our image is in the folder images, we have added its path as /images

- alt – alternative text

Our home section is complete now. Here is the full code for it.

*Code*

```
<section class="bg-dark text-light p-5 text-center
text-sm-start">
    <div class="container">
    <div class="d-sm-flex align-items-center
justify-content-between">
        <div>
        <h1 class="my-5">Lorem ipsum dolor sit
amet.</h1>
        <p class="lead my-5">Lorem ipsum dolor sit
amet consectetur adipisicing elit. Fugiat fuga
vitae,
        numquam eos iure distinctio facere eum
odio obcaecati! Nesciunt dolor minima porro qui
officiis.
        </p>
```

```
            <button class="btn btn-primary btn-lg">Read
More</button>
        </div>
        <img class="img-fluid w-50 d-sm-block d-none"
src="/images/home.svg" alt="a girl on her
computer">
        </div>
    </div>
  </section>
```

And this is what our blog will look like after finishing the section.

### Newsletter

As this is a blog template, we will be creating a newsletter section right below our home section.

First off, we will again use the <section> tag to create our newsletter section.

*Code*

```
<section class="bg-primary text-light p-5">
</section>
```

This will create a simple strip of blue color which is also the color code for primary in Bootstrap.

We will add a container to our section that will contain all the elements. We will add another <div> tag that we will turn into a flexbox within this container. This flexbox will turn the items inside into flex containers.

*Code*

```
<div class="container">
    <div class="d-md-flex justify-content-between
align-items-center">
</div>
    </div>
```

Now, it is time to add our content for our newsletter.

*Code*

```
<h3 class="mb-3 mb-md-0">Sign Up For Our
Newletter</h3>
```

We have added a heading tag <h3>.

mb-3 – margin bottom 3

mb-md-0 – margin 0 at breakpoint md

We will add our input group now. You can either check the link https://get-bootstrap.com/docs/5.0/forms/input-group/ or copy the following code.

*Code*

```
<div class="input-group">
        <input type="text" class="form-control"
placeholder="Enter Email">
        <button class="btn btn-dark btn-lg"
type="button">Sign Up</button>
        </div>
```

Since our input group is more prominent now, we will have to customize it. There are no custom classes available within Bootstrap to decrease the size of the input group. So, we will be doing that using CSS.

First, create a stylesheet with the name style.css in the same folder where your index.html file is.

We will then link our newly created stylesheet with our main index.ht ml page. Add the following code right below your Bootstrap CSS file.

*Code*

```
<link rel="stylesheet" href="/style.css">
```

Open up your stylesheet. We will be adding a media query to our stylesheet. Before that, we will have to create a class. We will create a class with the name news-input and add it to our <div> tag.

*Code*

```
<div class="input-group news-input">
```

After creating your class, go to your stylesheet that is your style.css file and the following media queries.

*Code*

```
@media(min-width: 768px){
  .news-input {
    width: 50%;
  }
}
```

The above code will decrease the width to 50% of its original width in screens more giant than 768px, which is the breakpoint for medium screens.

Our newsletter section is complete and here is the final code for it.

*Code*

```
<section class="bg-primary text-light p-5">
    <div class="container">
      <div class="d-md-flex justify-content-between
align-items-center">
        <h3 class="mb-3 mb-md-0">Sign Up For Our
Newletter</h3>
        <div class="input-group news-input">
          <input type="text" class="form-control"
placeholder="Enter Email">
          <button class="btn btn-dark btn-lg"
type="button">Sign Up</button>
        </div>
      </div>
    </div>
  </section>
```

*Note:* Do not forget to link the custom stylesheet with your HTML page.

Blog Section

We will now create our blog section. Add a <section> tag. Within that section, there is going to be a container class. We will be using the grid classes while creating our blog section; to do that, we will create a row class.

*Code*

```
<section class="p-5" id="blog">
<div class="container">
```

```
<div class="row text-center">
</div>
</div>
</section>
```

Now, we will create 3 <div> tags for displaying our three blog posts.

```
<div class="col-md mb-4">
</div>
```

Within this <div> tag, we will use a Bootstrap component called Card. Check out the link https://getbootstrap.com/docs/5.0/components/card/ or copy the following code.

*Code*

```
<div class="col-md mb-4">
        <div class="card bg-dark text-light">
          <div class="card-body text-center">
            <div class="h1 mb-3">
              <i class="bi bi-laptop">
            </div>
            <h3 class="card-title mb-3">
              Lorem
            </h3>
            <p class="card-text">
              Lorem ipsum dolor sit amet consectetur
adipisicing elit. Beatae temporibus excepturi
              voluptatem delectus molestias adipisci?
            </p>
            <a href="#" class="btn btn-primary">
Read More</a>
          </div>
        </div>
      </div>
```

*Note:* We have added icons in the code mentioned above. Add the following link right underneath your Bootstrap CSS stylesheet.

```
<link rel="stylesheet" href="https://cdn.jsdelivr
.net/npm/bootstrap-icons@1.3.0/font/bootstrap-icons
.css">
```

We have successfully created a card displaying our blog post. If we repeat the same code twice, we will get three similar blog post featurettes in a row. Paste the following code or copy the code mentioned above.

*Code*

```html
<div class="col-md mb-4">
        <div class="card bg-dark text-light">
          <div class="card-body text-center">
            <div class="h1 mb-3">
              <i class="bi bi-person-square"></i>
            </div>
            <h3 class="card-title mb-3">
              Ipsum
            </h3>
            <p class="card-text">
              Lorem ipsum dolor sit amet consectetur
adipisicing elit. Beatae temporibus excepturi
                voluptatem delectus molestias adipisci?
            </p>
            <a class="btn btn-primary">Read More</a>
          </div>
        </div>
      </div>
<div class="col-md mb-4">
        <div class="card bg-dark text-light">
          <div class="card-body text-center">
            <div class="h1 mb-3">
              <i class="bi bi-people"></i>
            </div>
            <h3 class="card-title mb-3">
              Dolor
            </h3>
            <p class="card-text">
              Lorem ipsum dolor sit amet consectetur
adipisicing elit. Beatae temporibus excepturi
                voluptatem delectus molestias adipisci?
            </p>
            <a class="btn btn-primary">Read More</a>
          </div>
        </div>
      </div>
```

*Note:* We have changed the card-title and icon for each post. You can customize the posts accordingly.

We will create another row with three cards like the one we made above. We need to copy the same container class that we created above and paste the same. We can then change the card-title and icons in each. Remember, these two rows are part of the same section. Within this section, there are two container classes, and each container has three cards.

*Code*

```
<div class="container">
    <div class="row text-center">
      <div class="col-md mb-4">
        <div class="card bg-dark text-light">
          <div class="card-body text-center">
            <div class="h1 mb-3">
              <i class="bi bi-bootstrap"></i>
            </div>
            <h3 class="card-title mb-3">
              Sit
            </h3>
            <p class="card-text">
              Lorem ipsum dolor sit amet consectetur
adipisicing elit. Beatae temporibus excepturi
              voluptatem delectus molestias adipisci?
            </p>
            <a class="btn btn-primary">Read More</a>
          </div>
        </div>
      </div>
      <div class="col-md mb-4">
        <div class="card bg-dark text-light">
          <div class="card-body text-center">
            <div class="h1 mb-3">
              <i class="bi bi-broadcast"></i>
            </div>
            <h3 class="card-title mb-3">
              Amet
            </h3>
            <p class="card-text">
              Lorem ipsum dolor sit amet consectetur
adipisicing elit. Beatae temporibus excepturi
```

```
            voluptatem delectus molestias
adipisci?
            </p>
            <a class="btn btn-primary">Read More</a>
          </div>
        </div>
      </div>
      <div class="col-md mb-4">
        <div class="card bg-dark text-light">
          <div class="card-body text-center">
            <div class="h1 mb-3">
              <i class="bi bi-files"></i>
            </div>
            <h3 class="card-title mb-3">
              Elis
            </h3>
            <p class="card-text">
            Lorem ipsum dolor sit amet consectetur
adipisicing elit. Beatae temporibus excepturi
            voluptatem delectus molestias adipisci?
            </p>
            <a class="btn btn-primary">Read More</a>
          </div>
        </div>
      </div>
    </div>
  </div>
```

We will create another part of our blog section based on the examples given on Bootstrap's official website. We will change it according to our needs. Check out the link https://getbootstrap.com/docs/5.1/examples/ to see different kinds of examples available.

The rest of our blog section will be divided into parts, and all of it will be within the <main> tag with the class container.

*Code*

```
<main class="container">
</main>
```

Within this main container we will have our different sections. Let us start off with our featured post section.

*Code*

```
<div class="p-4 p-md-5 mb-4 text-white rounded
bg-dark">
    <div class="col-md-6 px-0">
        <h1 class="display-4 fst-italic">Featured
blog post</h1>
        <p class="lead my-3">Lorem ipsum dolor sit amet
consectetur adipisicing elit. Praesentium sunt quam
        illum quaerat impedit atque ad quibusdam
veniam tempora officiis, provident quis sed
similique ut
        quos illo blanditiis odio vero!</p>
        <p class="lead mb-0"><a href="#" class="text-
white fw-bold">Continue reading...</a></p>
    </div>
</div>
```

Next up, we will create two cards with their thumbnail to display a blog post with pictures.

*Code*

```
<div class="row mb-2">
    <div class="col-md-6">
        <div
        class="row g-0 border rounded overflow-
hidden flex-md-row mb-4 shadow-sm h-md-250
position-relative">
            <div class="col p-4 d-flex flex-column
position-static">
                <strong class="d-inline-block mb-2 text-
primary">World</strong>
                <h3 class="mb-0">Blog post</h3>
                <div class="mb-1 text-muted">Nov 12</div>
                <p class="card-text mb-auto">Lorem ipsum
dolor, sit amet consectetur adipisicing elit.
                Consequuntur omnis accusamus quae!
Nostrum similique adipisci odit expedita odio.</p>
                <a href="#" class="stretched-
link">Continue reading</a>
            </div>
            <div class="col-auto d-none d-lg-block">
```

```
            <svg class="bd-placeholder-img"
width="200" height="250" xmlns="http://www.w3.org/
2000/svg"
            role="img" aria-label="Placeholder:
Thumbnail" preserveAspectRatio="xMidYMid slice"
            focusable="false">
            <title>Placeholder</title>
            <rect width="100%" height="100%"
fill="#55595c"></rect><text x="50%" y="50%"
fill="#eceeef"
            dy=".3em">Thumbnail</text>
          </svg>
        </div>
      </div>
    </div>
    <div class="col-md-6">
      <div
        class="row g-0 border rounded overflow-
hidden flex-md-row mb-4 shadow-sm h-md-250
position-relative">
        <div class="col p-4 d-flex flex-column
position-static">
          <strong class="d-inline-block mb-2 text-
success">Design</strong>
          <h3 class="mb-0">Post title</h3>
          <div class="mb-1 text-muted">Nov 11</div>
          <p class="mb-auto">Lorem ipsum dolor sit
amet consectetur adipisicing elit. Quidem ex
          voluptatibus excepturi et quam illo,
natus deleniti in voluptas quibusdam magnam.</p>
          <a href="#" class="stretched-
link">Continue reading</a>
        </div>
        <div class="col-auto d-none d-lg-block">
          <svg class="bd-placeholder-img"
width="200" height="250" xmlns="http://www.w3.org
/2000/svg"
            role="img" aria-label="Placeholder:
Thumbnail" preserveAspectRatio="xMidYMid slice"
            focusable="false">
            <title>Placeholder</title>
```

```
                <rect width="100%" height="100%"
fill="#55595c"></rect><text x="50%" y="50%"
fill="#eceeef"
                dy=".3em">Thumbnail</text>
              </svg>
            </div>
          </div>
        </div>
      </div>
```

Now we will be creating three sample blog posts with sticky navbar to the side. The blog posts will take up 8 column width, and the sticky bar on the side will take up 4 column width. We will use the <article> tag to write blog posts.

First, we will create a row with gutter 5.

*Code*

```
<div class="row g-5">
    <div class="col-md-8">
</div>
</div>
```

The <div> tag with class col-md-8 will contain all the sample blog posts within the <article> tag.

Blog Post 1
*Code*

```
<article class="blog-post">
        <h2 class="blog-post-title">Sample blog
post</h2>
        <p class="blog-post-meta">January 1, 2022
by <a href="#">Someone</a></p>
  <p>
  I love my country</p>
        <p>
  HELLO WORLD
        </p>
        <blockquote class="lead fw-bold">Sub
Heading</blockquote>
        <p>
```

```
Paragarph 1</p>
        <h3>A list</h3>
        <p>
Paragraph 2</p>
        <ul>
          <li>First list item</li>
          <li>Second list item</li>
          <li>Third list item</li>
        </ul>
      </article>
  <hr>
```

## Blog Post 2

*Code*

```
<article class="blog-post">
        <h2 class="blog-post-title">Another blog
post</h2>
        <p class="blog-post-meta">January 10, 2022
by <a href="#">Someone Else</a></p>
        <p>
  Text 1</p>
        <blockquote>
          <p>
Text 2</p>
        </blockquote>
        <p>
  Text 3</p>
        <p>
  Text 3</p>
      </article>
      <hr>
```

## Blog Post 3

*Code*

```
<article class="blog-post">
        <h2 class="blog-post-title">And another
blog post</h2>
        <p class="blog-post-meta">December 23, 2021
by <a href="#">Someone Else</a></p>
      <p>Lorem ipsum dolor sit amet, consectetur
adipisicing elit. Quod dolor sed maiores. Vero, qui
sequi
```

```
        voluptate tempore voluptatum quae sed
molestias eligendi accusamus dignissimos dolores
        veritatis? Totam nisi voluptate iste,
commodi eius ab perspiciatis eligendi culpa eaque
        exercitationem. Cupiditate, consectetur.</p>
        <blockquote>
        <p>Lorem ipsum dolor, sit amet
consectetur adipisicing elit. Deleniti vero delectus
illum
        excepturi eligendi maxime.</p>
        </blockquote>
        <p>Lorem ipsum dolor sit amet consectetur
adipisicing elit. Enim fugiat dolorum eos maxime
rerum
        natus, officiis, nesciunt blanditiis
repellat cum quibusdam. Molestias praesentium
asperiores
        repudiandae, libero commodi error hic ipsa
sunt quasi expedita eius dolorum ex incidunt quidem
        aut consectetur debitis minima nam.
Exercitationem, vel?</p>
        <p>Lorem ipsum dolor sit amet consectetur
adipisicing elit. Incidunt totam, adipisci fuga
dolores
        sapiente non nemo, rem esse voluptatum
officiis nulla eos? Labore modi dignissimos
temporibus
        reprehenderit nemo? Sapiente beatae quo
blanditiis voluptas aut. Quam quibusdam eveniet
amet,
        repellat reiciendis quasi reprehenderit ut
dolor architecto numquam? Necessitatibus eveniet
quam
        unde?</p>
        </article>
```

The end of this blog post marks the end of our sample blog posts. We will close the <div> tag pertaining to the class .col-md-8. After closing this, we will start another <div> tag with the class .col-md-4 that will take up the remaining space on our screen.

We will create three parts within this sticky part: some content, archives, and socials, respectively.

*Code*

```
<div class="col-md-4">
        <div class="position-sticky" style="top:
2rem;">
        </div>
</div>
```

The rest of our parts will go inside the <div> tag with class position-sticky.

## Some Content

*Code*

```
<div class="p-4 mb-3 bg-light rounded">
          <h4 class="fst-italic">Some Content</h4>
          <p class="mb-0">Lorem ipsum dolor, sit
amet consectetur adipisicing elit. Consequuntur
eaque,
          porro pariatur odit dignissimos nulla
saepe ipsa blanditiis assumenda ipsam?</p>
      </div>
```

rounded – create a box with rounded corners
fst-italic – changes the font size to italic
Next part on our sticky sidebar is the archives.
Archives:

*Code*

```
<div class="p-4">
          <h4 class="fst-italic">Archives</h4>
          <ol class="list-unstyled mb-0">
            <li><a href="#">January 2022</a></li>
            <li><a href="#">December 2021</a></li>
            <li><a href="#">November 2021</a></li>
            <li><a href="#">October 2021</a></li>
            <li><a href="#">September 2021</a></li>
            <li><a href="#">August 2021</a></li>
            <li><a href="#">July 2021</a></li>
            <li><a href="#">June 2021</a></li>
            <li><a href="#">May 2021</a></li>
            <li><a href="#">April 2021</a></li>
            <li><a href="#">March 2021</a></li>
```

```
            <li><a href="#">February 2021</a></li>
          </ol>
        </div>
```

list-unstyled – creates an ordered list without any numbering

The last element on our sticky sidebar is socials.

Socials:

*Code*

```
<div class="p-4">
        <h4 class="fst-italic">Socials</h4>
        <ol class="list-unstyled">
          <li><a href="#">Instagram</a></li>
          <li><a href="#">Twitter</a></li>
          <li><a href="#">Facebook</a></li>
          <li><a href="#">YouTube</a></li>
        </ol>
      </div>
```

This marks the end of our main section, which included our three sample blog posts and a sticky bar on the side that contains space for some content, archives, and socials.

Now, we will move toward our about section.

## About Section

The about section usually contains info about the creators of the content hosted on the website. We will have an illustrated image toward our left side and some dummy text on the right side for this section. At the end, there would be a button.

We will start off by creating a section and give class names so as to provide margin and padding to the section.

*Code*

```
<section id="about" class="p-5 mt-5">
</section>
```

Within this section, we will create a container class, and within that class, we will have another <div> tag to create a flexbox.

*Code*

```
<div class="container">
   <div class="row align-items-center
justify-content-between">
</div>
   </div>
```

We have created our flexbox. It will have two flex items inside it: one is the image, and the other is the text. Let us start with our image class.

*Code*

```
<div class="col-md">
        <img src="/images/about.svg" class="img-
fluid d-sm-block d-none" alt="about-us">
      </div>
```

The second flex item is our text. There are four <p> tags within our text: a heading, two paragraphs, and a button at the end.

*Code*

```
<div class="col-md p-5">
        <h2>About Us</h2>
        <p class="lead">Lorem ipsum dolor sit amet
consectetur adipisicing elit. Omnis fugiat quod
eligendi
          modi delectus sint!</p>
        <p>Lorem ipsum dolor sit amet, consectetur
adipisicing elit. Sit molestiae id reprehenderit,
nostrum
          possimus aliquid doloremque numquam, iusto
enim sed facere repellat quam quo accusantium dicta
          incidunt veritatis illum! Et!</p>
        <a class="btn btn-light mt-3">
          <i class="bi bi-chevron-right"></i>
          Read More
        </a>
      </div>
```

Here is the complete code of the about section.

*Code*

```
<section id="about" class="p-5 mt-5">
    <div class="container">
      <div class="row align-items-center
justify-content-between">
        <div class="col-md">
          <img src="/images/about.svg" class="img-
fluid d-sm-block d-none" alt="about-us">
        </div>
        <div class="col-md p-5">
          <h2>About Us</h2>
          <p class="lead">Lorem ipsum dolor sit amet
consectetur adipisicing elit. Omnis fugiat quod
eligendi
            modi delectus sint!</p>
          <p>Lorem ipsum dolor sit amet, consectetur
adipisicing elit. Sit molestiae id reprehenderit,
nostrum
            possimus aliquid doloremque numquam, iusto
enim sed facere repellat quam quo accusantium dicta
            incidunt veritatis illum! Et!</p>
          <a class="btn btn-light mt-3">
            <i class="bi bi-chevron-right"></i>
            Read More
          </a>
        </div>
      </div>
    </div>
  </section>
```

Now, we will move toward our contact section.

## Contact Section

The contact section would follow a similar pattern to the about section. It will have an image on the right and a form on the left. We will create a <section> tag, add a container class, and create a flexbox within.

*Code*

```
<section class="p-5" id="contact">
    <div class="container">
      <div class="row align-items-center
justify-content-between">
```

In order to add a form, you can copy the following code or check out the Bootstrap component for forms on their website: https://getbootstrap.com/docs/5.1/forms/overview/

*Code*

```
<div class="col-md">
        <h2 class="text-center mb-4">Contact Us</h2>
        <form>
          <div class="mb-3">
            <label for="exampleInputEmail1"
class="form-label">Name</label>
            <input type="email" class="form-control"
id="exampleInputEmail1"
              aria-describedby="emailHelp">
          </div>
          <div class="mb-3">
            <label for="exampleInputEmail1"
class="form-label">Email address</label>
            <input type="email" class="form-control"
id="exampleInputEmail1"
              aria-describedby="emailHelp">
          </div>
          <div class="mb-3">
            <label for="exampleInputEmail1"
class="form-label">Enter your message</label>
            <textarea class="form-control" name=""
id="" cols="90" rows="7"></textarea>
          </div>
          <button type="submit" class="btn
btn-primary">Submit</button>
        </form>
      </div>
```

Let us add the image now.

*Code*

```
<div class="col-md">
        <img src="/images/contact.svg" class=
"img-fluid d-sm-block d-none" alt="contact-us">
      </div>
```

Our contact section is complete. Here is the complete code for it.

*Code*

```
<section class="p-5" id="contact">
    <div class="container">
      <div class="row align-items-center
justify-content-between">
              <div class="col-md">
          <h2 class="text-center mb-4">Contact Us</h2>
          <form>
            <div class="mb-3">
              <label for="exampleInputEmail1"
class="form-label">Name</label>
              <input type="email" class="form-control"
id="exampleInputEmail1"
                aria-describedby="emailHelp">
            </div>
            <div class="mb-3">
              <label for="exampleInputEmail1"
class="form-label">Email address</label>
              <input type="email" class="form-control"
id="exampleInputEmail1"
                aria-describedby="emailHelp">
            </div>
            <div class="mb-3">
              <label for="exampleInputEmail1"
class="form-label">Enter your message</label>
              <textarea class="form-control" name=""
id="" cols="90" rows="7"></textarea>
            </div>
            <button type="submit" class="btn btn-
primary">Submit</button>
          </form>
        </div>
        <div class="col-md">
          <img src="/images/contact.svg" class="img-
fluid d-sm-block d-none" alt="contact-us">
        </div>
      </div>
    </div>
  </section>
```

Footer

We will create a footer that will have the copyright and an arrow that will take us straight to the top.

*Code*

```
<footer class="p-5 bg-dark text-white text-center
position-relative">
   <div class="container">
      <p class="lead">Copyright &copy; 2022 Blog
template</p>
      <a href="#" class="position-absolute bottom-0
end-0 p-5">
         <i class="bi bi-arrow-up-circle h1"></i>
      </a>
   </div>
</footer>
```

## CREATING A PORTFOLIO TEMPLATE

We will be creating a portfolio template by first creating a folder with the name "portfolio" and then opening up that folder in your code editor. Create another folder within your existing folder with the name of "images". We will be keeping all our images in that folder. Now we will create a file named index.html; here, we will be writing our code.

Now that we have created our folder and file and set everything up, we can get the starter template. To use the starter template, go to Bootstrap's official website https://getbootstrap.com/ and click on Get started.

From here on, you can either copy the starter template or place the CSS and JS files accordingly.

*Code*

```
<!DOCTYPE html>
<html lang="en">
<head>
  <meta charset="UTF-8">
  <meta http-equiv="X-UA-Compatible"
content="IE=edge">
  <meta name="viewport" content="width=device-width,
initial-scale=1.0">
  <title>Portfolio</title>
  <!-- Bootstrap CSS -->
  <link href="https://cdn.jsdelivr.net/npm/bootstrap
@5.1.3/dist/css/bootstrap.min.css" rel="stylesheet"
    integrity="sha384-1BmE4kWBq78iYhFldvKuhfTAU6a
uU8tT94WrHftjDbrCEXSU1oBoqyl2QvZ6jIW3"
crossorigin="anonymous">
</head>
```

```
<body>
  <!-- Bootstrap JS and Popper Bundle -->
  <script src="https://cdn.jsdelivr.net/npm/
bootstrap@5.1.3/dist/js/bootstrap.bundle.min.js"
    integrity="sha384-ka7Sk0Gln4gmtz2MlQnikT1wXgY
sOg+OMhuP+IlRH9sENBO0LRn5q+8nbTov4+1p"
    crossorigin="anonymous">
  </script>
</body>
</html>
```

*Note:* We will be using a separate CDN for our icons. You can get the CDN link from https://cdnjs.com/libraries/font-awesome, or you can paste the following code right below your Bootstrap CSS in the <head> tag.

*Code*

```
<!-- Font Awesome CDN -->
  <link rel="stylesheet" href="https://cdnjs.
cloudflare.com/ajax/libs/font-awesome/6.0.0-beta3/
css/all.min.css"
    integrity="sha512-Fo3rlrZj/k7ujTnHg4CGR2D7kSs0v
4LLanw2qksYuRlEz0+tcaEPQogQ0KaoGN26/zrn20ImR1DfuLW
nOo7aBA=="
    crossorigin="anonymous" referrerpolicy="no-
referrer" />
```

Navbar

You can copy the navbar code from https://getbootstrap.com/docs/5.1/ components/navbar/, or you can use the following code.

*Code*

```
<!-- navbar starts here -->
  <nav class="navbar navbar-light bg-light
shadow-sm">
    <div class="container-lg">
      <a class="navbar-brand text-primary fw-bold
fs-4" href="#">Portfolio</a>
      <div class="dropdown">
        <button class="btn btn-primary px-3"
type="button" id="dropdownMenuButton1"
data-bs-toggle="dropdown"
          aria-expanded="false">
```

```
    <i class="fas fa-bars"></i>
  </button>
  <ul class="dropdown-menu dropdown-menu-end"
aria-labelledby="dropdownMenuButton1">
    <li><a class="dropdown-item"
href="#home">Home</a></li>
    <li><a class="dropdown-item"
href="#about">About</a></li>
        <li><a class="dropdown-item" href=
"#portfolio">Portfolio</a></li>
    <li><a class="dropdown-item"
href="#contact">Contact</a></li>
    </ul>
  </div>
 </div>
</nav>
<!-- navbar ends here -->
```

## Home Section

Our home section is going to have two sections: one section will be the text, and the other will be an image.

*Code*

```
<!-- home section starts here -->
  <section id="home" class="home py-5">
    <div class="container-lg">
      <div class="row min-vh-100 align-items-center
align-content-center">
        <div class="col-md-6 mt-5 mt-md-0">
          <div class="home-img text-center">
            <img src="/images/Personal site-cuate.
svg" alt="profile image">
          </div>
        </div>
        <div class="col-md-6 mt-5 mt-md-0
order-md-first">
          <div class="home-text">
            <p class="text-muted mb-1">Hello, I'm a</p>
            <h1 class="text-primary text-uppercase
fs-1 fw-bold">Web Designer</h1>
            <h2 class="fs-4">Jhon Smith</h2>
```

```
        <p class="mt-4 text-muted">Lorem ipsum
dolor sit amet consectetur adipisicing elit. Facilis
ea modi saepe? Commodi sunt obcaecati dolor dolorum
vero quae facere voluptates, incidunt, tempore qui
nisi.</p>
        <a href="#portfolio" class="btn btn-
primary px-3 mt-3">My Work</a>
      </div>
    </div>
    </div>
  </div>
 </section>
  <!-- home section ends here -->
```

## About Section

We would use Bootstrap's progress bar component to describe our skills in this section. We would also have our socials and a *Download CV* button.

*Code*

```
<!-- about section starts here -->
 <section class="about py-5" id="about">
  <div class="container-lg py-4">
   <div class="row justify-content-center">
    <div class="col-lg-8">
     <div class="section-title text-center">
      <h2 class="fw-bold mb-5">About Me</h2>
     </div>
    </div>
   </div>
   <div class="row">
    <div class="col-md-6">
     <div class="about-text">
      <h3 class="fs-4 mb-3">Lorem ipsum, dolor sit
amet consectetur adipisicing elit</h3>
      <p class="text-muted">Lorem ipsum dolor, sit
amet consectetur adipisicing elit. Reprehenderit
odit ratione
        quidem dolore amet, dolorem fugiat rerum
delectus vitae, illum optio quos autem, sint
corrupti. Lorem
        ipsum dolor sit amet consectetur adipisicing
elit. In nisi non excepturi quidem explicabo
quaerat?</p>
```

```
    </div>
    <div class="row text-center text-uppercase my-3">
     <div class="col-sm-4">
      <div>
       <h4 class="fs-1 fw-bold">x</h4>
       <p class="text-muted">Projects</p>
      </div>
     </div>
     <div class="col-sm-4">
      <div>
       <h4 class="fs-1 fw-bold">y</h4>
       <p class="text-muted">Clients</p>
      </div>
     </div>
     <div class="col-sm-4">
      <div>
       <h4 class="fs-1 fw-bold">z</h4>
       <p class="text-muted">Reviews</p>
      </div>
     </div>
    </div>
    <div class="row">
     <div class="col-lg-12 d-flex
align-items-center">
      <a href="#" class="btn btn-primary me-5
px-3">Download CV</a>
      <div class="socials">
       <a href="#" class="text-dark me-2">
<i class="fab fa-linkedin"></i></a>
       <a href="#" class="text-dark me-2">
<i class="fab fa-github"></i></a>
       <a href="#" class="text-dark me-2">
<i class="fab fa-twitter"></i></a>
       <a href="#" class="text-dark me-2">
<i class="fab fa-instagram-square"></i></a>
      </div>
     </div>
    </div>
   </div>
   <div class="col-md-6 mt-5 mt-md-0">
    <div class="skills mb-4">
     <h3 class="fs-6">Skill 1</h3>
     <div class="progress" style="height: 5px;">
```

```
      <div class="progress-bar bg-primary"
role="progressbar" style="width: 25%;" aria-
valuenow="25" aria-valuemin="0" aria-
valuemax="100"></div>
    </div>
  </div>
  <div class="skills mb-4">
   <h3 class="fs-6">Skill 2</h3>
   <div class="progress" style="height: 5px;">
     <div class="progress-bar bg-primary"
role="progressbar" style="width: 50%;" aria-
valuenow="50" aria-valuemin="0" aria-
valuemax="100"></div>
    </div>
  </div>
  <div class="skills mb-4">
   <h3 class="fs-6">Skill 3</h3>
   <div class="progress" style="height: 5px;">
     <div class="progress-bar bg-primary"
role="progressbar" style="width: 75%;" aria-
valuenow="75" aria-valuemin="0" aria-
valuemax="100"></div>
    </div>
  </div>
  <div class="skills">
   <h3 class="fs-6">Skill 4</h3>
   <div class="progress" style="height: 5px;">
     <div class="progress-bar bg-primary"
role="progressbar" style="width: 100%;" aria-
valuenow="100" aria-valuemin="0" aria-
valuemax="100"></div>
    </div>
   </div>
  </div>
 </div>
</div>
</section>
<!-- about section ends here -->
```

Portfolio Section

The portfolio section is used to display the projects undertaken by the developer. You can add your project images and link them to show a live demo to whoever is visiting your website.

*Code*

```
<!-- portfolio section starts here -->
 <section class="portfolio py-5" id="portfolio">
  <div class="container-lg py-4">
   <div class="row justify-content-center">
    <div class="col-lg-8">
     <div class="section-title text-center">
      <h2 class="fw-bold mb-5">Latest Works</h2>
     </div>
    </div>
   </div>
   <div class="row">
    <div class="col-md-6 col-lg-4">
     <div class="portfolio-item">
      <img src="/images/project.jpg" class="w-100
img-thumbnail" alt="">
      <h3 class="text-capitalize fs- my-2">dolor
sit</h3>
      <p class="mb-4"><a class="text-primary text-
decoration-none" href="#">Live Demo</a></p>
     </div>
    </div>
    <div class="col-md-6 col-lg-4">
     <div class="portfolio-item">
      <img src="/images/project.jpg" class="w-100
img-thumbnail" alt="">
      <h3 class="text-capitalize fs- my-2">amet
ilis</h3>
      <p class="mb-4"><a class="text-primary text-
decoration-none" href="#">Live Demo</a></p>
     </div>
    </div>
    <div class="col-md-6 col-lg-4">
     <div class="portfolio-item">
      <img src="/images/project.jpg" class="w-100
img-thumbnail" alt="">
      <h3 class="text-capitalize fs- my-2">elis
cconsect</h3>
      <p class="mb-4"><a class="text-primary text-
decoration-none" href="#">Live Demo</a></p>
     </div>
    </div>
```

```
    <div class="col-md-6 col-lg-4">
      <div class="portfolio-item">
      <img src="/images/project3.jpg" class="w-100
img-thumbnail" alt="">
        <h3 class="text-capitalize fs- my-2">mdian
garced</h3>
        <p class="mb-4"><a class="text-primary text-
decoration-none" href="#">Live Demo</a></p>
      </div>
      </div>
      <div class="col-md-6 col-lg-4">
        <div class="portfolio-item">
        <img src="/images/project3.jpg" class="w-100
img-thumbnail" alt="">
          <h3 class="text-capitalize fs- my-2">lorem
ipsum</h3>
          <p class="mb-4"><a class="text-primary text-
decoration-none" href="#">Live Demo</a></p>
        </div>
        </div>
        <div class="col-md-6 col-lg-4">
          <div class="portfolio-item">
          <img src="/images/project3.jpg" class="w-100
img-thumbnail" alt="">
            <h3 class="text-capitalize fs- my-2">poratsio
wericb</h3>
            <p class="mb-4"><a class="text-primary text-
decoration-none" href="#">Live Demo</a></p>
          </div>
          </div>
        </div>
      </div>
    </section>
    <!-- portfolio section ends here -->
```

## Contact Section

The contact section will contain all the contact details of the developer.
It will also contain a form that you can send a message to the developer.

*Code*

```
<!-- contact section starts here -->
  <section class="contact py-5" id="contact">
```

```
<div class="container-lg py-4">
 <div class="row justify-content-center">
  <div class="col-lg-8">
   <div class="section-title text-center">
    <h2 class="fw-bold mb-5">Contact Me</h2>
   </div>
  </div>
 </div>
 <div class="row">
  <div class="col-md-5">
   <div class="contact-item d-flex mb-3">
    <div class="icon fs-4 text-primary">
     <i class="fas fa-envelope"></i>
    </div>
    <div class="text ms-3">
     <h3 class="fs-5">Email</h3>
     <p class="text-muted">example@gmail.com</p>
    </div>
   </div>
   <div class="contact-item d-flex mb-3">
    <div class="icon fs-4 text-primary">
     <i class="fas fa-phone"></i>
    </div>
    <div class="text ms-3">
     <h3 class="fs-5">Phone</h3>
     <p class="text-muted">+91 9876 543 210</p>
    </div>
   </div>
   <div class="contact-item d-flex">
    <div class="icon fs-4 text-primary">
     <i class="fas fa-map-marker-alt"></i>
    </div>
    <div class="text ms-3">
     <h3 class="fs-5">Location</h3>
     <p class="text-muted">101 Street,
City - 001245</p>
    </div>
   </div>
  </div>
  <div class="col-md-7">
   <div class="contact-form">
    <form>
     <div class="row">
```

```
        <div class="col-lg-6 mb-4">
         <input type="text" placeholder="Your Name"
class="form-control form-control-lg fs-6 border-0
shadow-sm">
        </div>
        <div class="col-lg-6 mb-4">
         <input type="text" placeholder="Your Email"
class="form-control form-control-lg fs-6 border-0
shadow-sm">
        </div>
       </div>
       <div class="row">
        <div class="col-lg-12 mb-4">
         <input type="text" placeholder="Subject"
class="form-control form-control-lg fs-6 border-0
shadow-sm">
        </div>
       </div>
       <div class="row">
        <div class="col-lg-12 mb-4">
         <textarea rows="5" placeholder="Your
Message" class="form-control form-control-lg fs-6
border-0 shadow-sm">
         </textarea>
        </div>
       </div>
       <div class="row">
        <div class="col-lg-12">
         <button type="submit" class="btn btn-primary
px-3">Send Message</button>
        </div>
       </div>
      </form>
     </div>
    </div>
   </div>
  </section>
  <!-- contact section ends here -->
```

## Footer Section

Lastly, we have our footer section, which contains the copyright details about the website and its contents.

*Code*

```
<!-- footer section starts here -->
 <footer class="bg-dark footer border-top py-4">
  <div class="container-lg">
   <div class="row">
    <div class="col-lg-12">
     <p class="m-0 text-center text-muted">Copyright
&copy; 2022 Portfolio Template</p>
    </div>
   </div>
  </div>
 </footer>
 <!-- footer section ends here -->
```

## MOBILE-FRIENDLY DESIGN

Mobile phones are everywhere. Every other person has a mobile phone these days. Everyone is constantly accessing the internet for communicating, learning new information, and much more. Mobile phones have created an easy and accessible way to stay connected with the world when you are on the go. There are many countries where mobile users are way more than the number of users who access the internet using a personal computer or a laptop. When there are so many mobile users across the globe, it becomes necessary to create a website that works well on mobile devices to increase your reach.

To increase the number of unique visitors to your website, it is essential to have a website that works well on mobile phones. Considering the number of mobile users in the world today, there would be a lot of users who would be visiting the site using a mobile device. Failing to create a mobile-friendly design will result in a decrease of unique visitors from those devices, which will, in turn, decrease the overall reach of the website. A mobile-friendly design is customized according to the mobile devices so that the content of the website is displayed in an optimal way to the user.

The success and popularity of any website depend on how high it can rank on the Google Search Algorithm. Around 2018, Google changed its previous policies regarding search and came up with a new version of its search algorithm. Google specifically built this version for mobile searches, and it was called mobile-first indexing. With the onset of this version, Google changed how it used to rank websites. Before this new search algorithm, Google used methods like crawling and indexing to create its ranking systems. This system would look for content relevant to the search based on the desktop version of the website. Now, with mobile-first indexing, Google ranks its websites based on how mobile-friendly they are and how well they display content on mobile devices.

This change in search algorithm created a massive difference because your website would not even show up in searches done from mobile phones or tablets if Google did not think it was mobile-friendly to display. The ranking of any page in Google Searches depends on various factors, but being mobile-friendly remains a primary factor. Creating a mobile-friendly website is the essential requirement for a mobile-friendly design.

## TYPES OF MOBILE-FRIENDLY DESIGN

There are two types of mobile-friendly designs:

1. Responsive

2. Adaptive

When a website is responsively designed, the components would expand and shrink based on the user's screen size. The design will be fluid and transform itself depending on the user's needs.

Adaptive design is more like having two different websites. It is also called progressive enhancement. In adaptive design, there are two different versions of the same website: one is designed for mobile screens, and the other is designed for laptops and desktops.

### Responsive Design

In a website with responsive design, the website's layout would grow or shrink based on the screen resolution. Whether it is the text or the images, the content will grow and shrink to adapt itself to the space available. The same applies to all the elements as well. They will also grow and shrink respectively with the screen size.

### Advantages

- **Decrease in development time:** You do not need to develop multiple sites, significantly reducing development time. You only need to create one website that will fit various devices rather than make multiple websites according to different devices.

- **Reduces maintenance:** Responsive websites are comparatively less complex than adaptive websites. Even if you have to change, you need to only change in one place. With adaptive designs, you need to make multiple changes.

- **Recommended by Google:** For search engine ranking, Google recommends the responsive design pattern.

- **Works better with medium screens:** Adaptive design has only two versions – one for mobile and one for desktop. Devices with medium screens such as tablets or an iPad get left out and receive a mobile version that may or may not fit well. That is not an issue with responsive design, as it will automatically shift based on the screen resolution.

### Disadvantages

- **Expensive:** Creating a responsive design is more costly compared to an adaptive design. That is because the responsive design requires additional work. However, after its completion, the maintenance cost is low. This results in an overall long-term saving in the development of any website.

- **Redesign:** If you suddenly choose to make your website responsive, you might need to redesign your whole website so that the layout remains functional on a mobile device. You cannot simply add a mobile template. However, a long-term benefit is creating a consistent user experience, and both your mobile and desktop sites will look great.

### Adaptive Design

Opting for an adaptive design feels like having two different websites. One of them would work well on your phone, and the other would be for your desktop. Facebook is one of the prime examples of an adaptive design. In an adaptive design, JavaScript and other elements are used to know what kind of device you are on, and then the server will serve the type of website corresponding to the user's screen resolution.

### Advantages

- Mobile sites are usually kept lighter so that they load faster. Since you need to build two different designs, you can leave out the resource-intensive components like logos, images, etc., for your mobile site. Doing this will ensure that the mobile site is faster, lighter, and comprises only the essential components.

- You can create different versions and improve upon your existing mobile version without making any changes to your desktop site.

- You can also let the users choose which site they would like to access by providing them with a link to your desktop site.

- The design can be custom-made for mobile users keeping their preferences in mind. With responsive design, you have to create a one size fits all approach; but with adaptive design, you can change depending on what works better and for which version.

*Disadvantages*

- It takes longer to develop a website using an adaptive design because you have to design two websites: one for the mobile and one for the desktop. And in some cases, you choose a different layout and template for both; then, it might take even longer. In a way, it is like developing two websites that would take longer.

- Adaptive design is usually more complex compared to responsive. Even the maintenance required is more adaptive because if you decide to make a change, you have to change it in two different places instead of one.

- Adaptive designs only cater to two types of users – desktop and mobile. This leaves the users with medium-sized screens, tablets, and iPad users. They will see one of the versions: either mobile or desktop. None of it was designed explicitly for its resolution.

## CHAPTER SUMMARY

In this chapter, we learned how to create a template from scratch. We used different classes of Bootstrap that we had learned about in the previous chapter. We also learned about mobile-friendly design and its types and the advantages disadvantages of each type. In the next chapter, we will create another template and dive deeper into creating a better user experience.

## CHAPTER 4

# Creating Admin Panels

## IN THIS CHAPTER

➢ Designing an Admin Panel

➢ Creating a Backend UI

➢ Difference between UI and UX

In the previous chapter, we created a blog and a resume template. We also created a blog template and a portfolio template. We learned about mobile-friendly design and its types with their advantages and disadvantages. In this chapter, we will learn how to design an admin panel. We will discuss the user interface and the user experience in-depth and why it is so important.

## CREATING AN ADMIN PANEL IN BOOTSTRAP

We will create an "admin panel" folder as we did in the previous chapter. Open up this folder in your code editor. Create two files within that folder named "index.html" and "style.css."

Copy the starter template from Bootstrap's official website or paste the following code.

DOI: 10.1201/9781003309383-4

Code

```
<!DOCTYPE html>
<html lang="en">
<head>
  <meta charset="UTF-8">
  <meta http-equiv="X-UA-Compatible"
content="IE=edge">
  <meta name="viewport" content="width=device-width,
initial-scale=1.0">
  <title>Admin Panel</title>
  <!-- Bootstrap's CSS -->
  <link href="https://cdn.jsdelivr.net/npm/bootstrap
@5.1.3/dist/css/bootstrap.min.css" rel="stylesheet"
    integrity="sha384-1BmE4kWBq78iYhFldvKuhfTAU6au
U8tT94WrHftjDbrCEXSU1oBoqyl2QvZ6jIW3"
crossorigin="anonymous">
  <!-- Bootstrap Icons -->
  <link rel="stylesheet" href="https://cdn.jsdelivr.net/
npm/bootstrap-icons@1.7.2/font/bootstrap-icons.css">
  <!-- Custom Stylesheet -->
  <link rel="stylesheet" href="/style.css">
</head>
<body>
<!-- Bootstrap's JS and Popper Bundle -->
  <script src="https://cdn.jsdelivr.net/npm/
bootstrap@5.1.3/dist/js/bootstrap.bundle.min.js"
    integrity="sha384-ka7Sk0Gln4gmtz2MlQnikT1wXgYs
Og+OMhuP+IlRH9sENBO0LRn5q+8nbTov4+1p"
    crossorigin="anonymous"></script>
</body>
</html>
```

We have also included our custom stylesheet and the link to Bootstrap icons in the <head> tag in the code above.

Here is the link for Bootstrap icons:

Code

```
<!-- Bootstrap Icons -->
  <link rel="stylesheet" href="https://cdn.jsdelivr.net/
npm/bootstrap-icons@1.7.2/font/bootstrap-icons.css">
```

Paste this right below Bootstrap's stylesheet.

## Navbar

After setting everything up, we can create our navbar. We will have two navbars within our admin panel. One would be horizontal, and the other would be vertical. A vertical navbar is also called an offcanvas component in Bootstrap.

### Horizontal Navbar

We are going to add mainly three components to our horizontal navbar. One of them is the name; second, there will be a search bar; and lastly, there will be a dropdown menu. You can copy the navbar component from https://getbootstrap.com/docs/5.1/components/navbar/ and customize it, or you can copy the following code:

## Code

```
<!-- navbar starts here -->
  <nav class="navbar navbar-expand-lg navbar-dark
bg-dark">
    <div class="container-fluid">
      <a class="navbar-brand fw-bold text-uppercase"
href="#">Admin Panel</a>
      <button class="navbar-toggler" type="button"
data-bs-toggle="collapse"
        data-bs-target="#navbarSupportedContent"
aria-controls="navbarSupportedContent"
aria-expanded="false"
        aria-label="Toggle navigation">
        <span class="navbar-toggler-icon"></span>
      </button>
      <div class="collapse navbar-collapse"
id="navbarSupportedContent">
        <form class="d-flex ms-auto">
          <div class="input-group">
            <input type="text" class="form-control"
placeholder="Search" aria-label="Search"
              aria-describedby="button-addon2">
            <button class="btn btn-primary"
type="button" id="button-addon2">
              <i class="bi bi-search">
            </button>
          </div>
        </form>
```

```
      <ul class="navbar-nav mb-2 mb-lg-0">
        <li class="nav-item dropdown">
          <a class="nav-link dropdown-toggle"
 href="#" id="navbarDropdown" role="button"
          data-bs-toggle="dropdown"
 aria-expanded="false">
            <i class="bi bi-person-fill"></i>
          </a>
          <ul class="dropdown-menu dropdown-menu-
 end" aria-labelledby="navbarDropdown">
            <li><a class="dropdown-item"
 href="#">Action</a></li>
            <li><a class="dropdown-item"
 href="#">Another action</a></li>
            <li>
              <hr class="dropdown-divider">
            </li>
            <li><a class="dropdown-item"
 href="#">Something else here</a></li>
          </ul>
        </li>
      </ul>
    </div>
  </div>
</nav>
<!-- navbar ends here -->
```

*Note:* You can use icons of your own choice from Bootstrap here – https://
icons.getbootstrap.com/

*Vertical Navbar*

Now we will create a vertical navbar, also called offcanvas in Bootstrap.
Our vertical navbar is going to be a sticky navbar. As the offcanvas component generally tends to get activated using a button, we need to add
some custom CSS to modify it according to our needs.

Check out the offcanvas component here: https://getbootstrap.com/
docs/5.1/components/offcanvas/

Code

```
<!-- sidebar starts here -->
  <div class="offcanvas offcanvas-start bg-dark
text-white sidebar-nav" tabindex="-1"
id="offcanvasExample"
```

```
        aria-labelledby="offcanvasExampleLabel">
        <div class="offcanvas-body p-0">
          <nav class="navbar-dark">
            <ul class="navbar-nav">
              <li>
                <div class="text-muted small fw-bold
text-uppercase px-3">
                  Admin
                </div>
              </li>
              <li>
                <a href="#" class="nav-link px-3 active">
                  <span class="me-2">
                    <i class="bi bi-speedometer2"></i>
                  </span>
                  <span>Dashboard</span>
                </a>
              </li>
              <li class="my-4">
                <hr class="dropdown-divider">
              </li>
              <li>
                <div class="text-muted small fw-bold
text-uppercase px-3">
                  Interface
                </div>
              </li>
              <li>
                <a class="nav-link px-3 sidebar-link"
data-bs-toggle="collapse" href="#collapseExample"
role="button"
                  aria-expanded="false"
aria-controls="collapseExample">
                  <span class="me-2">
                    <i class="bi bi-layout-split"></i>
                  </span>
                  <span>Layouts</span>
                  <span class="right-icon ms-auto">
                    <i class="bi bi-chevron-down"></i>
                  </span>
                </a>
                <div class="collapse" id="collapseExample">
                  <div>
                    <ul class="navbar-nav ps-3">
```

```
          <li>
            <a href="#" class="nav-link px-3">
              <span class="me-2">
              <i class="bi bi-layout-split"></i>
              </span>
              <span>Layouts</span>
            </a>
          </li>
        </ul>
      </div>
    </div>
  </li>
</ul>
</nav>
</div>
</div>
<!-- sidebar ends here -->
```

For our sidebar component to be sticky, we need to add custom CSS.

Code

```
:root {
--offcanvas-width: 270px;
--topNavbar: 56px;
}
.sidebar-nav {
width: var(--offcanvas-width);
}
.sidebar-link {
display: flex;
align-items: center;
}
.sidebar-link .right-icon {
display: inline-flex;
transition: all ease 0.25s;
}
.sidebar-link[aria-expanded="true"] .right-icon {
transform: rotate(180deg);
}
@media (min-width: 992px){
 body {
  overflow: auto !important;
 }
```

```
.offcanvas-backdrop::before {
display: none;
}
main {
margin-left: var(--offcanvas-width);
}
.sidebar-nav {
transform: none;
visibility: visible !important;
top: var(--topNavbar);
height: calc(100% - var(--topNavbar));
}
}
```

*Note:* We need to create an offcanvas trigger so that our sidebar works appropriately on small devices. The following code would be used right after the container fluid class in the navbar. This would create a navbar toggle icon for the sidebar in devices with low screen resolution.

Code

```
<!-- offcanvas trigger -->
    <button class="navbar-toggler" type="button"
data-bs-toggle="offcanvas"
data-bs-target="#offcanvasExample"
     aria-controls="offcanvasExample">
     <span class="navbar-toggler-icon" data-bs-ta
rget="#offcanvasExample"></span>
     </button>
     <!-- offcanvas trigger -->
```

Main Section

The main section contains our dashboard and all our required elements for working on an admin panel.

Code

```
<!-- main content starts here -->
  <main class="mt-5 pt-3">
    <div class="container-fluid">
      <div class="row">
        <div class="col-md-12 fw-bold fs-3">
         Dashboard
        </div>
```

```
      </div>
      <div class="row">
        <div class="col-md-3 mb-3">
          <div class="card text-dark bg-light h-100">
            <div class="card-header">Customers</div>
            <div class="card-body">
              <h5 class="card-title">Card title</h5>
              <p class="card-text">
Text 1.</p>
            </div>
          </div>
        </div>
        <div class="col-md-3 mb-3">
          <div class="card text-dark bg-light h-100">
            <div class="card-header">Revenue</div>
            <div class="card-body">
              <h5 class="card-title">Card title</h5>
              <p class="card-text">,sit amet
consectetur adipisicing elit. Natus amet
              consectetur optio!</p>
            </div>
          </div>
        </div>
        <div class="col-md-3 mb-3">
          <div class="card text-dark bg-light h-100">
            <div class="card-header">Purchases</div>
            <div class="card-body">
              <h5 class="card-title">Card title</h5>
              <p class="card-text">Lorem ipsum dolor
sit, amet consectetur adipisicing elit. Repellendus
              aliquid consequuntur facere.</p>
            </div>
          </div>
        </div>
        <div class="col-md-3 mb-3">
          <div class="card text-dark bg-light h-100">
            <div class="card-header">Traffic</div>
            <div class="card-body">
              <h5 class="card-title">Card title</h5>
              <p class="card-text">Lorem ipsum dolor
sit, amet consectetur adipisicing elit. Suscipit
              voluptas non porro.</p>
            </div>
```

```
        </div>
      </div>
    </div>
    <div class="row">
      <div class="col-md-6 mb-3">
        <div class="card">
          <div class="card-header">
            Charts
          </div>
          <div class="card-body">
            <canvas id="myChart" class="chart"
width="400" height="200"></canvas>
          </div>
        </div>
      </div>
      <div class="col-md-6 mb-3">
        <div class="card">
          <div class="card-header">
            Active Users Per Month
          </div>
          <div class="card-body">
            <div class="progress mb-4 mt-1">
              <div class="progress-bar bg-success
progress-bar-striped progress-bar-animated"
                role="progressbar" style="width: 25%"
aria-valuenow="25" aria-valuemin="0"
                aria-valuemax="100">January</div>
            </div>
            <div class="progress mb-4">
              <div class="progress-bar bg-info
progress-bar-striped progress-bar-animated"
                role="progressbar" style="width: 80%"
aria-valuenow="80" aria-valuemin="0"
                aria-valuemax="100">February</div>
            </div>
            <div class="progress mb-4">
              <div class="progress-bar bg-warning
progress-bar-striped progress-bar-animated"
                role="progressbar" style="width: 40%"
aria-valuenow="40" aria-valuemin="0"
                aria-valuemax="100">March</div>
            </div>
            <div class="progress mb-4">
```

```
            <div class="progress-bar bg-primary
progress-bar-striped progress-bar-animated"
                role="progressbar" style="width: 70%"
aria-valuenow="75" aria-valuemin="0"
                aria-valuemax="100">April</div>
        </div>
        <div class="progress mb-4">
            <div class="progress-bar bg-danger
progress-bar-striped progress-bar-animated"
                role="progressbar" style="width: 80%"
aria-valuenow="80" aria-valuemin="0"
                aria-valuemax="100">May</div>
        </div>
        <div class="progress mb-4">
            <div class="progress-bar bg-warning
progress-bar-striped progress-bar-animated"
                role="progressbar" style="width: 75%"
aria-valuenow="75" aria-valuemin="0"
                aria-valuemax="100">June</div>
        </div>
        <div class="progress mb-4">
            <div class="progress-bar bg-info
progress-bar-striped progress-bar-animated"
                role="progressbar" style="width: 60%"
aria-valuenow="60" aria-valuemin="0"
                aria-valuemax="100">July</div>
        </div>
        </div>
      </div>
     </div>
    </div>
 </main>
 <!-- main content ends here -->
```

*Note:* We need to add some JavaScript code and a chart.js CDN for charts to work. Link the following scripts in the <body> tag below the popper and Bootstrap links.

Code

```
<script src="https://cdn.jsdelivr.net/npm/chart.js
@3.7.0/dist/chart.min.js"></script>
<script src="/script.js"></script>
```

We also have to create a script.js file and the chart.js code. Check out the following link for creating a chart (https://www.chartjs.org/docs/latest/ ), or paste the code below onto your JavaScript file.

Code

```
const ctx = document.getElementById('myChart').getCo
ntext('2d');
const myChart = new Chart(ctx, {
  type: 'bar',
  data: {
    labels: ['Red', 'Blue', 'Yellow', 'Green',
'Purple', 'Orange'],
    datasets: [{
      label: '# of Votes',
      data: [12, 19, 3, 5, 2, 3],
      backgroundColor: [
        'rgba(255, 99, 132, 0.2)',
        'rgba(54, 162, 235, 0.2)',
        'rgba(255, 206, 86, 0.2)',
        'rgba(75, 192, 192, 0.2)',
        'rgba(153, 102, 255, 0.2)',
        'rgba(255, 159, 64, 0.2)'
      ],
      borderColor: [
        'rgba(255, 99, 132, 1)',
        'rgba(54, 162, 235, 1)',
        'rgba(255, 206, 86, 1)',
        'rgba(75, 192, 192, 1)',
        'rgba(153, 102, 255, 1)',
        'rgba(255, 159, 64, 1)'
      ],
      borderWidth: 1
    }]
  },
  options: {
    scales: {
      y: {
        beginAtZero: true
      }
    }
  }
});
```

## WHAT WE LEARNED

Our admin panel is up and ready. We learned about the new components of Bootstrap. We also combined several different components to create a comprehensive dashboard. The admin panel contains a lot of various parts. It includes a horizontal navbar that is fixed on the top. It has a vertical navbar, also called an offcanvas component. The offcanvas would stick to the sides of large screens. However, it would get hidden toward the left side on small screens. We need to click on the menu toggle button on the horizontal dashboard to access the vertical dashboard on screens with smaller resolutions.

We also learned about several other components like the progress bar and cards. A card component can be incredibly versatile as you can use it in various formats. A card can be used with images, text, list groups, links, and more. We have used a card to feature multiple things in this admin panel that we created.

The first type of card displayed in the main content part of our admin panel is a basic card with a card header. The card header shows what type of information is within the card. It provides a quick view to the admin or the dashboard user. Then the other part of the card is a card body. A card body contains a card title and a card text. A card title elaborates on the information of the card. And the card text provides us with detailed info concerning the header and title of the card. We have created four similar-looking cards on the top in which each card displays different types of information like customers, revenue, purchases, and traffic.

Then we have another card component that displays a chart. The chart is made using chart.js. To use chart.js, you need to first download or paste the CDN link in your file. Then you can copy the <canvas> tag from the official website. The official website contains all the information about setting up and working with chart.js. After pasting the CDN link, you need to copy the JavaScript code and paste it in a separate .js file or put it in the same index.html file using a <script> tag.

Then lastly, we created a similar card to the one we used to display our chart. In that card, we used another Bootstrap component named progress bars. A progress bar component is used to show the progress of any particular task using horizontal lines. These horizontal lines have a specific width and height that resemble a bar. To create a progress bar, usually, two classes are used, .progress and .progress-bar. These two classes work in tandem to create a progress bar.

We have also used two additional classes within our progress bar: .progress-bar-striped and .progress-bar-animated. The striped class would create stripes onto the progress bar. The lines create an effect that makes the bars look visually appealing. The strips are done diagonally. The animated class within a progress bar takes it up a notch by making it look like a bar is moving forward in its place. The animated class progress bar should be used with the striped class. Without using the striped class, the animated effect would not take place. To change the color of a progress bar, simply use the .bg-color class. The color corresponds to the color codes available within the Bootstrap. The color codes available within the Bootstrap are as follows:

- **primary:** blue

- **secondary:** gray

- **success:** green

- **warning:** yellow

- **danger:** red

- **info:** light blue

- **dark:** black

- **light:** light gray

- **white:** white

As the color of the progress bar can be changed, in the same way, the width can also be easily changed. You need to change two values to change the width of a progress bar; first change the value of width contained within the style attribute in the <div> tag. Next up, you need to change the value of area now. Make sure that the values in both of these are equal. A mismatched value can produce unexpected results on the dashboard. Now that we have discussed all the new things we have learned about in this admin panel template we created, it is time to make another back end–based UI. Creating another UI will cement those concepts and help us create complex layouts and templates using a simple framework like Bootstrap.

## BACKEND UI

Before jumping onto creating a Backend UI, it is essential to understand what it even means and its basics. So, to begin with, any website or application consists of mainly two parts: the front end and the back end. Both serve their purposes and are essential to sustain a website or a web application. These parts need to work efficiently to achieve the best user experience.

Front-end development is mainly focused on what is in front of the user. Front-end developers work on making a website look visually appealing for the web. The front end is the part that any user interacts with. It is also called the client-side. The user is referred to as the client here. The client asks for that data, whether it is a website, image, etc., and the server fetches it for them. For the most part, HTML, CSS, and JavaScript are the most used languages for the front end. They are what you could call the building blocks of the front end.

The front end includes everything that the user can access directly while using the website: anything that the user directly interacts with, whether it is an image, a text, a graph, or a table. It could also be a button, color schemes, or even the navigation menu. All of it form the front-end part of any website. The front-end developers create everything that you get access to. From the content to the structure, the layout, and the design pattern, they are all designed by front-end developers. The front-end developers essentially work on the behavior of a website on a screen. Managing the behavioral aspect comes with two significant challenges. One is maintaining responsiveness, and the other is not compromising on the performance in any way. For a website to work efficiently and smoothly and for the user to have the best user experience, it becomes crucial that the website is responsive and works smoothly throughout. Responsiveness refers to the ability of any website to grow and shrink its components according to the screen resolution it encounters. It does not matter how big or small the screen is, everything should function properly.

As mentioned before, the front end is essentially built up of three languages:

1. **HTML:** The full form of HTML is HyperText Markup Language. It is a combination of Hypertext and Markup language. Hypertext creates a link between the web pages, whereas the markup language is used to define the content of a web page in the form of text. This is done by wrapping the text within tags. The tags in any HTML document are used to provide the structure to any web page. HTML is a standard markup language and is used to create web pages. It is one of the first things that any web developer must learn. It is an

essential and indispensable component of the web. HTML is used to give some form of structure to the front end of a website.

2. **CSS:** The complete form of CSS is Cascading Style Sheets. It is used to make the web pages look presentable. The primary function of CSS is to add styling to any web page and make it look presentable. With CSS, you can separate the styling and structure of any web page. This leads to a cleaner and more manageable code.

3. **JavaScript:** JavaScript is a scripting language used to add functionality to any web page. JavaScript makes the website interactive for the users. JavaScript is also one of the most popular programming languages in the world. It is also called the programming language of the web. It is even estimated that more than 97% of websites use JavaScript to manage the behavior of a web page on the client-side of any website. Without JavaScript, no website can function smoothly and interact with the users. There are lots of frameworks available nowadays that use JavaScript, the popular ones being Angular, React, and Vue.js

There are lots of other programming languages that help with front-end development using different frameworks, e.g., Flutter is a framework that makes use of Dart, Django is a framework that makes use of Python, and so many more.

Popular Front-end Frameworks and Libraries

- **AngularJS:** Angular is a JavaScript-based front-end framework. It is also open-source. Angular is used to create web applications. These web applications are also called SPAs. SPA stands for a single-page web application. Angular has gained immense popularity over the years and continues to grow tremendously. It is a steadily growing framework that provides a great way to develop a web application. Because it is a free, open-source project, the community for Angular has also grown over the years. Angular changes the static HTML of any web page to dynamic HTML. Data is bound within HTML while also simultaneously extending the HTML attributes with the help of directives.

- **React.js:** React is a JavaScript library used to build a user interface. React is a declarative library that is also incredibly efficient. Just like Angular, ReactJS is also an open-source library. It is a flexible component-based library used for the front end. The basic methodology behind the working of React is that it builds components. Everything you see on the screen is a component that can be reused again by the developer. A page created with React is essentially a collection of components. It is responsible for the view layer of any web application. React.js was created and is currently maintained by Facebook.

- **Bootstrap:** Bootstrap is also a free and open-source framework for creating websites and web applications. Bootstrap focuses on mobile-first development and is increasingly responsive. It is also one of the most popular CSS-based frameworks.

- **jQuery:** jQuery is also an open-source library based on JavaScript. It simplifies the interactions between the Document Object Model (DOM) and JavaScript. Using jQuery makes HTML document traversal and manipulation much more accessible. It also simplifies event handling, an essential part of JavaScript and other things like animation and Ajax. It provides incredible versatility and extensibility and is easy to work across many browsers.

- **Sass:** Sass stands for Syntactically Awesome Style Sheets. It is a stable and robust CSS extension language. It is a preprocessor scripting language compiled into Cascading Style Sheets (CSS). It is incredibly reliable and powerful and is used to extend the functionality provided by an existing CSS-based site. Sass functionality includes everything – variables, inheritance, and even nesting – and does the same with ease.

- **Flutter:** Flutter is an open-source software development kit (SDK). It is used for creating the user interface (UI). It was created by Google and used the Dart programming language. Flutter is used for creating natively compiled applications for multiple devices with just a single code base. It can develop good-looking applications for iOS and Android mobile devices, web, and desktop. One of the most noteworthy things about Flutter is that it made flat development much more manageable and expressive. It also creates a flexible user interface while also maintaining native performance. The latest version of Flutter, Flutter 2, was announced in March 2021.

- **Other Libraries:** Many other libraries and frameworks are equally good and offer some fantastic features. The popular ones are Foundation, Backbone.js, Ember.js, Materialize, etc.

The client at the front end does not usually know what is going on behind the scenes. The user remains unaware of how a website is fetched and displayed. This is where the back end comes into play. The back-end part of any website focuses on the data and the processes hidden from the user's eyes. The back end is also called as the server-side.

Back end is involved with the part of the website that the user has no access to. All the processes happening at the back end are why a website works and runs smoothly. If a back-end issue occurs, the whole site will be down, leaving the users unable to access the website's content. In a computer system network, the back end corresponds to the data access layer of any piece of software or hardware. The rear end of any software includes functionality that would ease the user's burden and make it easier for them to access or navigate the website.

On the server-side, any website mainly works on storing and arranging the data. The back end also makes sure that everything is up and running on the front end of the website. The back end is the software part that never comes in direct contact with the users. The users indirectly access all the features of a website that a back-end developer develops with the help of a front-end application. A back-end developer usually writes APIs, creates libraries, and works with system components.

Many programming languages help build the back-end portion of any website or web application.

## Popular Back-end Programming Languages

- **PHP:** PHP is a server-side scripting language because PHP code is executed. It was specifically designed for web development. All of the PHP code is executed at the server-side, and then it sends the result in the form that can be displayed on the browser to be accessed by the client.

- **C++:** It is a widely used general-purpose programming language. Nowadays, it is increasingly used for competitive programming. It is also a popular language used for the back end.

- **Java:** It is one of the most popular programming languages on the planet. It provides exceptional customer service and an active online forum. James Gosling created this high-level object-oriented programming language. It is a highly scalable language, and its components are readily available.

- **Python:** Python is also a popular programming language used for back-end services. It is a high-level, general-purpose programming language. The readability of Python is high because of its use of specific indentation. It enables programmers to write clear, clean, and logical code.

- **JavaScript:** JavaScript is a universal programming language used for both the front end and back end. It is a multi-paradigm, object-oriented programming language.

- **Node.js:** Node.js is an open-source run-time environment for executing JavaScript code outside a browser. It is also a cross-platform. However, NodeJS is in another category because it is neither a framework nor a programming language. NodeJS is primarily used for building back-end services like APIs. Those can further be used in a web app or a mobile app. NodeJS is used by some top-rated companies like PayPal, Uber, Netflix, to name but a few.

Popular Back-end Frameworks

- **Express.js:** Express.js is a web application framework based on NodeJS. It is a free and open-source software.

- **Django:** Django is a free and open-source web framework based in Python. It follows the model-template-architectural pattern. It is a high-level web framework. It encourages rapid development, helps write clean code, and builds a pragmatic design.

- **Ruby on Rails:** Ruby on Rails or simply Rails is a server-side web application framework. It is written in Ruby. It is an MVC framework and provides default structures database, web service, and web pages. MVC stands for Model View Controller.

- **Laravel:** Laravel is a free and open-source web framework based on PHP. It used the model-view-controller architectural pattern. Taylor Otwell created it.

- **Flask:** Flask is a micro web framework that is written in Python. It is considered a microframework because it does not require a particular tool or library. It does not have a data abstraction layer, form validation, or other components where third-party libraries provide standard functions.

## CREATING A BACKEND UI IN BOOTSTRAP

Now that we have talked about the back end at length, it is time to create a Bootstrap user interface. It is essential to know the data analytics of any website to make the required changes according to the prominent demographic of the website. To keep track of the inner workings of any website, the admin of any website needs a dashboard. A dashboard would let the admin do a quick check of the analytics on the go without doing anything complex.

We will be creating an admin dashboard interface with the following:

1. A navigation bar

2. A sidebar

3. Breadcrumb for the current page

4. Main content area with widget cards

5. Footer

Before we start building the interface, we first need a folder with the name Backend UI. Open up that folder in your code editor and create an index.ht ml file. We will be using CDN links to pull in all of the dependencies. Before adding the CDN links, let us add the basic boilerplate code to our file.

Code

```
<!DOCTYPE html>
<html lang="en">
<head>
  <meta charset="UTF-8">
  <meta http-equiv="X-UA-Compatible" content="IE=edge">
  <meta name="viewport" content="wide=device-wide,
initial-scale=1.0">
  <title>Backend UI</title>
  <!-- insert stylesheets here -->
</head>
<body>
    <!-- insert scripts here -->
</body>
</html>
```

Paste the following stylesheet in your <head> tag.

## Code

```
<!-- Bootstrap's Stylesheet -->
  <link href="https://cdn.jsdelivr.net/npm/bootstrap
@5.1.3/dist/css/bootstrap.min.css" rel="stylesheet"
integrity="sha384-1BmE4kWBq78iYhFldvKuhfTAU6auU8tT
94WrHftjDbrCEXSU1oBoqyl2QvZ6jIW3"
crossorigin="anonymous">
```

Paste the following Bootstrap script file bundle for JavaScript and Popper .js in your <body> tag.

## Code

```
<!-- Bootstrap Bundle -->
  <script src="https://cdn.jsdelivr.net/npm/
bootstrap@5.1.3/dist/js/bootstrap.bundle.min.js"
integrity="sha384-ka7Sk0Gln4gmtz2MlQnikT1wXgYsOg+O
MhuP+IlRH9sENBOOLRn5q+8nbTov4+1p"
crossorigin="anonymous"></script>
```

Now that we have set up Bootstrap 5, it is time to build our user interface.

## Navbar

Our horizontal navbar will have three main parts

1. Brand name or logo

2. Search bar

3. Admin button

Paste the following code right after the beginning of the <body> tag.

## Code

```
<!-- navbar starts here -->
  <nav class="navbar navbar-info bg-light p-3">
    <div class="d-flex col-12 col-md-3 col-lg-2 mb-2
mb-lg-0 flex-wrap flex-md-nowrap
justify-content-between">
      <a class="navbar-brand" href="#">
        Backend UI
      </a>
```

```
        <button class="navbar-toggler d-md-none
collapsed mb-3" type="button" data-toggle="collapse"
        data-target="#sidebar" aria-
controls="sidebar" aria-expanded="false" aria-
label="Toggle navigation">
            <span class="navbar-toggler-icon"></span>
        </button>
    </div>
    <div class="col-12 col-md-4 col-lg-2">
        <input class="form-control form-control-dark"
type="text" placeholder="Search" aria-label="Search">
    </div>
    <div class="col-12 col-md-5 col-lg-8 d-flex align-
items-center justify-content-md-end mt-3 mt-md-0">
        <div class="dropdown">
            <button class="btn btn-secondary dropdown-
toggle" type="button" id="dropdownMenuButton"
            data-toggle="dropdown"
aria-expanded="false">
            Hello, Admin
            </button>
            <ul class="dropdown-menu" aria-labelledby="dr
opdownMenuButton">
                <li><a class="dropdown-item"
href="#">Settings</a></li>
                <li><a class="dropdown-item" href="#">Log
out</a></li>
            </ul>
        </div>
    </div>
</nav>
<!-- navbar ends here -->
```

The above code will create a horizontal navigation bar that will span across the whole width of the viewport. It currently has the title/logo on the left side of the navbar, a search bar, and an admin settings dropdown button. A hamburger menu will appear for mobile devices.

Sidebar

The sidebar will contain additional navigation items of the dashboard. In a way, the sidebar will have all the main navigation parts. We will first create a container class that will contain all our main items.

Code

```
<div class="container-fluid">
   <div class="row">
      <nav id="sidebar" class="col-md-3 col-lg-2
d-md-block bg-light sidebar collapse">
         <!-- sidebar content goes in here -->
      </nav>
      <main class="col-md-9 ml-sm-auto col-lg-10
px-md-4 py-4">
         <h1 class="h2">Dashboard</h1>
      </main>
   </div>
   </div>
```

Now we need to add the sidebar content within the <nav> tag.

Code

```
<!-- sidebar content goes in here -->
   <div class="position-sticky pt-md-5">
    <ul class="nav flex-column">
     <li class="nav-item">
      <a class="nav-link active" aria-current="page"
href="#">
      <svg xmlns="http://www.w3.org/2000/svg"
width="24" height="20" viewBox="0 0 22 22" fill="solid"
      stroke="currentColor" stroke-width="4"
stroke-linecap="round" stroke-linejoin="round"
      class="feather feather-home">
      <path d="M3 9l9-7 9 7v11a2 2 0 0 1-2 2H5a2 2
0 0 1-2-2z"></path>
      <polyline points="9 22 9 12 15 12 15 22">
</polyline>
      </svg>
      <span class="ml-2">Dash</span>
      </a>
     </li>
     <li class="nav-item">
      <a class="nav-link" href="#">
      <svg xmlns="http://www.w3.org/2000/svg"
width="20" height="20" viewBox="0 0 24 24"
fill="none"
```

```
        stroke="currentColor" stroke-width="2"
stroke-linecap="round" stroke-linejoin="round"
        class="feather feather-file">
        <path d="M13 2H6a2 2 0 0 0-2 2v16a2 2 0 0 0
2 2h12a2 2 0 0 0 2-2V9z"></path>
        <polyline points="13 2 13 9 20 9"></polyline>
        </svg>
        <span class="ml-2">Orders</span>
       </a>
      </li>
      <li class="nav-item">
       <a class="nav-link" href="#">
        <svg xmlns="http://www.w3.org/2000/svg"
width="24" height="24" viewBox="0 0 24 24" fill="none"
        stroke="currentColor" stroke-width="2"
stroke-linecap="round" stroke-linejoin="round"
        class="feather feather-shopping-cart">
        <circle cx="9" cy="21" r="1"></circle>
        <circle cx="20" cy="21" r="1"></circle>
        <path d="M1 1h4l2.68 13.39a2 2 0 0 0 2
1.61h9.72a2 2 0 0 0 2-1.61L23 6H6"></path>
        </svg>
        <span class="ml-2">Products</span>
       </a>
      </li>
      <li class="nav-item">
       <a class="nav-link" href="#">
        <svg xmlns="http://www.w3.org/2000/svg"
width="24" height="24" viewBox="0 0 24 24" fill="none"
        stroke="currentColor" stroke-width="2"
stroke-linecap="round" stroke-linejoin="round"
        class="feather feather-users">
        <path d="M17 21v-2a4 4 0 0 0-4-4H5a4 4 0 0
0-4 4v2"></path>
        <circle cx="9" cy="7" r="4"></circle>
        <path d="M23 21v-2a4 4 0 0 0-3-3.87"></path>
        <path d="M16 3.13a4 4 0 0 1 0 7.75"></path>
        </svg>
        <span class="ml-2">Customers</span>
       </a>
      </li>
      <li class="nav-item">
       <a class="nav-link" href="#">
```

```
        <svg xmlns="http://www.w3.org/2000/svg"
width="24" height="24" viewBox="0 0 24 24"
fill="none"
        stroke="currentColor" stroke-width="2"
stroke-linecap="round" stroke-linejoin="round"
        class="feather feather-bar-chart-2">
        <line x1="18" y1="20" x2="18" y2="10"></line>
        <line x1="12" y1="20" x2="12" y2="4"></line>
        <line x1="6" y1="20" x2="6" y2="14"></line>
        </svg>
        <span class="ml-2">Reports</span>
      </a>
    </li>
   </ul>
  </div>
  <!-- sidebar ends here -->
```

We have to design a style.css file to add our custom styles. We will add our custom stylesheet right after our bootstrap stylesheet.

```
<!-- custom stylesheet -->
<link rel="stylesheet" href="/style.css">
```

Now, it is time to add some styles to our stylesheet so that we get a fixed sidebar.

## Code

```
@media (max-width: 760.98px) {
  .sidebar {
   top: 10.5rem;
   padding: 0;
  }
}
  .navbar {
  box-shadow: inset 0 -2px 0 rgba(0, 0, 0, .1);
}
  @media (min-width: 767.98px) {
  .navbar {
   top: 0;
   position: sticky;
```

```
 z-index: 999;
 }
}
 .sidebar .nav-link {
 color: #333;
 }
 .sidebar .nav-link.active {
 color: #0d6efd;
 }
```

*Note:* The custom styles we have added would make the sidebar stay fixed when we scroll down. It will also take the full height of the viewport. The active navigation items will be highlighted.

### Breadcrumb

Now, it is time to add our <main> section. We have created two main components: the horizontal navbar and the sidebar. We will add the following code within the <main> tag to make our breadcrumb navigation.

### Code

```
<main class="col-md-9 ml-sm-auto col-lg-15 px-md-4
py-4">
    <nav aria-label="breadcrumb">
     <ol class="breadcrumb">
     <li class="breadcrumb-item"><a href="#">Home</a>
</li>
     <li class="breadcrumb-item active" aria-
current="page">view</li>
     </ol>
     </nav>
     <h1 class="h2">Dash</h1>
     <p>Lorem ipsum dolor sit amet consectetur
adipisicing elit. Ducimus, illo!
     </p>
</main>
```

A breadcrumb is used to navigate the current location within a website. It is like a secondary navigation system to quickly show a user's location hierarchically.

## Main Content

Our main content area also has a few widgets or card items, called Bootstrap. You can put any type of information within these card items. It could be a chart, statistics, a to-do list, etc. These dashboard interfaces displayed with the help of a card help us organize and give us a bird's eye view of all the different metrics involved. Let us start by creating our first card.

## Code

```
<div class="row my-4">
    <div class="col-12 col-md-6 col-lg-3 mb-4 mb-lg-0">
     <div class="card">
      <h5 class="card-header bg-dark text-light">
Customers</h5>
        <div class="card-body">
         <h5 class="card-title">345k</h5>
         <p class="card-text">Oct 1 - Dec 31, India</p>
         <p class="card-text text-success">8.2%
increase since last quarter</p>
        </div>
       </div>
      </div>
</div>
```

Now we will add three more cards right where our first card ends. We will put all our card in the "row my-4" class.

## Code

```
<div class="col-12 col-md-6 mb-4 mb-lg-0 col-lg-3">
    <div class="card">
     <h5 class="card-header bg-dark text-light">
Revenue</h5>
       <div class="card-body">
        <h5 class="card-title">$25.4k</h5>
        <p class="card-text">Oct 1 - Dec 31, India</p>
        <p class="card-text text-success">
4.6% increase since last quarter</p>
       </div>
      </div>
     </div>
     <div class="col-12 col-md-6 mb-4 mb-lg-0
col-lg-3">
```

```
    <div class="card">
     <h5 class="card-header bg-dark text-light">
Purchases</h5>
       <div class="card-body">
        <h5 class="card-title">643</h5>
        <p class="card-text">Oct 1 - Dec 31, India</p>
        <p class="card-text text-danger">2.7%
decrease since last quarter</p>
       </div>
      </div>
     </div>
          <div class="col-12 col-md-6 mb-4 mb-lg-0
col-lg-3">
       <div class="card">
       <h5 class="card-header bg-dark text-
light">Traffic</h5>
       <div class="card-body">
        <h5 class="card-title">64k</h5>
        <p class="card-text">Oct 1 - Dec 31, India</p>
        <p class="card-text text-success">5.5%
increase since last quarter</p>
       </div>
      </div>
     </div>
```

The complete code for all four widget cards is given below.

Code

```
<!-- widget cards -->
    <div class="row my-4">
     <div class="col-12 col-md-6 col-lg-3 mb-4 mb-lg-0">
      <div class="card">
       <h5 class="card-header bg-dark text-
light">Customers</h5>
       <div class="card-body">
        <h5 class="card-title">345k</h5>
        <p class="card-text">Oct 1 - Dec 31, India</p>
        <p class="card-text text-success">8.2%
increase since last quarter</p>
       </div>
      </div>
     </div>
```

```
        <div class="col-12 col-md-6 mb-4 mb-lg-0
col-lg-3">
     <div class="card">
     <h5 class="card-header bg-dark text-
light">Revenue</h5>
        <div class="card-body">
        <h5 class="card-title">$25.4k</h5>
        <p class="card-text">Oct 1 - Dec 31, India</p>
        <p class="card-text text-success">
5.6% increase since last quarter</p>
        </div>
      </div>
     </div>
     <div class="col-12 col-md-6 mb-4 mb-lg-0
col-lg-3">
      <div class="card">
      <h5 class="card-header bg-dark text-
light">Purchases</h5>
      <div class="card-body">
      <h5 class="card-title">643</h5>
      <p class="card-text">Oct 1 - Dec 31, India</p>
      <p class="card-text text-danger">
3.6% decrease since last quarter</p>
      </div>
      </div>
     </div>
         <div class="col-12 col-md-6 mb-4 mb-lg-0
col-lg-3">
     <div class="card">
     <h5 class="card-header bg-dark text-
light">Traffic</h5>
      <div class="card-body">
      <h5 class="card-title">64k</h5>
      <p class="card-text">Oct 1 - Dec 31, India</p>
      <p class="card-text text-success">
5.5% increase since last quarter</p>
      </div>
      </div>
     </div>
    </div>
    <!-- widget cards end here -->
```

After the widget card, we will have a table that will show our latest trans-actions. This table will also be part of our <main> tag, and you need to add it right after that widget cards end.

Code

```
<div class="row">
    <div class="col-12 col-xl-8 mb-4 mb-lg-0">
    <div class="card">
    <h5 class="card-header bg-dark
text-light">Latest Transactions</h5>
    <div class="card-body">
     <div class="table-responsive">
      <table class="table">
       <thead>
        <tr>
         <th scope="col">Order</th>
         <th scope="col">Product</th>
         <th scope="col">Customer</th>
         <th scope="col">Total</th>
         <th scope="col">Date</th>
         <th scope="col"></th>
        </tr>
       </thead>
       <tbody>
        <tr>
         <th scope="row">17371705</th>
         <td>Lorem ipsum dolor sit amet</td>
         <td>someone@gmail.com</td>
         <td>$45.11</td>
         <td>Jul 19 2021</td>
         <td><a href="#" class="btn-sm
btn-primary">View</a></td>
        </tr>
        <tr>
         <th scope="row">17370540</th>
         <td>consectetur adipisicing elit</td>
         <td>you.yourname@company.com</td>
         <td>$153.11</td>
         <td>Aug 28 2021</td>
         <td><a href="#" class="btn-sm
btn-primary">View</a></td>
```

```
        </tr>
        <tr>
         <th scope="row">17371705</th>
         <td>Voluptatibus unde odit sed ipsa</td>
         <td>you@gmail.com</td>
         <td>$61.11</td>
         <td>Sept 15 2021</td>
         <td><a href="#" class="btn-sm btn-
primary">View</a></td>
        </tr>
        <tr>
         <th scope="row">17370540</th>
         <td>Molestiae dicta quo dolorem
adipisci</td>
         <td>someone@company.com</td>
         <td>$15.11</td>
         <td>Oct 20 2021</td>
         <td><a href="#" class="btn-sm btn-
primary">View</a></td>
        </tr>
       </tbody>
      </table>
     </div>
     <a href="#" class="btn-block btn-light">
View all</a>
      </div>
     </div>
    </div>
```

Right where our <div> tag for our table ends, we will add another card that will be a chart displaying our website traffic for the last six months. We need to add a CDN for the chartist to create our traffic chart. Add the following stylesheet in your <head> tag right after the Bootstrap stylesheet to include a chartist.

Code

```
<!-- chartist stylesheet -->
 <link rel="stylesheet" href="https://cdn.jsdelivr.
net/chartist.js/latest/chartist.min.css">
```

You will also add a <script> tag toward the end of your <body> tag. Also, create a script.js file and link it right below the chartist script. Add the following <script> tags right below the Bootstrap bundle <script> tag.

Code

```
<!-- chartist script -->
<script src="https://cdn.jsdelivr.net/chartist.js/
latest/chartist.min.js"></script>
<!-- custom script -->
<script src="/script.js"></script>
```

Now that we have included all our scripts, it is time to include our chart. Add the following code right after your table ends.

Code

```
<!-- traffic chart goes here -->
    <div class="col-12 col-xl-4">
     <div class="card">
      <h5 class="card-header bg-dark text-light">
Traffic For First Half</h5>
      <div class="card-body">
       <div id="traffic-chart"></div>
      </div>
     </div>
    </div>
```

Add the following code in your script.js file.

Code

```
new Chartist.Line('#traffic-chart', {
  labels: ['January', 'Februrary', 'March', 'April',
'May', 'June'],
  series: [
   [23000, 25000, 19000, 34000, 56000, 64000]
  ]
}, {
low: 0,
showArea: true
});
```

Here is the complete code for the table and chart that you need to include right after your widget code. All of this is going to be within the <main> tag.

Code

```
<!-- table -->
    <div class="row">
```

```
        <div class="col-12 col-xl-8 mb-4 mb-lg-0">
         <div class="card">
         <h5 class="card-header bg-dark
  text-light">Latest Transactions</h5>
           <div class="card-body">
            <div class="table-responsive">
             <table class="table">
              <thead>
               <tr>
                <th scope="col">Order</th>
                <th scope="col">Product</th>
                <th scope="col">Customer</th>
                <th scope="col">Total</th>
                <th scope="col">Date</th>
                <th scope="col"></th>
               </tr>
              </thead>
              <tbody>
               <tr>
                <th scope="row">17371705</th>
                <td>Lorem ipsum dolor sit amet</td>
                <td>someone@gmail.com</td>
                <td>$45.11</td>
                <td>Jul 19 2021</td>
                <td><a href="#" class="btn-sm btn-
  primary">View</a></td>
               </tr>
               <tr>
                <th scope="row">17370540</th>
                <td>consectetur adipisicing elit</td>
                <td>you.yourname@company.com</td>
                <td>$153.11</td>
                <td>Aug 28 2021</td>
                <td><a href="#" class="btn-sm btn-
  primary">View</a></td>
               </tr>
               <tr>
                <th scope="row">17371705</th>
                <td>Voluptatibus unde odit sed ipsa</td>
                <td>you@gmail.com</td>
                <td>$61.11</td>
                <td>Sept 15 2021</td>
                <td><a href="#" class="btn-sm
  btn-primary">View</a></td>
```

```
        </tr>
        <tr>
        <th scope="row">17370540</th>
        <td>Molestiae dicta quo dolorem
adipisci</td>
        <td>someone@company.com</td>
        <td>$15.11</td>
        <td>Oct 20 2021</td>
        <td><a href="#" class="btn-sm
btn-primary">View</a></td>
        </tr>
        </tbody>
        </table>
        </div>
        <a href="#" class="btn-block btn-light">
View all</a>
      </div>
      </div>
      </div>
      <!-- traffic chart goes here -->
      <div class="col-12 col-xl-4">
      <div class="card">
        <h5 class="card-header bg-dark
text-light">Traffic For First Half</h5>
        <div class="card-body">
        <div id="traffic-chart"></div>
        </div>
        </div>
        </div>
        </div>
```

## Footer

The last thing left to build is the footer for our back-end user interface. Add the footer code right after the chart code within the <main> tag. Apart from our navbar and sidebar, every section will be part of our main content.

## Code

```
<!-- footer starts here -->
    <footer class="pt-5 d-flex justify-content-between">
    <span>Copyright &copy; 2022 Backend UI</span>
    <ul class="nav m-10">
```

```
    <li class="nav-item">
    <a class="nav-link text-second" aria-
current="page" href="#">Privacy Policies</a>
    </li>
    <li class="nav-item">
    <a class="nav-link text-secondary" href="#">
Terms and condition</a>
    </li>
    <li class="nav-item">
    <a class="nav-link text-secondary" href="#">
Contacts</a>
    </li>
    </ul>
    </footer>
    <!-- footer ends here -->
```

## What We Learned

Now that we have finished working on our Backend UI, we learned a couple of things. Let us do a quick recap and see what new things we learned after designing the user interface for a back end–based dashboard. First, we started by creating an index.html file, and then we set it up by adding Bootstrap's stylesheets and the script files. Bootstrap contains two script files: one is for JavaScript, and the other includes links for Popper. We had the bundle, which contains both JavaScript and Popper; however, if you choose to add both of them separately, make sure to add Popper first and then the JavaScript link. There are lots of JavaScript components that require JavaScript to function, like modals, offcanvas, etc. These components specifically need the JavaScript plugins and Popper to work smoothly. Always make sure that you add the <script> tag near the end of the page, right before closing the <body> tag.

Since we chose to add a bundle, both JavaScript and Popper are included within our file in one go. Including the bundle will ensure that the Bootstrap JavaScript plugin and all its dependencies are added within the file. Popper is used to adding tooltips. It is also used as a popover and positioning engine. Check out the official Popper website: https://popper .js.org/ . Popper helps in placing a tooltip on any object or element. Popper provides us with 12 different placement positions for any tooltip. It also has features that help in preventing the tooltip container from overflowing. It also contains a feature called flipping which will change the direction of the tooltip within an object container to the opposite side. Flipping happens when there is an overflow from the visible area. If enough space is detected on the other side, it will flip back again.

To summarize what Popper does, it places the tooltips relative to the reference object. It changes the context of the tooltip close to the reference object. Last but not least, it keeps the tooltip and popover in view.

After adding our CDN links, we created our horizontal navbar. Bootstrap is all about adding classes according to our needs. We added a few classes within the <nav> tag to create our horizontal navbar, which contains our brand name, a search bar right next to our brand name, and lastly, a dropdown button for the admin settings. Here is a breakdown of the few classes and what we used to create our horizontal navbar:

- **navbar:** used to create a navbar

- **navbar-info:** change the color of navbar items to color code info which is light blue

- **bg-light:** changes the background of the navbar to Bootstrap color code light

- **p-3:** provides padding of 3 in all directions

- **navbar-brand:** used to highlight the brand name on the navbar

- **d-flex:** changes the display of any container to flex

- **col-12:** initiates the 12-column grid system in Bootstrap

- **flex-wrap:** wraps the flex items within the container

- **navbar-toggler:** helps in toggling the navbar for small screens

- **d-md-none:** makes the display to none for the toggle button in screens with a higher resolution than medium.

- **collapsed:** collapses the navbar as screen resolution gets smaller.

- **navbar-toggler-icon:** provides a navbar toggling icon for smaller screen resolutions. The navbar toggling icon is also called the hamburger menu.

- **form-control:** used for input tags within a form

- **align-items-center:** helps in aligning all the items in the center of the cross axis

- **justify-content-end:** arranges the items at the end of the flex container – in this case, the dropdown button is set at the end of the flexbox, which is the right-hand side of the navbar

- **mt-3:** provides a margin-top value of 3

- **dropdown:** creates a dropdown button

- **btn:** helps in creating a button

- **btn-secondary:** creates a button of the secondary color

- **dropdown-toggle:** creates a dropdown toggle button

- **dropdown-menu:** creates a dropdown-menu

- **dropdown-item:** lists each of the items within the dropdown-menu.

The classes written above provide a comprehensive list of all the classes used to create our navbar. Now, we will take a look at our sidebar.

Our sidebar has five components: dashboard, orders, products, customers, and reports. For this tutorial of ours, we only created the dashboard page. Our sidebar is also a sticky navbar, which means the sidebar is present for the whole width of the screen. While using the dashboard from a smaller screen, a hamburger icon would appear to help us access the sidebar. For larger screens, the sidebar will always be present. Bootstrap classes were not enough to create an ever-present sidebar, and we had to add some custom styles to make sure the sidebar component was available throughout the larger screens. We first created a style.css page and then used the <link> tag within our index.html page. Let us first look at all the Bootstrap classes that we used to create our sidebar, and then we will talk about the custom styles that we put into our stylesheet.

- **container-fluid:** creates a fluid container that spreads the entire width of the viewport

- **row:** creates a row that activates the grid system in Bootstrap

- **sidebar:** used to create a sidebar

- **d-md-block:** used to change the display to block in medium screens and above

- **bg-light:** used to change the sidebar background to light

- **collapse:** used to collapse the sidebar in screens with smaller resolution
- **position-sticky:** makes the navbar stick onto the screen throughout
- **pt-md-5:** gives a padding-top value of 5 for medium screens and above
- **nav:** creates a nav
- **flex-column:** creates a flex with the flex-direction column.
- **nav-item:** used to generate nav items within a navbar
- **nav-link:** used to create a link for a nav item
- **active:** used to make the current link functional
- **ml-2:** provides a margin-left value of 2
- **svg:** used to add the Bootstrap icon; check out the website https://icons.getbootstrap.com/ for more

After linking our custom stylesheet, we used the CSS properties.

- **@media:** media queries are used to add CSS properties according to the screen resolution
- **max-width:** signifies the maximum width up to which an element or a particular property is applied
- **top:** used to set the top edge of any element
- **padding:** used to set the padding of any element
- **box-shadow:** used to provide a shadow to the box
- **position:** used to establish how an element is positioned within a document
- **z-index:** used to specify the stack level of an item within a box
- **color:** used to select the color

The classes written above provide a comprehensive list of all the classes used to create our sidebar. Now, take a look at our main section.

Our main section contains several items. Everything apart from our horizontal navbar and sidebar is part of our main section. It includes a breadcrumb, widget cards, a table, a graph-based chart, and a footer. Here is a breakdown of all the classes and their use.

- **ml:** used to apply the margin-left value

- **px:** padding in the $x$-axis

- **py:** padding in the $y$-axis

- **breadcrumb:** used to create breadcrumb navigation

- **breadcrumb-item:** used to create an item in a breadcrumb-based navigation bar

- **h2:** Bootstrap has special classes based on HTML heading tags – using the class h2 would make any text of size h2

- **my-4:** provides a margin of 4 on the $y$-axis

- **card:** used to create a widget card

- **card-header:** used to create a header for a widget card

- **bg-dark:** change the background color to dark

- **text-light:** change the text color to light

- **card-body:** used to create the body of any card

- **card-title:** used to specify the title of any card

- **card-text:** used to specify the main text of any widget card

- **text-success:** change the color of the text to green – success is the color code of green in Bootstrap

- **text-danger:** change the color of the text to red – the danger is the color code of red in Bootstrap

- **table-responsive:** used to create a responsive table

- **pt-5:** used to give a padding-top value of 5 to any element

- **m-0:** used to give a margin of 0 to any element

We have discussed most of the Bootstrap classes that we used to create our main section within our back-end user interface. Moving onto the next part, we will be talking about user interface and user experience, and their differences.

## ADDITIONAL CONSIDERATIONS AND UX

We have created several templates up until now. The ones we made in our previous chapter focused on the front-end aspect. We created a blog template and a portfolio template. The templates we created in this chapter gave us a look at how things are managed in the back end. We made an admin panel and a user interface for the back end depicting those things. While items on the front end are focused more on the way things look and are presented to the client in the back end, the technical aspects are the primary focus.

However, whether a template or website is used to display the front end or manage services at the back end, it is essential to focus on the UX. UI and UX are pretty popular terms on the web, but it is easy to get confused between these two. First, we will learn about how UX is different than UI, and then we will talk about how we can create a better user experience by using frameworks like Bootstrap.

At an elemental level, the user interface contains all the things the user can interact with on the screen. It could be anything ranging from the visual elements like the button or icons or the number of different pages available. It essentially encapsulates everything a client can interact with on the web page. On the other hand, user experience refers to the client's internal experience interacting with the website.

There are lots of people who use these terms interchangeably or sometimes even incorrectly. Even though there is a very subtle difference between these two, it is essential to know it.

UI or User Interface refers to anything that a user can interact with. Back in the days before the graphical user interface was developed, the only way to use a computer was through a command-line interface. Any user who would use the computer would need to communicate with it using a programming language. Even a single task would require writing seemingly infinite lines of code.

After the first GUI was developed, the users could interact with their computers by visual commands like clicking a button, using checkboxes, etc. This created a massive shift in the way computers are used, as now people could use computers without knowing how to code. This is how the personal computer revolution began. Personal computers started becoming a norm from here onward, and then different types of devices started coming in.

Apple released the first Macintosh computer in 1984. This was the very first computer that included a point-and-click mouse. Apple created a league of its own after putting out a computer like this in the market for the very first time. Macintosh became the first commercially successful home computer that used this interface type.

Decades have passed since the first computer with a graphical user interface was introduced. A lot has changed regarding technology and what our devices can do. But using a graphical interface gave birth to the role of a UI designer. A UI designer creates designs keeping in mind the user's visual experience. The primary goal of any UI designer is to prioritize the user's needs. The need for a UI designer is even more considering the prevalence of personal computers. The interface needs to be designed keeping in mind the variety of users that computers and other devices have these days. The role of a UI designer has evolved with technology. Like our systems, choices, expectations, and accessibility change, making our demands regarding what we want to have in our devices. The job of a UI designer was born out of designing simple user interfaces for computers has now evolved into something much bigger than that. Nowadays, UI designers work not just on computer interfaces but things like mobile phones, tablets, and augmented and virtual reality. There is also a new interface that is screenless or invisible, and they are referred to as zero UI. A zero UI works by using voice, gesture, or light controls. In today's world, a UI designer has limitless opportunities. They can work on websites, web apps, mobile devices, wearable devices, innovative home technology, etc. Designers will have to create interfaces that enable users of all ages, backgrounds, and technical experiences to use the product and have a seamless experience.

As long as computers are a part of our daily life, the user interface will be an essential component to create a great user experience. We will look at what user experience or UX is and what it entails.

User experience, also referred to as UX or UE, is defined by how users interact with any product, system, or service. User experience involves a person's perception and experience after using a product or service. It contains how easily and efficiently any user can use a product and how satisfying that interaction was.

UX came into being because of UI. As significant improvements were made in creating a UI, it became essential to know if creating said UI was beneficial to the user somehow. The evolution of UX happened as a result of improvements in UI. Once the user had several ways to interact with a product, it became necessary to know their experience to improve the UI to provide a better experience. The experience after any interaction with a product can range from positive, negative, or simply neutral.

The term User Experience was first coined by cognitive scientist Don Norman. He did so in the early 1990s while he was working at Apple. According to Don Norman, User Experience can be defined as encompassing all aspects of the end-users interaction with a company or its services and products.

Don Norman gave a broad definition that could contain every possible interaction a person could have, no matter how big or small with a product or service. This interaction does not have to be limited to a digital experience. Some people also refer to this field as experience design. Irrespective of the device or the product, it always depends on the user's experience. A positive user experience points toward an excellent user interface.

The designers are the ones that are responsible for ensuring that any company delivers the kind of product or service that would satisfy the users and meet their needs. Both UX and UI designers work closely to understand the users' needs through repeated research and experimentation in the working of their products. The insights gained from this research help them to improve the experience continually.

User Experience Research is a prevalent practice in big companies whose products rely on people's opinions and their terms of usage. Essentially, user experience research means studying interactions of users of a particular product or service and using those insights to help create people-first products and experiences.

There are different types of User Experience research methods available, and they are used depending upon the need and the goals of the company.

## Qualitative versus Quantitative Research

Qualitative research is a behavioral research method that uses observations and recordings of human behavior from the perspective of a subject to conclude. Qualitative researchers try to understand the how and why of human behavior. They do so by studying the subjects in their natural environment and obtaining information about their opinions and values concerning a particular situation. Commonly three methods are used for qualitative research.

1. **Participant observation:** This method is used to collect data from a participant while they are in their natural state.

2. **In-depth interviews:** This type of research method makes a detailed analysis of each individual, including their personal history, life-altering experiences, and opinions on sensitive topics. In this type of approach, particular focus is paid to each participant, and follow-up questions are asked quite often.

3. **Focus groups:** This research method is a collaborative venture in which lots of information is gathered at once from multiple participants. After that, a broad and generic overview of all the key points is made. A specific demographic is researched at once to determine where the consensus lies and avoid outliers that push the findings in one direction.

Each of these research methods has a unique approach to extracting the data and is used for obtaining a specific type of data.

The research method that focuses on numerical data is quantitative research. It collects and analyzes the numerical data and tries to find patterns within the said data. The patterns could be anything from averages to predictions based on previous results. The data, however, is generalized as it uses a numerical value to express data concerning a wide variety of people.

Both qualitative and quantitative have their use cases. Quantitative data helps you see the bigger picture, whereas qualitative data adds context and perspective to each experience.

These research methods help you gather detailed information about any topic in the form of upcoming trends and previous patterns. You can even combine these methods to attain a more understandable perspective. Quantitative data will help you find the trends, and based on that trend, you can do your qualitative research and learn more about your potential customer base. Quantitative data answers the question about "what" users want, whereas qualitative data answers the "why": why users are doing what they are doing.

## Attitudinal versus Behavioral Research

Attitudinal Research involves pre-assessment of users' beliefs and attitudes toward a specific experience. On the other hand, behavioral research is focused on what the user does. Behavioral research is great for telling you what's happening, whereas attitudinal reason helps assess why something is happening.

Sometimes, these two research methods are said to be the same thing. Even though they can be synonymous, both of these have subtle differences. If those differences are analyzed and approached correctly, the findings from this type of research could be insightful.

### Generative versus Evaluation Research

The goals of generative and evaluation base research are quite the opposite. Generative Research helps define the problem you would like to design a solution for. Evaluation research is based on making an existing design better. That current design could be in prototype, final, or other forms.

Even though it is essential to find a distinction between both UX and UI, however, UX is an extension of UI. UX came into being because of UI, but that does not mean both are co-related. As Jason Ogle said, "UI is the bridge that gets us where we want to go; UX is the feeling we get when we arrive."

## CHAPTER SUMMARY

This chapter taught us how to create an admin dashboard and its user interface. We learned about the differences between UI and UX and how they impact how a user accesses any website. In the next chapter, we will talk about Bootstrap and its different components that use JavaScript. We will talk about Bootstrap components that use JavaScript, like carousels and transitions. We would also discuss various attributes, alerts, and functions and work with React and Angular within Bootstrap.

# Bootstrap and JavaScript

## IN THIS CHAPTER

> ➤ Introduction to JavaScript

> ➤ Attributes

> ➤ Alerts

> ➤ Carousel

We created admin panels using Bootstrap in the previous chapter and talked about UI and UX. This chapter will talk about JavaScript and its influence on Bootstrap. JavaScript is, in fact, a recent addition to Bootstrap. In the previous versions of Bootstrap, jQuery was used. The latest version of Bootstrap 5 removed all of its dependency on jQuery and entirely switched to JavaScript. In this chapter, we will talk about how JavaScript is used on the web and the different components in Bootstrap that use JavaScript.

## INTRODUCTION TO JAVASCRIPT

JavaScript is a text-based, interpreted programming or scripting language that allows us to implement complex features on any web page. JavaScript is incredibly lightweight and is mainly used for scripting web pages. It is also used to create web apps that interact with clients without having to reload the page every time – most dynamic websites you see on the internet employ JavaScript in some form. JavaScript is used whenever a website displays timely content updates, interactive maps,

DOI: 10.1201/9781003309383-5

2D or 3D graphics, a scrolling movie, or even a simple button that does something when you click on it. The DOM API is used to change the user interface with JavaScript. It accomplishes this by dynamically altering the HTML and CSS.

DOM stands for Document Object Model. The DOM is a cross-platform, language-independent interface for creating a tree structure from an HTML content. Each tree node is an object that represents a section of the document. A document is represented as a logical tree in the document object model. Each branch of the tree terminates in a node, and each node contains an item. DOM gives us programmatic access to a tree, which we may utilize to change the structure of the tree. Changing the structure of the tree necessarily changes the document's basic behavior. The DOM is used to manipulate a page and change its behavior. Not only can the DOM be used to change the document's structure, but it can also be used to change the document's style and content. Attaching event handlers to nodes allows you to control the DOM. An event handler is called whenever an event is triggered.

JavaScript has a massive impact on the internet. More than 97% of all websites on the internet are expected to employ some form of JavaScript on the client side to show any type of web page functionality. JavaScript is considered one of the essential stepping stones toward learning web development. The prerequisites for learning JavaScript are a basic understanding of HTML and CSS. One of the things about JavaScript that make it so popular is that it is versatile and flexible enough to be used on both the client-side and server-side.

DOM is used in real-life applications by rendering a document, an HTML page, and creating a tree-like structure within the web browser. The nodes present in every copy are organized in a tree structure called a DOM tree. The node at the top of the tree is called the "document object." Whenever an HTML page is rendered in any browser, the browser downloads the HTML code into its local memory and then automatically parses it to display the page on the screen. The browser constructs a page DOM after a web page is loaded. The document object model that was constructed would represent the HTML document in an object-oriented manner. It would then act as a bridge between JavaScript and the document. This is how you make a dynamic web page. Any element or its characteristics can be changed, added, or removed using JavaScript. Any element's CSS style can be changed. It can also produce new events while also reacting to existing ones.

A DOM tree is mainly used to display an HTML document, but it is unnecessary. Some browsers do not represent a document as a tree and use other internal models. These models are unique to a browser.

## WHAT IS JAVASCRIPT USED FOR?

Even though JavaScript is an incredibly versatile language that can be used for almost anything, it is mainly used for creating web-based applications and adding functionality to websites. Other than web apps and web browsers, it is used in servers, software, and other hardware controls. JavaScript can be used for the following things:

1. **Adding interactive behavior to any web page**: The primary reason for which JavaScript is used is that it adds interactivity to any web page. It allows the user to interact with the page. You can do a lot with JavaScript that can transform a web page. You can add event handlers that get triggered when a specific event occurs. You can either show or hide the information just with the simple click of a button. It can also change the color of a button when the mouse hovers over it, making it easier for the user to know when they are clicking on a button. This feature can help in many different ways. For example, let us say you are making a purchase; you could accidentally click on the buy button, which will lead you to buy something that you did not even need in the first place. You can also use JavaScript to create a carousel of images on the homepage of your website. A carousel is a principal component in lots of websites. It can change the look and feel of any website.

2. **You can zoom in and zoom out of an image by using JavaScript**: Again, this is a ubiquitous feature among shopping websites where you hover over the product's image. The image automatically zooms, making you see the product that you wish to buy a little closer so that you can inspect it accordingly. It will also automatically zoom out if you remove the mouse cursor from the image, making the image go back to its standard size. JavaScript can also help you display things like timers and countdowns on your website. Creating a counter app is one of the most popular projects that beginners undertake when learning JavaScript. You can play an audio clip or a video within your web page with the help of JavaScript. It also helps in displaying animations. You can create a functional dropdown hamburger

menu using JavaScript. The hamburger menu will remain hidden on larger screens. Still, when the website encounters a screen with a smaller resolution, it will automatically switch to the hamburger menu, making navigation of the website easier for the users.

3. **Creating web applications**: JavaScript is used for making robust web applications. There are lots of JavaScript frameworks available these days, like Angular, React, and Vue.js, that make it very easy to build complex SPAs. SPA stands for single-page web applications. Developers can easily use these JavaScript frameworks to create mobile apps. A JavaScript framework is nothing but a collection of a JavaScript code library that would provide the developer with pre-written code. This pre-written framework will help them create features and tasks in regular programming. There are lots of popular apps made using JavaScript, like Netflix, Uber, LinkedIn, etc. There are lots of companies that use Node.js, which is a JavaScript-based run-time environment. It is built on Google Chrome's JavaScript V8 engine.

4. **Creating mobile apps**: Mobile devices are everywhere these days, and they are the ones that are used for accessing the internet by a vast majority of the population. These days most of the internet users use their mobile devices to surface the web. JavaScript is so versatile that we can create apps with it that are not even web-based in the first place. We can quickly build an application for non-web context using JavaScript. JavaScript has such varied features that it can be a powerful tool for creating web applications. One of the most popular JavaScript-based frameworks used for developing mobile applications is React Native. React Native allows you to build mobile apps for both Android and iOS natively rendered. By using React Native, you can create an application for various platforms by using the same codebase for all of them. We do not need to have a different codebase for Android and iOS. React Native follows "WORA," which stands for Write Once, Run Anywhere. WORA is used to describe the ability of a program to be just written once and then run on any platform. Sun Microsystems first coined this term about Java.

5. **Building web servers**: A web server can easily be created using Node.js. Node.js is an open-source, cross-platform, back end–based run-time environment in JavaScript. It runs on Google Chrome's JavaScript V8 engine and helps us to execute JavaScript code outside

of a web browser. With node.js, you can write command-line tools. And when you are doing server-side scripting, you can run your script on the server-side and produce dynamic web page content. You can do all of this without even sending the page to the user's web browser. Using node.js also helps maintain the "JavaScript everywhere" paradigm for developers. This paradigm is based on the notion that all of the web application's fundamental components are unified and written in a single language rather than separate languages for server-side and client-side scripts.

6. **NodeJS:** It has an event-driven architecture that is also capable of asynchronous I/O. Asynchronous I/O refers to a form of input/output processing in which processing of other stuff continues before the transmission has finished. Asynchronous I/O is also called non-sequential I/O. The need for asynchronous I/O arises because input and output operations (I/O) on any computer can be prolonged compared to data processing. This is a simple approach to I/O that leaves the processor idle. Asynchronous I/O, also called a blocking I/O, starts an operation first and then waits for it to complete fully to move on to the next task. But using this method blocks the progress of any program while the communication is still in progress as the system resources sit idle.

7. **I/O Operations:** When any program makes lots of I/O operations, it means that, for the most part, the processor is just sitting idle waiting for the input/output processes to complete. This is why asynchronous input/output is the preferred method of input/output processing because it is faster and saves a lot of time and resources. As mentioned before, Node.js is an event-driven architecture that does not wait for the response sent by the previous call. It just moves on and starts processing the next call. The servers created using Node .js are fast and transfer chunks of data in one go without constantly buffering. If you wish to make a server in Node.js, you can use the HTTP module and create a server using the createServer() method. The HTTP module contains the function used to create a web server. This method gets executed whenever someone tries to access port 8080. As a response to this, the HTTP server displays HTML. Also, it should be included in the HTTP header. As we already know, a web server accepts requests from clients such as web browsers. To interact with a web server, we need to enter a domain name, which

gets translated to an IP address (IP stands for Internet Protocol) by a DNS server (DNS stands for Domain Name System). An IP address is a unique number that is used to identify a machine on the internet. Like your fingerprint, each device accessing the internet has an individual IP address.

8. **Developing server applications**: Most of the web applications that we use these days have a server-side. A server is functional when it comes to dynamically display data as required. For example, let us assume there is an online shopping website; now imagine how many products are available on any shopping website. If we start displaying all the data for each product using static pages, it would be incredibly inefficient and highly time-consuming. So instead, most of the sites demonstrate static templates built using HTML, CSS, and JavaScript, and they dynamically update the data inside those templates as per their requirement. When you want to view another product than the one you have initially been considering, the data inside the template will change as it would pull data from the server to display data of the product that you want to see. JavaScript helps in generating content and handling HTTP requests.

9. **Server runtime:** JavaScript can run on servers as well by using Node .js. Node.js provides an environment that contains all the necessary tools required to run JavaScript on a web server. Whenever you view a web page in your web browser, you are essentially making a request to another computer on the internet. That other computer you are requesting is called the web server. You are asking the server to access some of the files it contains in its system. So, as a response, the server provides you with a web page containing the information you requested. A web server receives an HTTP request from a client. A client in this scenario is the browser that the user operates. After receiving the request, the server would then process it and send it back as an HTTP response. The HTTP response that is sent back by the server could be anything, like an HTML page or JSON from an API. API stands for Application Programming Interface, and it acts as a software intermediary between two applications and helps them talk to each other. You can see API as the middle man. They are used to perform a specified function or execute predefined processes. Every time you check the weather on your phone or use Facebook to send an instant message, you use an API.

10. **Server Processes:** Even though the process of a client requesting data and then receiving it within seconds sounds like a straightforward task, in reality, a lot goes into it. A lot of software make all of this look so easy. Many software processes are involved, from the client requesting a web page to the end of a server returning a web page. This software can be primarily divided into two categories: front end and back end. The front is concerned with how the content is presented to the user, like the color, layout, and theme of a webpage, the styling of the text, the color of the navigation bar, etc.

11. **Backend:** On the other hand, the back end is concerned with how data is exchanged between the server and the client and processed and stored within a database. The back end also handles network requests from the browser and communicates with the database to fulfill the said client request. Initially, JavaScript was created to write front-end code, but with the help of Node.js, developers can now easily use it to write back-end code. Having both the front end and the back end in one language reduces the effort it takes to create a web server considerably. This is one of the significant reasons Node.js is a prevalent choice for writing back-end code. Using Node.js, you can easily create a web server that can return different data types like CSV files, HTML web pages, and even JSON data.

12. **Developing games**: JavaScript can also be used for creating games. You can easily create a browser game using JavaScript. Creating a game using JavaScript is an excellent way for beginners to test their skills. JavaScript has lots of libraries and frameworks that can be used for creating a game. You can easily create a 2D or a 3D game using JavaScript. You can also create a top-quality game with JavaScript. It is the kind of language with so many libraries and frameworks, so it is somewhat expected that it would have tons of game engine options. You can choose from all these different game engine options to fit your programming skills and needs. These game engines are not just free and open-source, but many of them even work well within a web editor and provide incredibly fast rendering for 2D and 3D elements. Fast rendering of the graphics is an essential aspect of any type of game. Popular JavaScript game engines are Phaser, Babylon.js, Cocos2D, PlayCanvas, Kiwi.js, Panda Engine, Pixi.js, etc.

- **Phaser:** It allows you to create HTML 5–based games for both desktop and mobile devices. It has lots of features like sprites, images, and control inputs. Phaser has three main physics engines. Phaser is a kind of framework that uses both Canvas and WebGL renderers. Phaser can use both these renderers internally. It can also automatically switch between canvas and WebGL, depending on the browser support. Phaser has a substantial online community of developers, so you can easily find the solutions to all your doubts through forums, newsletters, and social media. The massive online community support system is one of the most significant advantages of using Phaser. To use this game engine, one of the first things you need to keep in mind is using a web browser that fully supports the HTML tag <canvas>. Besides using JavaScript, Phaser also supports TypeScript code. Check out the official website https://phaser.io/ for more information.

- **Babylon.js:** Babylon is a popular library that also happens to be supported by Microsoft. Babylon offers in-depth elements that help build and render 3D games using WebGL. Babylon also has a massive community of developers online. One of the most significant advantages of having a solid online community is that it becomes effortless to find tutorials and guidelines. Even deploying the code and how to go about that whole process also gets simplified.

  Additionally, you do not need to install Babylon onto your computer. You can efficiently work with it on your browser or code editor. Check out the official website https://www.babylonjs.com/ for more information.

- **Cocos2d:** Cocos2d is seen as a unified package consisting of all the game development tools. By using Cocos2d, a developer can code an entire game using JavaScript and export it to multiple different platforms. Cocos2d-x is an incredibly versatile platform capable of doing many things like resource management, scene editing, game previewing, etc. It is an open-source framework that also helps debug and publish various game features. The Cocos2d game engine is available for both Windows and Mac. It also has a large forum of developers to discuss your projects and find help about the same. Check out the official website https://www.cocos.com/en/ for more information.

- **PlayCanvas:** PlayCanvas has a complete set of tools that help in building 3D games. This game engine has light features, light-maps, meshes, and many other elements that prove immensely helpful while making any game. It also has an impressive graphics infrastructure and supports physical rendering and WebGL 3D rendering. One of the most significant advantages of using PlayCanvas that sets it apart from its counterparts is that it is a tool that entirely operates in the cloud. Because of that, it is not necessary to have plugins when you are running or to test your game in the browser. PlayCanvas is an open-source game development tool offering a paid version. The paid version provides signatures so that the developers can migrate their projects to a private server. The paid services are also used to offer more storage capacity. Check out the official website https://playcanvas.com/ for more information.

- **Kiwi.js:** Kiwi is an open-source framework based on JavaScript. It is also one of the most accessible frameworks that can be used to make mobile and desktop HTML 5 games. The Kiwi.js game engine uses both WebGL and Canvas rendering for game development. It can also easily publish games and apps using CocoonJS and the Chrome Webstore. One of the significant highlights of Kiwi is that it has a massive collection of plugins. There is a plugin that includes an achievement engine that helps create and customize achievements based on the user's progress in the game. It also has a quest management plugin that helps keep track of the different quests that the character in the game has gone through. There are also sprites and shades. There is even a social media connector plugin that can connect the game to social media so that the user can share their progress on their preferred social media app. Kiwi also has an artificial intelligence algorithm that you can explore. In addition to all of the plugins and various features that we discussed, Kiwi also has plenty of tutorials that help beginners create their first game and guide them in publishing their first game very quickly. Check out the official website https://www.kiwijs.org/ for more information.

- **Panda Engine:** Panda Engine works in tandem with Pixi and helps in rendering 2D games for mobile and desktop at an incredible speed. Besides the integration of Panda Engine with

Kiwi, this tool comes in a tiny package. It supports many libraries and algorithms that you can choose to work with based on your convenience. One feature that differentiates Panda Engine is that it can track Google Analytics events inside a game. Using analytics is a great way to determine the usage and measure its performance to make the necessary changes. Check out the official website https://www.panda3d.org/ for more information.

- **Pixi.js:** Pixi is a 2D renderer that is incredibly easy to use. You can create interactive digital content using Pixi, including HTML 5 games. Pixi is a prevalent library with some fantastic features used by massive names like Spotify, Marvel, Google, Adobe, etc. Pixi has a WebGL renderer, but it also uses Canvas if a browser does not support WebGL rendering. To start using Pixi, you need to download a prebuilt build. You can either choose CDN, or you can use an NPM install. If you are curious about Pixi and want to check how it works without downloading it first, Pixi also has an online playground where you can test its features. Check out the official website https://pixijs.com/ for more information.

We talked about WebGL and canvas for rendering graphics in all of the above game development engines. But what exactly are WebGL and Canvas rendering. Let us dive deeper into that.

WebGL stands for Web Graphics Library, and it is JavaScript API used for rendering interactive 2D and 3D graphics on compatible browsers without using any additional plugins to do so. WebGL is one of the versions of OpenGL, which is a 3D engine. It essentially helps the users in performing 3D manipulation in web browsers. The original authors attributed for the development of WebGL components is the Mozilla Foundations. However, the developers for this are the Kronos WebGL working group. WebGL first came into existence in the year 2011. WebGL is said to be the successor of Canvas, and it evolved out of Canvas 3D experiments. WebGL browsers are Google Chrome, Mozilla Firefox, Safari, Opera, Internet Explorer, Edge, and Vivaldi. For purchasing the license, the market value of WebGL is more than that of Canvas. The speed of WebGL is greater than Canvas. WebGL is mainly preferred and used for rendering 3D graphics, although it can also work on 2D graphics.

On the other hand, Canvas is a part of HTML5 that allows its users to use dynamic 2D shapes that are rendered using a script. Canvas does not have a built-in scene graph and can be seen as low, but it can update bitmap images. Canvas was first introduced by Apple for their internal uses and then later on for their MAC OS. It came into existence in the year 2004, and it is considered the predecessor of WebGL. Canvas is supported by many web browsers like Mozilla Firefox, Google Chrome, Internet Explorer, Safari, Opera, Edge, etc. Canvas also happens to have a lesser market value when purchasing the license. Canvas is somewhat slower than its counterparts and is generally preferred for 2D rendering or anything related to that.

13. **Web development:** JavaScript is one the most critical step for anyone who wants to become a web developer. JavaScript is most popularly used for making interactive web pages. It helps us in adding dynamic behavior to a web page. It also allows us to add special effects to any type of web page. On most websites, JavaScript helps with validation purposes. JavaScript helps us execute some complex actions that make the clients easily interact with the websites. A website can load content into a document without even loading the web page by using JavaScript.

14. **Presentations:** JavaScript is also capable of creating presentations as a website. Various such libraries are available that can help us create a web-based slide deck like RevealJS, BespokeJS, etc. They are relatively easy to use, so you can easily create something incredible in a brief period. Reveal.js is mainly used to create interactive and beautiful slide decks. It works with some help from HTML. These presentations work not only well on desktops but also on mobile devices and tablets. It also supports all kinds of CSS color formats. On the other hand, BespokeJS includes many features like bullet lists, responsive scaling, etc.

## HOW DOES JAVASCRIPT WORK?

JavaScript is a scripting language that can work on both the client-side and server-side. Some additional tools and languages help JavaScript when working on the server-side. So, in this part, we will focus on learning how JavaScript works on the client-side as JavaScript is primarily used for that. JavaScript is incredibly efficient and is one of the most commonly used scripting languages. The word client-side scripting language refers to any language that works. The term client-side could also be referred to as client machine. The scripting language works inside web browsers. However, for a scripting language to work in a web browser, the web browser needs to support JavaScript or be JavaScript enabled. Most web browsers these days support JavaScript or have their JavaScript engine. For example, Google Chrome has its JavaScript engine called V8. Node.js is also built on the V8 engine of Google Chrome. Microsoft Edge has a JavaScript engine named Chakra, Safari has JavaScript Core, and the JavaScript engine of Firefox is called Spidermonkey. JavaScript can be used in many ways; it depends on how the web developers want to use it and for what purpose. One of the most common ways JavaScript is used is for validating data given by the user in the form fields.

Whenever we run a JavaScript code in our web browser, the JavaScript engine about that web browser understands the code and then eventually runs it. JavaScript also happens to be an interpreted language, which means that each line of the code gets executed one by one instead of compiling the whole program all at once. So, the JavaScript engine will take each line of the code, convert it, and then run it in the same order.

Whenever a JavaScript program runs inside the web browser, the JavaScript code is received by the browser engine, and then the engine runs that code to obtain the output. In any standard JavaScript engine, the source code needs to go through several steps to get executed. A JavaScript engine has different parts that help us in running the code. Let us look at those other parts and understand what function each performs.

1. **Parser:** Whenever we run a piece of JavaScript code, our code first gets to the parser inside the JS engine. The parser checks the code for syntactic errors, going through each line because it is interpreted. So, whenever an error is detected, the execution stops right there and is thrown.

2. **AST:** It stands for Abstract Syntax Tree. After the parser checks the code and there are no mistakes, a data structure is created called AST.

3. **Machine Code Conversion:** Once the parser creates the syntax tree, the JS engine converts the JavaScript code into machine code. Machine code is the language that the machine can understand.

4. **Machine Code:** When the program is finally converted into machine code, it is sent to the system for execution, and then that machine code is run by our system.

## ATTRIBUTES

An attribute is a unique keyword that provides additional information about an element. Each tag can have features that define the behavior of that particular element. All attributes are applied within the start tag. Attributes always come in name–value pairs. Both the name and the value for an attribute are case-sensitive. So, it is advised to always write them in lowercase. Multiple attributes can be written within one HTML element, but you need to give space between those two attributes.

Syntax

<element attribute_name="value"> content </element>

The following is a list of all available attributes within HTML.

### Global Attributes

Global attributes are those attributes that can be used with all HTML elements.

- accesskey: The accesskey attribute in HTML is used to either activate or focus on a specific element. The access key attribute working depends on the browser. The way it works might differ from browser to browser.

Syntax

<element accesskey = "single_character">

As this is a browser-dependent attribute, each browser has a different shortcut. In windows, if you are using Chrome, Safari, or Opera, use the shortcut Alt + single_character. Whereas for Firefox in Windows, you need to use Alt + Shift + single_character.

- **class:** An attribute used to refer to a class in a stylesheet

- **contenteditable:** Specifies whether the content of any element is editable or not

- **data-\*:** Used to store custom data private to a page

- **Dir:** Specifies the direction of text for the content in an element

- **Draggable:** Determines whether an element is draggable or not

- **Hidden:** Hides an element, showing that an element is no longer relevant

- **Id:** Used to set a unique id for an element

- **Lang:** Specifies the language of the content within an element

- **Spellcheck:** Used to determine if the component needs to have its spelling or grammar checked or not

- **Style:** Determines inline CSS style for any element

- **tabindex:** Determines the order of tabbing in an element

- **Title:** Sets extra information about a component and creates a make-shift tooltip

- **Translate:** Determines whether the content of a part should be translated or not

## Global Event Attributes

Event attributes are used to define event actions. All the event attributes have a common value of the script.

- **Onafterprint:** Script to be run after the document is printed

- **Onbeforeprint:** Script to be run before the document is printed

- **onbeforeunload:** When the document is about to be unloaded

- **Onerror:** When an error occurs

- **Onhashchange:** When there is a change in the anchor part of the URL

- **Onload:** After the page has finished loading

- **Onmessage:** When the message is triggered

- **onoffline:** When the browser starts to work offline

- **Ononline:** When the browser starts to work online

- **Onpagehide:** When a user navigates away from the page

- **Onpageshow:** When a user navigates to a page

## All Attributes in Bootstrap
*For modals*

- Data-toggle = "modal"
- Data-target = "element"
- Data-target = "target-element"
- Data-dismiss = "modal"

*For dropdowns*

- Data-toggle = "dropdown"
- Data-target = "#"

*ScrollSpy*

- Data-spy = "scroll"
- Data-target = "target-element"
- Data-offset = "X"

*Toggleable tabs*

- Data-toggle = "tab"
- Data-target = "element"
- Data-toggle = "pill"

*Tooltip*

- Data-toggle = "tooltip"
- Data-toggle = "data-animation"
- Data-toggle = "data-container"
- Data-toggle = "data-delay"
- Data-toggle = "data-html"
- Data-toggle = "data-placement"

- Data-toggle = "data-selector"
- Data-toggle = "data-template"
- Data-toggle = "data-title"
- Data-toggle = "data-trigger"
- Data-toggle = "data-viewport"

*Popovers*

- Data-toggle = "popover"
- Data-toggle = "data-animation"
- Data-toggle = "data-container"
- Data-toggle = "data-content"
- Data-toggle = "data-delay"
- Data-toggle = "data-html"
- Data-toggle = "data-placement"
- Data-toggle = "data-selector"
- Data-toggle = "data-template"
- Data-toggle = "data-title"
- Data-toggle = "data-trigger"
- Data-toggle = "data-viewport"

*Alert messages*

- Data-dismiss = "alert"

*Buttons*

- Data-toggle = "button"

*Collapse*

- Data-toggle = "collapse"
- Data-target = "element"

*Carousel*

- Data-ride = "carousel"

- Data-keyboard = "true"

- Data-pause = "hover"

- Data-wrap = "true"

- Data-slide = "prev | next"

*Affix*

- Data-spy = "affix"

- Data-offset-top = "X"

- Data-offset-bottom = "X"

## ALERTS

Alert is a user message that is mostly used to display a message to the user based on prior user action.

- alert-primary

```
<div class="alert alert-primary" role="alert">
    A simple primary alert—check it out!
</div>
```

- alert-secondary

```
<div class="alert alert-secondary" role="alert">
    A simple secondary alert—check it out!
</div>
```

- alert-success

```
<div class="alert alert-success" role="alert">
    A simple success alert—check it out!
</div>
```

- alert-danger

```
<div class="alert alert-danger" role="alert">
    A simple danger alert—check it out!
</div>
```

- alert-warning

```
<div class="alert alert-warning" role="alert">
   A simple warning alert—check it out!
</div>
```

- alert-info

```
<div class="alert alert-info" role="alert">
   A simple info alert—check it out!
</div>
```

- alert-light

```
<div class="alert alert-light" role="alert">
   A simple light alert—check it out!
</div>
```

- alert-dark

```
<div class="alert alert-dark" role="alert">
   A simple dark alert—check it out!
</div>
```

- alert-link

Used to add a link in the alert class:

```
<div class="alert alert-primary" role="alert">
   A simple primary alert with <a href="#"
class="alert-link">an example link</a>. Give it a
click if you like.
</div>
```

- alert-dismissible

Can be used with any other alert color class like info, danger, success, etc. for styling:

```
<div class="alert alert-warning alert-dismissible
fade show" role="alert">
   <strong>Holy guacamole!</strong> You should
check in on some of those fields below.
   <button type="button" class="btn-close" data-bs-
dismiss="alert" aria-label="Close"></button>
</div>
```

- alert-heading

Can be used with any other alert color class like info, danger, success, etc. for styling:

```
<div class="alert alert-success" role="alert">
    <h4 class="alert-heading">Well done!</h4>
    <p>Aww yeah, you successfully read this
important alert message. This example text is going
to run a bit longer so
        that you can see how spacing within an alert
works with this kind of content.</p>
    <hr>
    <p class="mb-0">Whenever you need to, be sure to
use margin utilities to keep things nice and tidy.</p>
</div>
```

## CAROUSEL

Used to set up a slideshow that cycles through a series of slides, text, or images. It is built using CSS 3D and a little bit of JavaScript. It also has support for previous and next controls.

- carousel (slides only)

```
<div id="carouselSlidesOnly" class="carousel slide"
data-bs-ride="carousel">
    <div class="carousel-inner">
        <div class="carousel-item active">
            <img src="assets/images/bs-images/carousel-
slide-1.png" class="d-block w-100" alt="Slide 1">
        </div>
        <div class="carousel-item">
            <img src="assets/images/bs-images/carousel-
slide-2.png" class="d-block w-100" alt="Slide 2">
        </div>
        <div class="carousel-item">
            <img src="assets/images/bs-images/carousel-
slide-3.png" class="d-block w-100" alt="Slide 3">
        </div>
    </div>
</div>
```

- carousel with controls

```
<div id="carouselWithControls" class="carousel
slide" data-bs-ride="carousel">
   <div class="carousel-inner">
      <div class="carousel-item active">
         <img src="assets/images/bs-images/carousel-
slide-1.png" class="d-block w-100" alt="Slide 1">
      </div>
      <div class="carousel-item">
         <img src="assets/images/bs-images/carousel-
slide-2.png" class="d-block w-100" alt="Slide 2">
      </div>
      <div class="carousel-item">
         <img src="assets/images/bs-images/carousel-
slide-3.png" class="d-block w-100" alt="Slide 3">
      </div>
   </div>
   <a class="carousel-control-prev"
href="#carouselWithControls" role="button"
data-bs-slide="prev">
      <span class="carousel-control-prev-icon"
aria-hidden="true"></span>
      <span class="visually-hidden">Previous</span>
   </a>
   <a class="carousel-control-next"
href="#carouselWithControls" role="button"
data-bs-slide="next">
      <span class="carousel-control-next-icon"
aria-hidden="true"></span>
      <span class="visually-hidden">Next</span>
   </a>
</div>
```

- carousel-indicators

```
<div id="carouselWithIndicators" class="carousel
slide" data-bs-ride="carousel">
   <ol class="carousel-indicators">
      <li data-bs-target="#carouselWithIndicators"
data-bs-slide-to="0" class="active"></li>
      <li data-bs-target="#carouselWithIndicators"
data-bs-slide-to="1"></li>
```

```
    <li data-bs-target="#carouselWithIndicators"
data-bs-slide-to="2"></li>
    </ol>
    <div class="carousel-inner">
        <div class="carousel-item active">
            <img src="assets/images/bs-images/carousel-
slide-1.png" class="d-block w-100" alt="Slide 1">
        </div>
        <div class="carousel-item">
            <img src="assets/images/bs-images/carousel-
slide-2.png" class="d-block w-100" alt="Slide 2">
        </div>
        <div class="carousel-item">
            <img src="assets/images/bs-images/carousel-
slide-3.png" class="d-block w-100" alt="Slide 3">
        </div>
    </div>
    <a class="carousel-control-prev"
href="#carouselWithIndicators" role="button"
data-bs-slide="prev">
        <span class="carousel-control-prev-icon"
aria-hidden="true"></span>
        <span class="visually-hidden">Previous</span>
    </a>
    <a class="carousel-control-next"
href="#carouselWithIndicators" role="button"
data-bs-slide="next">
        <span class="carousel-control-next-icon"
aria-hidden="true"></span>
        <span class="visually-hidden">Next</span>
    </a>
</div>
```

- carousel-caption

```
<div id="carouselWithCaptions" class="carousel
slide" data-bs-ride="carousel">
    <ol class="carousel-indicators">
        <li data-bs-target="#carouselWithCaptions"
data-bs-slide-to="0" class="active"></li>
        <li data-bs-target="#carouselWithCaptions"
data-bs-slide-to="1"></li>
```

```
        <li data-bs-target="#carouselWithCaptions"
data-bs-slide-to="2"></li>
    </ol>
    <div class="carousel-inner">
        <div class="carousel-item active">
            <img src="assets/images/bs-images/carousel-
slide-1.png" class="d-block w-100" alt="Slide 1">
            <div class="carousel-caption d-none
d-sm-block">
                <h5>First slide label</h5>
                <p>Nulla vitae elit libero, a pharetra
augue mollis interdum.</p>
            </div>
        </div>
        <div class="carousel-item">
            <img src="assets/images/bs-images/carousel-
slide-2.png" class="d-block w-100" alt="Slide 2">
            <div class="carousel-caption d-none
d-sm-block">
                <h5>Second slide label</h5>
                <p>Lorem ipsum dolor sit amet,
consectetur adipiscing elit.</p>
            </div>
        </div>
        <div class="carousel-item">
            <img src="assets/images/bs-images/carousel-
slide-3.png" class="d-block w-100" alt="Slide 3">
            <div class="carousel-caption d-none
d-sm-block">
                <h5>Third slide label</h5>
                <p>Praesent commodo cursus magna, vel
scelerisque nisl consectetur.</p>
            </div>
        </div>
    </div>
    <a class="carousel-control-prev"
href="#carouselWithCaptions" role="button"
data-bs-slide="prev">
        <span class="carousel-control-prev-icon"
aria-hidden="true"></span>
        <span class="visually-hidden">Previous</span>
    </a>
```

```
    <a class="carousel-control-next"
href="#carouselWithCaptions" role="button"
data-bs-slide="next">
        <span class="carousel-control-next-icon"
aria-hidden="true"></span>
        <span class="visually-hidden">Next</span>
    </a>
</div>
```

- carousel-fade

```
<div id="carouselCrossfade" class="carousel slide
carousel-fade" data-bs-ride="carousel">
    <div class="carousel-inner">
        <div class="carousel-item active">
            <img src="assets/images/bs-images/carousel-
slide-1.png" class="d-block w-100" alt="Slide 1">
        </div>
        <div class="carousel-item">
            <img src="assets/images/bs-images/carousel-
slide-2.png" class="d-block w-100" alt="Slide 2">
        </div>
        <div class="carousel-item">
            <img src="assets/images/bs-images/carousel-
slide-3.png" class="d-block w-100" alt="Slide 3">
        </div>
    </div>
    <a class="carousel-control-prev"
href="#carouselCrossfade" role="button"
data-bs-slide="prev">
        <span class="carousel-control-prev-icon"
aria-hidden="true"></span>
        <span class="visually-hidden">Previous</span>
    </a>
    <a class="carousel-control-next"
href="#carouselCrossfade" role="button"
data-bs-slide="next">
        <span class="carousel-control-next-icon"
aria-hidden="true"></span>
        <span class="visually-hidden">Next</span>
    </a>
</div>
```

- carousel with intervals

```
<div id="carouselWithInterval" class="carousel
slide" data-bs-ride="carousel">
   <div class="carousel-inner">
      <div class="carousel-item active"
data-bs-interval="10000">
         <img src="assets/images/bs-images/carousel-
slide-1.png" class="d-block w-100" alt="Slide 1">
      </div>
      <div class="carousel-item"
data-bs-interval="2000">
         <img src="assets/images/bs-images/carousel-
slide-2.png" class="d-block w-100" alt="Slide 2">
      </div>
      <div class="carousel-item">
         <img src="assets/images/bs-images/carousel-
slide-3.png" class="d-block w-100" alt="Slide 3">
      </div>
   </div>
   <a class="carousel-control-prev"
href="#carouselWithInterval" role="button"
data-bs-slide="prev">
      <span class="carousel-control-prev-icon"
aria-hidden="true"></span>
      <span class="visually-hidden">Previous</span>
   </a>
   <a class="carousel-control-next"
href="#carouselWithInterval" role="button"
data-bs-slide="next">
      <span class="carousel-control-next-icon"
aria-hidden="true"></span>
      <span class="visually-hidden">Next</span>
   </a>
</div>
```

- carousel-dark

```
<div id="carouselDark" class="carousel carousel-
dark slide" data-bs-ride="carousel">
   <ol class="carousel-indicators">
      <li data-bs-target="#carouselDark" data-bs-
slide-to="0" class="active"></li>
      <li data-bs-target="#carouselDark" data-bs-
slide-to="1"></li>
```

```html
        <li data-bs-target="#carouselDark" data-bs-
slide-to="2"></li>
    </ol>
    <div class="carousel-inner">
        <div class="carousel-item active">
            <img src="assets/images/bs-images/carous
el-dark-slide-1.png" class="d-block w-100"
alt="Slide 1">
            <div class="carousel-caption d-none
d-sm-block">
                <h5>First slide label</h5>
                <p>Nulla vitae elit libero, a pharetra
augue mollis interdum.</p>
            </div>
        </div>
        <div class="carousel-item">
            <img src="assets/images/bs-images/carous
el-dark-slide-2.png" class="d-block w-100"
alt="Slide 2">
            <div class="carousel-caption d-none
d-sm-block">
                <h5>Second slide label</h5>
                <p>Lorem ipsum dolor sit amet,
consectetur adipiscing elit.</p>
            </div>
        </div>
        <div class="carousel-item">
            <img src="assets/images/bs-images/carous
el-dark-slide-3.png" class="d-block w-100"
alt="Slide 3">
            <div class="carousel-caption d-none
d-sm-block">
                <h5>Third slide label</h5>
                <p>Praesent commodo cursus magna, vel
scelerisque nisl consectetur.</p>
            </div>
        </div>
    </div>
    <a class="carousel-control-prev"
href="#carouselDark" role="button"
data-bs-slide="prev">
        <span class="carousel-control-prev-icon"
aria-hidden="true"></span>
```

```
        <span class="visually-hidden">Previous</span>
    </a>
    <a class="carousel-control-next"
href="#carouselDark" role="button"
data-bs-slide="next">
        <span class="carousel-control-next-icon"
aria-hidden="true"></span>
        <span class="visually-hidden">Next</span>
    </a>
</div>
```

## CHAPTER SUMMARY

In this chapter, we learned different components of Bootstrap that work in tandem with JavaScript. We learned about how JavaScript works and what we can do with it. We also saw several Bootstrap components that use JavaScript for their work. In the next chapter, we will learn about cod optimization and its importance.

## CHAPTER 6

# Code Optimization

## IN THIS CHAPTER

- ➤ What is Code Optimization
- ➤ Goals of Code Optimization
- ➤ Category of Optimization
- ➤ Code Optimization Techniques

In the previous chapter, we learned about JavaScript and its use within Bootstrap components. We talked about several Bootstrap components like attributes, alerts, transitions, carousels, etc. We also discussed jQuery plugins available in Bootstrap and how the previous versions of Bootstrap used jQuery as a dependency. We also learned how to use Bootstrap in conjunction with React and Angular. In this chapter, we will talk about code optimization. We would learn about the best practices for writing code, how to write cleaner and lighter code, and how to best optimize it.

## WHAT IS CODE OPTIMIZATION?

In this era when technology is changing rapidly, there has been a demand for lightweight, low power consuming, and responsive applications. Some examples of such applications include graphic editors on mobile devices, video calling/conferencing applications, live broadcasting stations, and many other devices just like that. This type of requirement is directly linked to the fact that applications should utilize the essential CPU resources like audio processing, video processing, computation engine, crypto engine,

DOI: 10.1201/9781003309383-6

etc., efficiently so that optimum result is obtained. However, this type of demand raises a unique challenge for developers, which forces them to write the program in a well-structured manner. This is done to utilize each CPU clock cycle to its full potential. The application program or the embedded software primarily runs on processors with minimal computational power. This limited power hence raises the evident need for Code Optimization.

Most of the compilers today optimize the program code at the lowest level. However, manual optimization remains essential for optimizing at the source code level. The compiler is often limited to general-purpose optimization so that it applies to many programs at once. This forces the programmer to become creative and use their knowledge and experience so that optimization is performed. It is often challenging to identify the areas where optimization is most required. This is even more so in the case of extensive and complex applications. In cases like that, we need to use the profiler to identify those areas that require optimization. After placing, the result of the optimization is verified. There are lots of different techniques by which a program can run faster, but it often increases the program's size.

Software applications, at their core, are designed to achieve a specified set of functionalities that the developers want. The performance consideration is also added to the design later in the development process. Several techniques can help any software to run faster. But to achieve speed improvement, there is also a downside: an increase in the size of the application. So, to solve this issue, the developers need to write the program code in such a way that optimizes both the memory and the speed. There are various ways to get performance data, but the best way is to use a good performance profiler, which shows the time spent in each function and analyzes the data.

Code Optimization refers to the process of improving the code in such a way that it consumes fewer resources and works faster than before. Modifying software or some part of it to make it work quicker and more efficiently is the primary goal of code optimization. Optimizing a computer program could consume less memory storage space or CPU, draw less power, etc. Code optimization is also referred to as program optimization and software optimization.

Any method of code modification could be termed code optimization if it ends up improving the quality and the efficiency of the code. There are multiple reasons why any program or computer software needs to be optimized; it could decrease its size to consume less memory. Optimization helps reduce the number of input and output operations so that the code executes more quickly.

All optimization methods should comply with one essential requirement, that is, the output for both optimized and non-optimized programs must be the same. This requirement can be ignored in exceptional cases where changes in the inherent behavior of the optimized code lead to better features. The consequences of changing the behavior of a program while optimizing it can be ignored if the changes end up creating a better result.

Different types and levels of optimization are used depending upon a case in point. Optimization can be performed manually by a programmer or by an automatic optimizer. An automated optimizer could be a specialized software, or it could be a built-in compiler. Most modern processors can also optimize the code based on their execution order or code instructions.

The optimizations are further classified into two types: high-level and low-level optimizations. Low-level optimizations are performed later on when the source code has already been compiled into a set of machine instructions. At this level, automated optimization comes into play. On the other hand, all the high-level optimizations are done by a programmer. A programmer is usually entrusted with that.

## GOALS OF CODE OPTIMIZATION

1. Remove repetitive code without changing the meaning of the program

2. Reduce execution speed

3. Reduce the consumption of memory

There are several points that you need to keep in mind before attempting to optimize the program code.

Time-based optimization will result in faster output, but it can also increase the size of the codebase. So, if you try to optimize the code for time-based performance, it may start conflicting with the memory and size consumption of the program. To avoid such a scenario, you need to find a delicate balance between the time taken and memory consumed while also keeping your requirement in mind. Trying to optimize the performance is a never-ending process. There are always different ways to improve your code and run it faster. Sometimes, we may feel tempted to use specific programming methods over others to make our code run faster at the expense of not following the best coding practices. Try to avoid any such kind of methods as much as possible. It will make it harder to maintain the code in the long run.

## CATEGORIES OF OPTIMIZATION

1. Space optimization

2. Time optimization

You can optimize your code by either reducing space or time because both space and time optimization categories are correlated. Space optimization is usually performed manually, which is an incredibly time-consuming process and may lead to results that are not optimal depending upon the programmer and their skills. For time-based optimization, always take some time to think about the proper algorithm to use. Always try to avoid type conversion and use the same variables as much as possible. Instead of making a loop run faster, make sure to make the loop run as little as possible. If a loop runs for lots of cycles in your code and takes up most of your execution time, redesign the code.

## CODE OPTIMIZATION TECHNIQUES

Some of the most critical code optimization techniques are as follows:

1. **Compile Time Evaluation:** Two methods fall under this category.

   i. **Constant folding:** This technique involves folding the constants. The expressions with constant value operands are evaluated at compile time. Those expressions are then replaced with their results.

   ii. **Constant propagation:** If a constant value is assigned to a variable, the variable would get replaced with the constant value during compilation.

2. **Common Sub-Expression Elimination:** It is the expression that has been computed before but somehow appears again during computation. In this technique, the common expressions are removed. The

common expressions are removed to avoid re-computing them all over again. The result that has already been computed is used in the program further.

3. **Code Movement:** This technique involves the movement of the code. The code within the loop is moved outside. This is done so that the code does not get executed again each time the loop runs. Removal of this code saves time and resources.

4. **Dead Code Elimination:** In this technique, the dead code is eliminated. The code statements whose outputs are never used are eliminated in this method.

5. **Strength Reduction:** In this technique, the strength of the expressions is reduced. In this technique, the expensive operators are replaced with cheap ones.

## CHAPTER SUMMARY

In this chapter, we learned about code optimization and the goals behind optimizing a piece of code. We also learned about the different categories of code optimization. In the end, we learned about the various techniques used for optimizing code. In the next chapter, we will learn how to integrate Bootstrap with Jekyll and ASP.NET; we will also learn how APIs work in Bootstrap.

## CHAPTER 7

# Integrations and API

## IN THIS CHAPTER

➢ Creating an HTTP Client

➢ Working with APIs in Bootstrap

➢ Integrating Bootstrap with Jekyll

➢ Integrating with ASP.NET

In the previous chapter, we learned about code optimization. We talked about how code optimization is done in compilers. We discussed the best tips and tricks for code optimization. We also learned how to write clean code and the best coding practices. In this chapter, we will learn how to create an HTTP client. We will also learn to work with Bootstrap APIs and integrate Bootstrap with Jekyll. We will also learn how to integrate Bootstrap with ASP.NET.

## CREATING AN HTTP CLIENT

Hypertext Transfer Protocol (HTTP) is considered the foundation of the World Wide Web (WWW) and is used to load web pages over the hypertext links on the internet. HTTP, also called Hypertext Transfer Protocol, is a protocol used in the application layer and is designed to transfer information between network devices. It runs at other network protocol stack layers. A typical data request from the client computer reaches the server, which sends a response message. HTTP requests allow internet communication platforms, such as web browsers, to request the information they

DOI: 10.1201/9781003309383-7

need to load a website. Each HTTP request sent over the internet contains a set of encrypted data containing different types of information. Typical HTTP requests include:

- HTTP version type
- URL
- HTTP method
- HTTP request header
- Optional HTTP body

Now let us look closely and see how requests work and how you can use the content of your request to share information.

HTTP methods, sometimes called HTTP verbs, specify the action expected from the server on which the HTTP request is queried. For example, two of the most common HTTP methods are GET and POST. A "GET" request expects information to be returned (usually in the form of a website). In contrast, a "POST" request usually indicates that the client sends data to a web server (form): information, sent a user name, password, etc.

HTTP headers contain text information stored in key-value pairs, and they are included in every HTTP request (and response, more on that later). These headers communicated core information, such as the client's browser and requested data.

The body of a request is the part that contains the "body" of information the request is transferring. The body of an HTTP request contains any information being submitted to the web server, such as a username and password or any other data entered into a form.

An HTTP response is what the web clients (often browsers) receive from an internet server to answer an HTTP request. These received responses communicate valuable information based on what was asked for in the HTTP request.

A typical HTTP response contains the following:

- An HTTP status code
- HTTP response headers
- Optional HTTP body

An HTTP Client can be used to send requests and retrieve the responses. An HTTP Client is made using a builder. A builder can be used for things like configuring per-client state, like the preferred protocol version (HTTP/1.1 or HTTP/2), whether to follow redirects, a proxy, an authenticator, etc. Once built, an HTTP Client is immutable and can send multiple requests. An HTTP Client provides configuration information, and resource sharing, for all requests sent through it.

## WORKING WITH APIS IN BOOTSTRAP

To work with an API in Bootstrap, we need to know an API first. API stands for Application Programming Interface. It acts as a software intermediary and allows two applications to talk to each other. We all use APIs in our day-to-day lives, like when we use Facebook, send a message, or even check the weather.

Whenever you use an application on your mobile phone, the application connects to the internet and sends the data to the server. The server retrieves this data, interprets it, takes the necessary actions, and sends it back to the mobile phone. The application then analyzes this data and presents the essential information in a human-readable format. This is an API; these actions are done via the API.

To better explain this, let's look at a well-known example. Imagine you are sitting at a restaurant table, and the waiter hands you a menu card so that you can order. The kitchen is part of the "system" that prepares the order. What's missing is an essential connection for sending orders to the kitchen and returning food to the table. This is where waiters or APIs come in handy. A waiter is a messenger (or API) that receives requests or orders and tells the kitchen (system) what to do. The waiter then returns and brings the answer to your question to you. In this case, it's food. Here is an example of a real API. You may be familiar with the process of searching for flights online. You can choose from various options with restaurants, including different cities, departure and return dates, and more. Suppose you book a flight on the airline's website. Select the departure city and date, return town and date, cabin class, and other variables. To book a flight, go to the airline's website to access the database and see if seats are available on those dates and how much it will cost.

But what if you are not using the airline's official website, which is also a channel that gives you direct access to information. Instead, you use an online travel service such as Make My Trip or Go Ibibo that collects various airline databases.

In this case, the travel service interacts with the API of the airline. The API is an interface that, like a convenient waiter, can ask this online travel service to retrieve information from the airline's database to book seats, luggage options, and more. The API receives the airline's response to the request and returns it directly to the online travel service. Online travel services provide up-to-date and relevant information to their users.

One of the added benefits of using an API is the extra layer of security. The data on your mobile phone will not be fully exposed to the server. Similarly, the server is never fully exposed to mobile phones. Instead, everyone communicates with small data packets and shares only what they need—for example, takeaway orders. You tell the restaurant what you want to eat, they tell you what they need for it, and finally, you get your food. The API is extremely valuable and accounts for most of the revenue of many enterprises. Large companies such as Google, eBay, Salesforce.com, Amazon, and Expedia are just a few companies that make money from APIs.

For years, an "API" often refers to any generic connection interface to an application. However, these days, modern APIs have some unique and valuable characteristics. The current API is easy for developers to use, easy to access, and adheres to commonly understood standards (usually HTTP and REST). They are treated more like products than codes. These are designed and documented for specific audiences (such as mobile developers) and are versioned to give particular maintenance and life cycle expectations.

They are much more standardized, so they have much stronger discipline regarding security and governance and are monitored and controlled for performance and scope. Like any productive software, modern APIs have their own software development life cycle (SDLC) for design, testing, building, managing, and versioning. Also, the latest APIs for consumption and version control are well documented. API originally referred to an interface dedicated to end-user-oriented programs, so-called application programs. Today, this origin is still reflected in the name "Application Programming Interface." Today, the term is broadened to include utility software and even hardware interfaces.

## UTILITY API IN BOOTSTRAP

The utility API of Bootstrap is a Sass tool used to generate utility classes. The utility API helps generate Bootstrap utilities which can be used to modify and extend the preexisting utility classes available in Bootstrap. Sass can do it. The utility API of Bootstrap is based on a series of Sass maps and functions. They are used for generating families of the bootstrap classes with various options. The $utilities map contains all the Bootstrap utilities, and it later gets merged with the user's custom $utilities map. The utility map lists utility groups based on a key, and they accept the following options.

- **Property:** The property's name can be a string or an array of strings. For example, it could be horizontal padding and margin. It is required.

- **Values:** If null is used as the map key, it would not be compiled. It contains a list of values, or it could also include a map if you don't want the class name to be the same as the value. It is required.

- **Class:** A variable is used for the class name if you don't want it to be the same as the property. If you omit, the class key and the property key are an array of strings, and the class name becomes the first element of the property array. It is optional.

- **State:** The state value is optional and does not have a default value. There is a list of pseudo-class variants like :hover and :focus that it can generate for the utility.

- **Responsive:** The Boolean value indicates if responsive classes should be generated or not. The default value is false, and it is an optional utility group.

- **rfs:** The default value is false. It is a Boolean value that enables fluid rescaling.

- **Print:** The default value is false. It is a Boolean value that indicates whether print classes need to be generated or not.

- **rtl:** The default value is true. It is a Boolean value that indicates if utility should be kept in RTL or not.

All the utilities variable are added to the $utilities variable available within the _utilities.scss stylesheet. Each utility group looks like this:

```
$utilities: ( "opacity": ( property:
opacity, values: ( 0: 0, 25: .25, 50: .5, 75:
.75, 100: 1, ) ));
```

The output for the above would look something like this:

```
.opacity-0 { opacity: 0; }.opacity-25 { opacity:
.25; }.opacity-50 { opacity: .5; }.opacity-75 {
opacity: .75; }.opacity-100 { opacity: 1; }
```

1. **Class:** You can also use the class option to change the class prefix used in the compiled CSS:

```
$utilities: ( "opacity": ( property:
opacity, class: o, values: ( 0: 0, 25:
.25, 50: .5, 75: .75, 100: 1, ) ));
```

The output for the above would look something like this:

```
.o-0 { opacity: 0 !important; }.o-25 { opacity: .25
!important; }.o-50 { opacity: .5 !important; }.o-75
{ opacity: .75 !important; }.o-100 { opacity: 1
!important; }
```

2. **States:** You can use the state option to generate pseudo-class variations. For example classes like :hover and :focus. When a list of states is provided, the class names are created for the specific pseudo class.

```
$utilities: ( "opacity": ( property:
opacity, class: opacity, state: hover, values:
( 0: 0, 25: .25, 50: .5, 75: .75, 100:
1, ) ));
```

Output:

```
.opacity-0-hover:hover { opacity: 0 !important; }
.opacity-25-hover:hover { opacity: .25 !important; }
.opacity-50-hover:hover { opacity: .5 !important; }
.opacity-75-hover:hover { opacity: .75 !important; }
.opacity-100-hover:hover { opacity: 1 !important; }
```

3. **Responsive utilities:** Add the responsive Boolean to generate responsive utilities across all breakpoints.

```
$utilities: ( "opacity": ( property:
opacity, responsive: true, values: ( 0: 0, 25:
.25, 50: .5, 75: .75, 100: 1, ) ));
```

Output:

```
.opacity-0 { opacity: 0 !important; }.opacity-25 {
opacity: .25 !important; }.opacity-50 { opacity: .5
!important; }.opacity-75 { opacity: .75 !important; }
.opacity-100 { opacity: 1 !important; }@media (min-
width: 576px) { .opacity-sm-0 { opacity: 0
!important; } .opacity-sm-25 { opacity: .25
!important; } .opacity-sm-50 { opacity: .5
!important; } .opacity-sm-75 { opacity: .75
!important; } .opacity-sm-100 { opacity: 1
!important; }}@media (min-width: 768px) {
.opacity-md-0 { opacity: 0 !important; }
.opacity-md-25 { opacity: .25 !important; }
.opacity-md-50 { opacity: .5 !important; }
.opacity-md-75 { opacity: .75 !important; }
.opacity-md-100 { opacity: 1 !important; }}@media
(min-width: 992px) { .opacity-lg-0 { opacity: 0
!important; } .opacity-lg-25 { opacity: .25
!important; } .opacity-lg-50 { opacity: .5
!important; } .opacity-lg-75 { opacity: .75
!important; } .opacity-lg-100 { opacity: 1
!important; }}@media (min-width: 1200px) {
.opacity-xl-0 { opacity: 0 !important; }
.opacity-xl-25 { opacity: .25 !important; }
.opacity-xl-50 { opacity: .5 !important; }
.opacity-xl-75 { opacity: .75 !important; }
.opacity-xl-100 { opacity: 1 !important; }}@media
(min-width: 1400px) { .opacity-xxl-0 { opacity: 0
!important; } .opacity-xxl-25 { opacity: .25
!important; } .opacity-xxl-50 { opacity: .5
!important; } .opacity-xxl-75 { opacity: .75
!important; } .opacity-xxl-100 { opacity: 1
!important; }}
```

4. **Changing utilities:** You can override the existing utilities by using the same key. Like if you want additional responsive overflow utility classes, then you can do the following:

```
$utilities: (
"overflow": (
responsive: true,
property: overflow,
values: visible hidden scroll auto,
),
);
```

5. **Print utilities:** You can also generate utility classes for print if you enable the print option.

```
$utilities: ( "opacity": ( property:
opacity, print: true, values: (  0: 0,    25:
.25,   50: .5,   75: .75,   100: 1, ) ));
```

Output:

```
.opacity-0 { opacity: 0 !important; }.opacity-25 {
opacity: .25 !important; }.opacity-50 { opacity: .5
!important; }.opacity-75 { opacity: .75 !important; }
.opacity-100 { opacity: 1 !important; }@media print {
.opacity-print-0 { opacity: 0 !important; } .opacity-
print-25 { opacity: .25 !important; } .opacity-
print-50 { opacity: .5 !important; }
.opacity-print-75 { opacity: .75 !important; }
.opacity-print-100 { opacity: 1 !important; }}
```

6. **Adding utilities:** You can add new utilities to the default $utilities map by using the map-merge function.

```
@import "bootstrap/scss/functions";@import
"bootstrap/scss/variables";@import "bootstrap/scss/
utilities";$utilities: map-
merge( $utilities, ( "cursor": ( property:
cursor,   class: cursor,   responsive:
true,   values: auto pointer grab, ) ));
```

7. **Modify utilities:** You can modify existing utilities in the default $utilities map with map-get and map-merge functions.

```
@import "bootstrap/scss/functions";@import
"bootstrap/scss/variables";@import "bootstrap/scss/
utilities";$utilities: map-
merge( $utilities, ( "width": map-merge(  map-
get($utilities, "width"),   (   values: map-merge(
map-get(map-get($utilities, "width"),
"values"),    (10: 10%),    ),  ),  ),  ));
```

8. **Enable responsive:** You can enable responsive classes for utilities that are not responsive by default. In the example given below, you can make the border classes responsive.

```
@import "bootstrap/scss/functions";@import
"bootstrap/scss/variables";@import "bootstrap/scss/
utilities";$utilities: map-merge( $utilities,
( "border": map-merge(  map-get($utilities,
"border"),   ( responsive: true ),  ),  ));
```

The generated CSS for responsive border variations will look something like this.

```
.border { ... }.border-0 { ... }@media (min-width:
576px) { .border-sm { ... } .border-sm-0 { ... }}@
media (min-width: 768px) { .border-md { ... }
.border-md-0 { ... }}@media (min-width: 992px) {
.border-lg { ... } .border-lg-0 { ... }}@media (min-
width: 1200px) { .border-xl { ... } .border-xl-0 { ...
}}@media (min-width: 1400px) { .border-xxl { ... }
.border-xxl-0 { ... }}
```

9. **Rename utilities:** You can rename the utilities by overriding the class.

```
@import "bootstrap/scss/functions";@import
"bootstrap/scss/variables";@import "bootstrap/scss/
utilities";$utilities: map-merge( $utilities,
( "margin-start": map-merge(  map-get($utilities,
"margin-start"),   ( class: ml ),  ),  ));
```

10. **Remove utilities:** You can also remove any utilities by removing the group key to null.

```
@import "bootstrap/scss/functions";@import
"bootstrap/scss/variables";@import "bootstrap/scss/
utilities";$utilities: map-
merge( $utilities, ( "width": null ));
```

11. **Remove utility in RTL:** You can remove the utility in RTL by setting the rtl option to false.

```
$utilities: ( "word-wrap": ( property: word-wrap
word-break, class: text, values: (break: break-
word), rtl: false ),);
```

## INTEGRATING BOOTSTRAP WITH JEKYLL

Jekyll is a static site builder. It is created in Ruby by GitHub co-founder Tom Preston Werner and distributed under the open-source MIT license. Tom Preston-Werner first published Jekyll in 2008. Parker Moore later acquired Jekyll. Parker Moore has been working on the release of Jekyll 1 and has been the new maintainer ever since.

Jekyll has launched a web development trend for static websites. Since 2017, Jekyll has been the most popular static website builder, primarily with the acquisition by GitHub. Jekyll renders Markdown or Textile and Liquid templates to create a completely static website ready to use with Apache HTTP Server, Nginx, or any other web server. Jekyll is a static site builder, so it doesn't use the database to generate pages dynamically. Jekyll supports loading content from YAML, JSON, CSV, and TSV files instead of using a database. The content of data files (YAML, JSON, CSV, and TSV files) can be accessed through the Liquid Templating system. Jekyll is the engine behind GitHub Pages, a feature of GitHub that allows users to host websites based on GitHub repositories at no additional cost.

Jekyll can be used with front-end frameworks such as Bootstrap and Semantic UI. The Jekyll website can connect to cloud-based CMS software such as CloudCannon, Forestry, Netlify, and Siteleaf, allowing content editors to modify the content of their website without knowing how to code it.

In theory, it's easy to put HTML, CSS, and JavaScript on your page. However, in reality, it quickly becomes complicated. You'll have to copy code from the header to each page unnecessarily, manually compile SCSS into CSS, and sort thousands of lines of iterative code. And when you or your client needs a blog, raise your hand and build a chunky WordPress site.

Jekyll is a static site framework that simplifies all these steps and allows developers to write meaningful code, the most critical part of development. Jekyll websites are simple, static, and blog-aware. You can build the structure and deploy the site on the same day. That's how fast it is. The Jekyll site is high-speed. At the end of the build process, the framework publishes a static-site folder. This folder can be added to any hosting provider via shell access, FTP, or cPanel.

Most importantly, the Jekyll website is easy to update and maintain. The framework separates design and data (like the latest JavaScript framework, but simpler). Therefore, it's easy to change menus, update lists, and add new posts.

The first step before working with Jekyll is to download Ruby. You do not need to learn Ruby, but the framework is built on the language, and Jekyll itself is a Ruby gem. Once you have set up this stuff, simply install the Jekyll and Bundler gems, and you are good to go.

```
gem install bundler jekyll
```

Jekyll projects start similarly to projects made with Ruby on Rails. The bundle init command helps create a Ruby Gemfile that manages different Jekyll dependencies. Ruby gems are analogous to WordPress plugins or npm packages.

```
jekyll new PROJECT_NAME --blank
cd PROJECT_NAMEbundle init
```

The last step is adding the Jekyll gem to the Gemfile anywhere below the first line. Then run the bundle command to add the gem to the site.

```
#Gemfile
gem "jekyll"
#terminal
bundle
```

Start the server, and your site is live.

```
jekyll serve --livereload
```

## INTEGRATING WITH ASP.NET

ASP.NET is an open-source and server-side web application framework designed for web development. It is used for creating dynamic web pages. Microsoft developed it to allow programmers to create dynamic websites, applications, and services. ASP stands for Active Server Pages. ASP is a development framework for building web pages. ASP and ASP.NET both are server-side technologies. Both of them enable computer code to be executed by the internet server. Whenever a browser requests an ASP or ASP.NET file, the ASP engine reads it, runs the code, and returns it to the browser.

ASP supports many different development models:

- **Classic ASP:** ASP was introduced in 1998 as Microsoft's first server-side scripting language. These pages have the final extension .asp and are usually written in VBScript.

- **ASP.NET Web Forms:** This is an event-driven application model. It is not a part of the new ASP.NET Core.

- **ASP.NET MVC:** It is an MVC application model. MVC stands for Model View Controller. It is being merged into the new ASP.NET Core.

- **ASP.NET Web Pages:** It is a SPA application model. SPA stands for Single Page Application. It is also being merged into the new ASP. NET Core.

- **ASP.NET API:** It is an API application model. API stands for Application Programming Interface. It is also being merged into the new ASP.NET Core.

- **ASP.NET Core:** It was released in 2016. This merges MVC, Web API, and Web Pages into one application framework.

Let's look at Bootstrap, a front-end framework now included in ASP.NET and MVC. This is a popular web application front-end toolkit that helps you create user interfaces using HTML, CSS, and JavaScript. Designed for personal use by Twitter web developers, it is now open-source and popular with designers and developers due to its flexibility and service. With Bootstrap, you can create a user interface that looks great on everything from large desktop displays to small mobile screens. This chapter also describes how Bootstrap works with Layout View to build the look of your application.

Bootstrap includes layouts, buttons, forms, menus, widgets, image carousels, labels, badges, typography, and all the parts you need for all sorts of features. Bootstrap is built entirely in HTML, CSS, and JavaScript and is an open standard, so it can be used with any CSS-based framework, including the ASP.NET MVC. Whenever you start a new MVC project, Bootstrap will be there. That is, the Project has Bootstrap.css and Bootstrap.js.

Start Visual Studio. Select the ASP.NET Web application (.NET Framework) and press the [OK] button.

Select the Blank icon in the Templates section on the New ASP.NET Web Application screen. Also, select MVC in the "Add Folder and Core References" section and press the OK button. You have now created an empty MVC project. Add the Bootstrap file to an open MVC project.

Download the Bootstrap-compiled CSS and JS files from http://getbootstrap.com. Unzip the downloaded Bootstrap file bootstrap5.1.0dist.zip. Copy the CSS and js folders from the downloaded zip file and paste them into your MVC project folder.

Go to Visual Studio and include the folder in your Project. Select the folders for CSS and JavaScript and right-click on them. From the rightclick menu, include those files in the Project. The folders are now included in the MVC project.

Now we will add the dependencies of Bootstrap. Include the file in your Project like you included the Bootstrap file. The Bootstrap framework is now ready to be used in the MVC project. To use Bootstrap in the Project, you must add a Bootstrap template. The Bootstrap template is nothing but the Bootstrap navigation bar and container.

In an MVC project, you can add the navigation bar and container in the Layout file and the Bootstrap grid and column system in the views.

## CHAPTER SUMMARY

In this chapter, we learned about integrating different stuff with Bootstrap. We learned about HTTP and HTTP Client. We also learned how to work with the Utility API of Bootstrap. We then went forward and learned how we could integrate Bootstrap with Jekyll, which is a static site generator. And then, we learned how we could incorporate Bootstrap with ASP.NET. In the next chapter, we will recap what we know until now in this book.

## CHAPTER 8

# Cheat Sheet 1

## IN THIS CHAPTER

➤ What is Bootstrap?

➤ Why Choose Bootstrap?

➤ Features of Bootstrap

➤ Bootstrap Cheat Sheet

In the previous chapter, we went over everything we have learned so far in this book. In this chapter, we will provide you with a cheat sheet that you can gloss over to remember concepts you have forgotten.

## WHAT IS BOOTSTRAP?

- Bootstrap is a free and open-source CSS-based framework.

- It contains HTML and CSS-based design templates for buttons, forms, typography, etc.

- It supports JavaScript plugins.

- It is used to make faster, mobile-friendly, and responsive websites.

- It is lightweight and has a wide variety of components available for use.

DOI: 10.1201/9781003309383-8

## WHY CHOOSE BOOTSTRAP?

- It is one of the most popular frameworks for front-end development.

- It is easy to learn and use.

- It has built-in classes, so you do not have to code most elements from scratch, saving time.

- It is open-source and has significant community support and documentation.

- It is versatile and scalable so that you can create any website quickly.

## FEATURES OF BOOTSTRAP

- There are no cross-browser issues and incompatibilities.

- It is customizable.

- It has a powerful grid system.

- It has a simple integration process.

- It has prestyled components.

## BOOTSTRAP CHEAT SHEET

This cheat sheet contains a brief description of every Bootstrap component.

## INITIAL SETUP (USING CDN)

To set up Bootstrap via CDN, you need to paste the following links.

## CSS

```
<link href="https://cdn.jsdeliver.net/npm/bootstrap
@5.1.3/dist/css/bootstrap.min.css" rel="stylesheet"
integrity="sha384-1BmE4kWBq78iYhFldvKuhfTAU6auU8tT
94WrHftjDbrCEXSUloBoqyl2QvZ6jIW3"
crossorigin="anonymous">
```

## Popper

```
<script src="https://cdn.jsdelivr.net/npm/@popper.
js/core@2.10.2/dist/umd/popper.min.js" integrity="sha3
84-7+zCNj/IqJ95wol6oMtfsKbZ9ccEh31eOz1HGyDuCQ6wgny
JNSYdrPa03rtR1zdB" crossorigin="anonymous"></script>
```

JavaScript

```
<script src="https://cdn.jsdeliver.net/npm/bootstrap
@5.1.3/dist/js/bootstrap.min.js" integrity="sha3
84-QJHtvGhmr9XOIpI6YVutG+2QOK9T+ZnN4kzFN1RtK3zEFEI
sxhlmW15/YESvpZ13" crossorigin="anonymous"></script>
```

Bundle (Popper + JavaScript)

```
<script src="https://cdn.jsdeliver.net/npm/
bootstrap@5.1.3/dist/js/bootstrap.bundle.min.js"
integrity="sha384-ka7Sk0Gln4gmtz2MlQnikT1wXgYsOg+O
MhuP+IlRH9sENBOOLRn5q+8nbTov4+1p"
crossorigin="anonymous"></script>
```

Bootstrap Icons

- https://icons.getbootstrap.com/ - Bootstrap Icon Library

## INITIAL SETUP (USING NPM)

To download Bootstrap via npm package, you need to use the following command.

Bootstrap

- $ npm install bootstrap – to install Bootstrap via npm

Bootstrap Icons

- $ npm i bootstrap-icons – to download Bootstrap icons via npm

## BOOTSTRAP SCREEN SIZING

| Breakpoint | Class infix | Dimensions |
|---|---|---|
| X-small | None | <576px |
| Small | sm | ≥576px |
| Medium | md | ≥768px |
| Large | lg | ≥992px |
| Extra large | xl | ≥1,200px |
| Extra extra-large | xxl | ≥1,400px |

## BOOTSTRAP GRID SYSTEM

Used to create a flexbox grid to build layouts. It has a 12 column system and 6 default responsive tiers.

*Note :* * refers to the value { sm | md | lg | xl | xxl } and # refers to the value from 1 to 12.

- container

```
<div class="container">Max width changes at each
breakpoint</div>
```

- container-*

```
<div class="container-sm">100% wide until small
breakpoint</div>
<div class="container-md">100% wide until medium
breakpoint</div>
<div class="container-lg">100% wide until large
breakpoint</div>
<div class="container-xl">100% wide until extra
large breakpoint</div>
<div class="container-xxl">100% wide until extra
extra large breakpoint</div>
```

- container-fluid

```
<div class="container-fluid">Always 100% wide</div>
```

- row

```
<div class="row">
  <!-- col- elements here -->
</div>
```

- col-#

```
<div class="row">
  <div class="col-3">col-3</div>
  <div class="col-5">col-5</div>
  <div class="col-4">col-4</div>
</div>
```

- col-sm-#

```
<div class="row">
  <div class="col-sm-3">col-sm-3</div>
  <div class="col-sm-5">col-sm-5</div>
  <div class="col-sm-4">col-sm-4</div>
</div>
```

- col-md-#

```
<div class="row">
  <div class="col-md-3">col-md-3</div>
  <div class="col-md-5">col-md-5</div>
  <div class="col-md-4">col-md-4</div>
</div>
```

- col-lg-#

```
<div class="row">
  <div class="col-lg-3">col-lg-3</div>
  <div class="col-lg-5">col-lg-5</div>
  <div class="col-lg-4">col-lg-4</div>
</div>
```

- col-xl-#

```
<div class="row">
  <div class="col-xl-3">col-xl-3</div>
  <div class="col-xl-5">col-xl-5</div>
  <div class="col-xl-4">col-xl-4</div>
</div>
```

- col-xxl-#

```
<div class="row">
  <div class="col-xxl-3">col-xxl-3</div>
  <div class="col-xxl-5">col-xxl-5</div>
  <div class="col-xxl-4">col-xxl-4</div>
</div>
```

- col

```
<div class="row">
  <div class="col">1 of 3</div>
  <div class="col">1 of 3</div>
  <div class="col">1 of 3</div>
</div>
```

- col-*

```
<div class="row">
  <div class="col-sm">1 of 3</div>
  <div class="col-sm">1 of 3</div>
  <div class="col-sm">1 of 3</div>
</div>
```

- col-*-auto

```
<div class="row justify-content-md-center">
  <div class="col col-lg-2">
    1 of 3
  </div>
  <div class="col-md-auto">
   Variable width content
  </div>
  <div class="col col-lg-2">
    3 of 3
  </div>
</div>
<div class="row">
  <div class="col">
    1 of 3
  </div>
  <div class="col-md-auto">
   Variable width content
  </div>
  <div class="col col-lg-2">
    3 of 3
  </div>
</div>
```

- row-cols-#

```
<div class="row row-cols-3">
  <div class="col">Column</div>
  <div class="col">Column</div>
  <div class="col">Column</div>
  <div class="col">Column</div>
</div>
```

- row-cols-*-#

```
<div class="row row-cols-1 row-cols-sm-2
row-cols-md-3 row-cols-lg-4 row-cols-xxl-6">
  <div class="col">Column</div>
  <div class="col">Column</div>
  <div class="col">Column</div>
  <div class="col">Column</div>
  <div class="col">Column</div>
  <div class="col">Column</div>
</div>
```

- nesting

```
<div class="row">
  <div class="col-sm-3">Level 1: .col-sm-3</div>
  <div class="col-sm-9">
    <div class="row">
      <div class="col-8 col-sm-6">Level 2: .col-8
.col-sm-6</div>
      <div class="col-4 col-sm-6">Level 2: .col-4
.col-sm-6</div>
    </div>
  </div>
</div>
```

- offset-#

```
<div class="row">
<  div class="col-3">col-3</div>
  <div class="col-3 offset-6">col-3 offset-6</div>
</div>
```

- offset-*-#

```
<div class="row">
  <div class="col-3">col-3</div>
  <div class="col-3 offset-md-6">col-3
offset-md-6</div>
</div>
```

- gx-{size}

```
<!-- Different sized gutters can be used with the
help of .gx-{0|1|2|3|4|5} class -->
<div class="row gx-5">
  <div class="col">
    <div class="p-3 border bg-light">Custom column
padding</div>
  </div>
  <div class="col">
    <div class="p-3 border bg-light">Custom column
padding</div>
  </div>
</div>
```

- gx-*-{size}

```
<!-- Different sized gutters can be used with the
help of .gx-*-{0|1|2|3|4|5} class -->
<div class="row gx-3 gx-xxl-5">
  <div class="col">
    <div class="p-3 border bg-light">Custom column
padding</div>
  </div>
  <div class="col">
    <div class="p-3 border bg-light">Custom column
padding</div>
  </div>
</div>
```

- gy-{size}

```
<!-- Different sized gutters can be used with the
help of .gy-{0|1|2|3|4|5} class -->
<div class="row gy-5">
  <div class="col">
    <div class="p-3 border bg-light">Custom column
padding</div>
  </div>
  <div class="col">
    <div class="p-3 border bg-light">Custom column
padding</div>
  </div>
</div>
```

- gy-*-{size}

```
<!-- Different sized gutters can be used with the
help of .gy-*-{0|1|2|3|4|5} class -->
<div class="row gy-3 gy-xxl-5">
  <div class="col">
    <div class="p-3 border bg-light">Custom column
padding</div>
  </div>
  <div class="col">
    <div class="p-3 border bg-light">Custom column
padding</div>
  </div>
</div>
```

- g-{size}

```
<!-- Different sized gutters can be used with the
help of .g-{1|2|3|4|5} class -->
<div class="row g-3">
  <div class="col">
    <div class="p-3 border bg-light">Custom column
padding</div>
  </div>
  <div class="col">
    <div class="p-3 border bg-light">Custom column
padding</div>
  </div>
</div>
```

- g-*-{size}

```
<!-- Different sized gutters can be used with the
help of .g-*-{0|1|2|3|4|5} class -->
<div class="row g-2 g-xl-4">
  <div class="col">
    <div class="p-3 border bg-light">Custom column
padding</div>
  </div>
  <div class="col">
    <div class="p-3 border bg-light">Custom column
padding</div>
  </div>
</div>
```

- g-0

```
<div class="row g-0">
  <div class="col-sm-6 col-md-8">.col-sm-6 .col-md-8</
div>
  <div class="col-6 col-md-4">.col-6 .col-md-4</div>
</div>
```

## TYPOGRAPHY

Used for typography like headings, body text, lists, etc.

- h1-h6

```
<p class="h1">h1. Bootstrap heading</p>
<p class="h2">h2. Bootstrap heading</p>
```

```
<p class="h3">h3. Bootstrap heading</p>
<p class="h4">h4. Bootstrap heading</p>
<p class="h5">h5. Bootstrap heading</p>
<p class="h6">h6. Bootstrap heading</p>
```

• text-muted

```
<h3>
  Fancy display heading
  <small class="text-muted">With faded secondary
text</small>
</h3>
```

• display-{size}

```
<h1 class="display-1">Display 1</h1>
<h1 class="display-2">Display 2</h1>
<h1 class="display-3">Display 3</h1>
<h1 class="display-4">Display 4</h1>
<h1 class="display-5">Display 5</h1>
<h1 class="display-6">Display 6</h1>
```

• lead

```
<p class="lead">
  Vivamus sagittis lacus vel faucibus dolor auctor.
Duis mollis, est non commodo luctus.
</p>
```

• mark

```
<p>You can use .mark class to <span
class="mark">highlight</span> text.</p>
```

• small
```
<p class="small">This line of text is meant to be
treated as fine print.</p>
```

• initialism

```
<p><abbr title="attribute"
class="initialism">attr</abbr></p>
```

• blockquote

```
<blockquote class="blockquote">
  <p>Lorem ipsum dolor sit amet, consectetur
adipiscing elit. Integer posuere erat a ante.</p>
</blockquote>
```

- blockquote-footer

```
<figure>
  <blockquote class="blockquote">
    <p>Lorem ipsum dolor sit amet, consectetur
adipiscing elit. Integer posuere erat a ante.</p>
  </blockquote>
  <figcaption class="blockquote-footer">
    Someone famous in <cite title="Source
Title">Source Title</cite>
  </figcaption>
</figure>
```

- list-unstyled

```
<ul class="list-unstyled">
  <li>Lorem ipsum dolor sit amet</li>
  <li>Consectetur adipiscing elit</li>
  <li>Nulla volutpat aliquam velit
    <ul>
      <li>Phasellus iaculis neque</li>
      <li>Purus sodales ultricies</li>
    </ul>
  </li>
  <li>Aenean sit amet erat nunc</li>
  <li>Eget porttitor lorem</li>
</ul>
```

- list-inline

```
<ul class="list-inline">
  <li class="list-inline-item">Lorem ipsum</li>
  <li class="list-inline-item">Phasellus iaculis</li>
  <li class="list-inline-item">Nulla volutpat</li>
</ul>
```

## UTILITY CLASSES

Used for showing, hiding, aligning, and spacing content.

### Utility: Colors

Used to convey meaning through color utility classes.

- text-{color}

```
<p class="text-primary">.text-primary</p>
<p class="text-secondary">.text-secondary</p>
<p class="text-success">.text-success</p>
<p class="text-danger">.text-danger</p>
<p class="text-warning">.text-warning</p>
<p class="text-info">.text-info</p>
<p class="text-light bg-dark">.text-light</p>
<p class="text-dark">.text-dark</p>
```

- text-body

```
<p class="text-body">.text-body</p>
```

- text-white

```
<p class="text-white">.text-white</p>
```

- text-black-50

```
<p class="text-black-50">.text-black-50</p>
```

- text-white-50

```
<p class="text-white-50 bg-dark">.text-white-50</p>
```

- bg-{color}

```
<div class="p-3 mb-2 bg-primary text-white">.
bg-primary</div>
<div class="p-3 mb-2 bg-secondary text-white">.
bg-secondary</div>
<div class="p-3 mb-2 bg-success text-white">.
bg-success</div>
<div class="p-3 mb-2 bg-danger text-white">.
bg-danger</div>
<div class="p-3 mb-2 bg-warning text-white">.
bg-warning</div>
<div class="p-3 mb-2 bg-info text-white">.bg-info</div>
<div class="p-3 mb-2 bg-light text-dark">.
bg-light</div>
<div class="p-3 bg-dark text-white">.bg-dark</div>
```

- bg-white

```
<div class="p-3 bg-white text-dark">.bg-white</div>
```

- bg-transparent

```
<div class="p-3 bg-transparent text-dark">
.bg-transparent</div>
```

- bg-gradient

```
<div class="p-3 bg-primary bg-gradient text-white">
.bg-primary.bg-gradient</div>
```

## Utility: Borders

Used to quickly style the border and border-radius of any element.

- border

```
<span class="border"></span>
```

- border-{direction}

```
<span class="border-top"></span>
<span class="border-end"></span>
<span class="border-bottom"></span>
<span class="border-start"></span>
```

- border-0

```
<span class="border-0"></span>
```

- border-{direction}-0

```
<span class="border-top-0"></span>
<span class="border-end-0"></span>
<span class="border-bottom-0"></span>
<span class="border-start-0"></span>
```

- border-{color}

```
<span class="border border-primary"></span>
```

- border-{size}

```
<span class="border border-1"></span>
<span class="border border-2"></span>
<span class="border border-3"></span>
<span class="border border-4"></span>
<span class="border border-5"></span>
```

- rounded

```
<img src="assets/images/bs-images/img-2x2.png"
class="rounded" alt="Rounded image">
```

- rounded-{corner}

```
<img src="assets/images/bs-images/img-2x2.png"
class="rounded-top" alt="Rounded top image">
<img src="assets/images/bs-images/img-2x2.png"
class="rounded-end" alt="Rounded end image">
<img src="assets/images/bs-images/img-2x2.png"
class="rounded-bottom" alt="Rounded bottom image">
<img src="assets/images/bs-images/img-2x2.png"
class="rounded-start" alt="Rounded start image">
<img src="assets/images/bs-images/img-2x2.png"
class="rounded-circle" alt="Rounded circle image">
<img src="assets/images/bs-images/img-2x1.png"
class="rounded-pill" height="200" alt="Rounded pill
image">
```

- rounded-{size}

```
<img src="assets/images/bs-images/img-2x2.png"
class="rounded-0" alt="Rounded 0 image">
<img src="assets/images/bs-images/img-2x2.png"
class="rounded-1" alt="Rounded 1 image">
<img src="assets/images/bs-images/img-2x2.png"
class="rounded-2" alt="Rounded 2 image">
<img src="assets/images/bs-images/img-2x2.png"
class="rounded-3" alt="Rounded 3 image">
```

## Utility: Flex

Used to manage the layout, alignment, and sizing of grid columns, navigation, components, and more using flexbox utilities.

*Note:* * refers to the value { sm | md | lg | xl | xxl }

- flex-*-row

```
<!-- Display flex can be used for responsive cases
as well with the help of .flex-{sm|md|lg|xl|xxl}-row
class -->
<div class="d-flex flex-row bd-highlight">
  <div class="p-2 bd-highlight">Flex item 1</div>
  <div class="p-2 bd-highlight">Flex item 2</div>
  <div class="p-2 bd-highlight">Flex item 3</div>
</div>
```

- flex-*-row-reverse

```
<!-- Display flex can be used for responsive cases
as well with the help of .flex-{sm|md|lg|xl|xxl}-
row-reverse class -->
<div class="d-flex flex-row-reverse bd-highlight">
  <div class="p-2 bd-highlight">Flex item 1</div>
  <div class="p-2 bd-highlight">Flex item 2</div>
  <div class="p-2 bd-highlight">Flex item 3</div>
</div>
```

- flex-*-column

```
<!-- Display flex can be used for responsive cases
as well with the help of .flex-{sm|md|lg|xl|xxl}-
column class -->
<div class="d-flex flex-column bd-highlight">
  <div class="p-2 bd-highlight">Flex item 1</div>
  <div class="p-2 bd-highlight">Flex item 2</div>
  <div class="p-2 bd-highlight">Flex item 3</div>
</div>
```

- flex-*-column-reverse

```
<!-- Display flex can be used for responsive cases
as well with the help of .flex-{sm|md|lg|xl|xxl}-
column-reverse class -->
<div class="d-flex flex-column-reverse
bd-highlight">
  <div class="p-2 bd-highlight">Flex item 1</div>
  <div class="p-2 bd-highlight">Flex item 2</div>
  <div class="p-2 bd-highlight">Flex item 3</div>
</div>
```

- justify-content-*-{option}

```
<!-- justify-content can be used for responsive
cases as well with the help of .justify-content-{sm
|md|lg|xl|xxl}-{start|end|center|between|around|ev
enly} class -->
<div class="d-flex justify-content-start
bd-highlight mb-2">
  <div class="p-2 bd-highlight">Flex item</div>
  <div class="p-2 bd-highlight">Flex item</div>
  <div class="p-2 bd-highlight">Flex item</div>
</div>
```

```
<div class="d-flex justify-content-end bd-highlight
mb-2">
  <div class="p-2 bd-highlight">Flex item</div>
  <div class="p-2 bd-highlight">Flex item</div>
<  div class="p-2 bd-highlight">Flex item</div>
</div>
<div class="d-flex justify-content-center
bd-highlight mb-2">
  <div class="p-2 bd-highlight">Flex item</div>
  <div class="p-2 bd-highlight">Flex item</div>
  <div class="p-2 bd-highlight">Flex item</div>
</div>
<div class="d-flex justify-content-between
bd-highlight mb-2">
<div class="p-2 bd-highlight">Flex item</div>
<div class="p-2 bd-highlight">Flex item</div>
<div class="p-2 bd-highlight">Flex item</div>
</div>
<div class="d-flex justify-content-around
bd-highlight mb-2">
  <div class="p-2 bd-highlight">Flex item</div>
  <div class="p-2 bd-highlight">Flex item</div>
  <div class="p-2 bd-highlight">Flex item</div>
</div>
<div class="d-flex justify-content-evenly
bd-highlight">
  <!-- New -->
  <div class="p-2 bd-highlight">Flex item</div>
  <div class="p-2 bd-highlight">Flex item</div>
  <div class="p-2 bd-highlight">Flex item</div>
</div>
```

- align-items-*-{option}

```
<!-- align-items can be used for responsive cases
as well with the help of .align-items-{sm|md|lg|xl
|xxl}-{start|end|center|baseline|stretch} class -->
<div class="d-flex align-items-start bd-highlight
mb-2" style="height: 100px;">
  <div class="p-2 bd-highlight">Flex item</div>
  <div class="p-2 bd-highlight">Flex item</div>
  <div class="p-2 bd-highlight">Flex item</div>
</div>
```

```
<div class="d-flex align-items-end bd-highlight
mb-2" style="height: 100px;">
  <div class="p-2 bd-highlight">Flex item</div>
  <div class="p-2 bd-highlight">Flex item</div>
  <div class="p-2 bd-highlight">Flex item</div>
</div>
<div class="d-flex align-items-center bd-highlight
mb-2" style="height: 100px;">
  <div class="p-2 bd-highlight">Flex item</div>
  <div class="p-2 bd-highlight">Flex item</div>
  <div class="p-2 bd-highlight">Flex item</div>
</div>
<div class="d-flex align-items-baseline
bd-highlight mb-2" style="height: 100px;">
  <div class="p-2 bd-highlight">Flex item</div>
  <div class="p-2 bd-highlight">Flex item</div>
  <div class="p-2 bd-highlight">Flex item</div>
</div>
<div class="d-flex align-items-stretch
bd-highlight" style="height: 100px;">
  <div class="p-2 bd-highlight">Flex item</div>
  <div class="p-2 bd-highlight">Flex item</div>
  <div class="p-2 bd-highlight">Flex item</div>
</div>
```

- align-self-*-{option}

```
<!-- align-self can be used for responsive cases as
well with the help of .align-self-{sm|md|lg|xl|
xxl}-{start|end|center|baseline|stretch} class -->
<div class="d-flex bd-highlight mb-2" style="height:
100px;">
  <div class="p-2 bd-highlight">Flex item</div>
  <div class="align-self-start p-2
bd-highlight">Aligned flex item</div>
  <div class="p-2 bd-highlight">Flex item</div>
</div>
<div class="d-flex bd-highlight mb-2" style="height:
100px;">
  <div class="p-2 bd-highlight">Flex item</div>
  <div class="align-self-end p-2
bd-highlight">Aligned flex item</div>
  <div class="p-2 bd-highlight">Flex item</div>
</div>
```

```
<div class="d-flex bd-highlight mb-2" style="height:
100px;">
  <div class="p-2 bd-highlight">Flex item</div>
  <div class="align-self-center p-2
bd-highlight">Aligned flex item</div>
  <div class="p-2 bd-highlight">Flex item</div>
</div>
<div class="d-flex bd-highlight mb-2" style="height:
100px;">
  <div class="p-2 bd-highlight">Flex item</div>
  <div class="align-self-baseline p-2
bd-highlight">Aligned flex item</div>
  <div class="p-2 bd-highlight">Flex item</div>
</div>
<div class="d-flex bd-highlight" style="height:
100px;">
  <div class="p-2 bd-highlight">Flex item</div>
  <div class="align-self-stretch p-2
bd-highlight">Aligned flex item</div>
  <div class="p-2 bd-highlight">Flex item</div>
</div>
```

- flex-*-fill

```
<!-- flex-fill can be used for responsive cases as
well with the help of .flex-{sm|md|lg|xl|xxl}-fill
class -->
<div class="d-flex bd-highlight">
  <div class="flex-fill p-2 bd-highlight">Flex item
with a lot of content</div>
  <div class="flex-fill p-2 bd-highlight">Flex
item</div>
  <div class="flex-fill p-2 bd-highlight">Flex
item</div>
</div>
```

- flex-grow-{option}

```
<!-- flex-grow can be used for responsive cases as
well with the help of .flex-{sm|md|lg|xl|xxl}-
grow-{0|1} class -->
<div class="d-flex bd-highlight">
  <div class="flex-grow-1 p-2 bd-highlight">Flex
item</div>
```

```
  <div class="p-2 bd-highlight">Flex item</div>
  <div class="p-2 bd-highlight">Third flex item</div>
</div>
```

- flex-shrink-{option}

```
<!-- flex-shrink can be used for responsive cases
as well with the help of .flex-{sm|md|lg|xl|xxl}-
shrink-{0|1} class -->
<div class="d-flex bd-highlight">
  <div class="w-100 p-2 bd-highlight">Flex item</div>
  <div class="flex-shrink-1 p-2 bd-highlight">Flex
item</div>
</div>
```

- flex-*-nowrap

```
<!-- flex-nowrap can be used for responsive cases
as well with the help of .flex-{sm|md|lg|xl|xxl}-
nowrap class -->
<div class="d-flex flex-nowrap bd-highlight"
style="width: 8rem;">
  <div class="p-2 bd-highlight">Flex item</div>
  <div class="p-2 bd-highlight">Flex item</div>
  <div class="p-2 bd-highlight">Flex item</div>
  <div class="p-2 bd-highlight">Flex item</div>
  <div class="p-2 bd-highlight">Flex item</div>
</div>
```

- flex-*-wrap

```
<!-- flex-wrap can be used for responsive cases as
well with the help of .flex-{sm|md|lg|xl|xxl}-wrap
class -->
<div class="d-flex flex-wrap bd-highlight">
  <div class="p-2 bd-highlight">Flex item</div>
  <div class="p-2 bd-highlight">Flex item</div>
  <div class="p-2 bd-highlight">Flex item</div>
  <div class="p-2 bd-highlight">Flex item</div>
  <div class="p-2 bd-highlight">Flex item</div>
  <div class="p-2 bd-highlight">Flex item</div>
  <div class="p-2 bd-highlight">Flex item</div>
  <div class="p-2 bd-highlight">Flex item</div>
  <div class="p-2 bd-highlight">Flex item</div>
```

```
  <div class="p-2 bd-highlight">Flex item</div>
  <div class="p-2 bd-highlight">Flex item</div>
  <div class="p-2 bd-highlight">Flex item</div>
  <div class="p-2 bd-highlight">Flex item</div>
  <div class="p-2 bd-highlight">Flex item</div>
</div>
```

- flex-*-wrap-reverse

```
<!-- flex-wrap-reverse can be used for responsive
cases as well with the help of .flex-
{sm|md|lg|xl|xxl}-wrap-reverse class -->
<div class="d-flex flex-wrap-reverse bd-highlight">
  <div class="p-2 bd-highlight">Flex item</div>
  <div class="p-2 bd-highlight">Flex item</div>
  <div class="p-2 bd-highlight">Flex item</div>
  <div class="p-2 bd-highlight">Flex item</div>
  <div class="p-2 bd-highlight">Flex item</div>
  <div class="p-2 bd-highlight">Flex item</div>
  <div class="p-2 bd-highlight">Flex item</div>
  <div class="p-2 bd-highlight">Flex item</div>
  <div class="p-2 bd-highlight">Flex item</div>
  <div class="p-2 bd-highlight">Flex item</div>
  <div class="p-2 bd-highlight">Flex item</div>
  <div class="p-2 bd-highlight">Flex item</div>
  <div class="p-2 bd-highlight">Flex item</div>
  <div class="p-2 bd-highlight">Flex item</div>
</div>
```

- order-*-{order-number}

```
<!-- order can be used for responsive cases as well
with the help of .order-
{sm|md|lg|xl|xxl}-{0|1|2|3|4|5} class -->
<div class="d-flex flex-nowrap bd-highlight">
  <div class="order-3 p-2 bd-highlight">First flex
item</div>
  <div class="order-2 p-2 bd-highlight">Second flex
item</div>
  <div class="order-5 p-2 bd-highlight">Third flex
item</div>
</div>
```

- order-*-{order-name}

```
<!-- order can be used for responsive cases as well
with the help of .order-{sm|md|lg|xl|xxl}-
{first|last} class -->
<div class="d-flex flex-nowrap bd-highlight">
  <div class="order-3 p-2 bd-highlight">First flex
item</div>
  <div class="order-last p-2 bd-highlight">Second
flex item</div>
  <div class="order-first p-2 bd-highlight">Third
flex item</div>
  <div class="order-1 p-2 bd-highlight">Fourth flex
item</div>
</div>
```

- align-content-*-{option}

```
<!-- align-content can be used for responsive cases
as well with the help of .align-content-{sm|md|lg|
xl|xxl}-{start|end|center|around|stretch} class -->
<div class="d-flex align-content-start flex-wrap
bd-highlight mb-3" style="height: 200px">
  <div class="p-2 bd-highlight">Flex item</div>
  <div class="p-2 bd-highlight">Flex item</div>
  <div class="p-2 bd-highlight">Flex item</div>
  <div class="p-2 bd-highlight">Flex item</div>
  <div class="p-2 bd-highlight">Flex item</div>
  <div class="p-2 bd-highlight">Flex item</div>
  <div class="p-2 bd-highlight">Flex item</div>
  <div class="p-2 bd-highlight">Flex item</div>
  <div class="p-2 bd-highlight">Flex item</div>
  <div class="p-2 bd-highlight">Flex item</div>
  <div class="p-2 bd-highlight">Flex item</div>
  <div class="p-2 bd-highlight">Flex item</div>
  <div class="p-2 bd-highlight">Flex item</div>
  <div class="p-2 bd-highlight">Flex item</div>
  <div class="p-2 bd-highlight">Flex item</div>
</div>
<div class="d-flex align-content-end flex-wrap
bd-highlight mb-3" style="height: 200px">
  <div class="p-2 bd-highlight">Flex item</div>
  <div class="p-2 bd-highlight">Flex item</div>
```

```
  <div class="p-2 bd-highlight">Flex item</div>
  <div class="p-2 bd-highlight">Flex item</div>
  <div class="p-2 bd-highlight">Flex item</div>
  <div class="p-2 bd-highlight">Flex item</div>
  <div class="p-2 bd-highlight">Flex item</div>
  <div class="p-2 bd-highlight">Flex item</div>
  <div class="p-2 bd-highlight">Flex item</div>
  <div class="p-2 bd-highlight">Flex item</div>
  <div class="p-2 bd-highlight">Flex item</div>
  <div class="p-2 bd-highlight">Flex item</div>
  <div class="p-2 bd-highlight">Flex item</div>
  <div class="p-2 bd-highlight">Flex item</div>
  <div class="p-2 bd-highlight">Flex item</div>
</div>
<div class="d-flex align-content-center flex-wrap
bd-highlight mb-3" style="height: 200px">
  <div class="p-2 bd-highlight">Flex item</div>
  <div class="p-2 bd-highlight">Flex item</div>
  <div class="p-2 bd-highlight">Flex item</div>
  <div class="p-2 bd-highlight">Flex item</div>
  <div class="p-2 bd-highlight">Flex item</div>
  <div class="p-2 bd-highlight">Flex item</div>
  <div class="p-2 bd-highlight">Flex item</div>
  <div class="p-2 bd-highlight">Flex item</div>
  <div class="p-2 bd-highlight">Flex item</div>
  <div class="p-2 bd-highlight">Flex item</div>
  <div class="p-2 bd-highlight">Flex item</div>
  <div class="p-2 bd-highlight">Flex item</div>
  <div class="p-2 bd-highlight">Flex item</div>
  <div class="p-2 bd-highlight">Flex item</div>
</div>
<div class="d-flex align-content-around flex-wrap
bd-highlight mb-3" style="height: 200px">
  <div class="p-2 bd-highlight">Flex item</div>
  <div class="p-2 bd-highlight">Flex item</div>
  <div class="p-2 bd-highlight">Flex item</div>
  <div class="p-2 bd-highlight">Flex item</div>
  <div class="p-2 bd-highlight">Flex item</div>
  <div class="p-2 bd-highlight">Flex item</div>
  <div class="p-2 bd-highlight">Flex item</div>
  <div class="p-2 bd-highlight">Flex item</div>
```

```
  <div class="p-2 bd-highlight">Flex item</div>
  <div class="p-2 bd-highlight">Flex item</div>
  <div class="p-2 bd-highlight">Flex item</div>
  <div class="p-2 bd-highlight">Flex item</div>
  <div class="p-2 bd-highlight">Flex item</div>
  <div class="p-2 bd-highlight">Flex item</div>
  <div class="p-2 bd-highlight">Flex item</div>
</div>
<div class="d-flex align-content-stretch flex-wrap
bd-highlight" style="height: 200px">
  <div class="p-2 bd-highlight">Flex item</div>
  <div class="p-2 bd-highlight">Flex item</div>
  <div class="p-2 bd-highlight">Flex item</div>
  <div class="p-2 bd-highlight">Flex item</div>
  <div class="p-2 bd-highlight">Flex item</div>
  <div class="p-2 bd-highlight">Flex item</div>
  <div class="p-2 bd-highlight">Flex item</div>
  <div class="p-2 bd-highlight">Flex item</div>
  <div class="p-2 bd-highlight">Flex item</div>
  <div class="p-2 bd-highlight">Flex item</div>
  <div class="p-2 bd-highlight">Flex item</div>
  <div class="p-2 bd-highlight">Flex item</div>
  <div class="p-2 bd-highlight">Flex item</div>
  <div class="p-2 bd-highlight">Flex item</div>
</div>
```

## Utility: Display

Used to quickly and responsively toggle the display value of components by using display utilities.

- d-*-none

```
<div class="d-none p-2 bd-highlight">d-none</div>
<div class="d-sm-none p-2 bd-highlight">d-sm-none</div>
<div class="d-md-none p-2 bd-highlight">d-md-none</div>
<div class="d-lg-none p-2 bd-highlight">d-lg-none</div>
<div class="d-xl-none p-2 bd-highlight">d-xl-none</div>
<div class="d-xxl-none p-2 bd-highlight">d-xxl-none</div>
```

- d-*-inline

```
<div class="d-inline p-2 bd-highlight">d-inline</div>
<div class="d-sm-inline p-2 bd-highlight">d-sm-inline</div>
```

```
<div class="d-md-inline p-2 bd-highlight">d-md-inline</div>
<div class="d-lg-inline p-2 bd-highlight">d-lg-inline</div>
<div class="d-xl-inline p-2 bd-highlight">d-xl-inline</div>
<div class="d-xxl-inline p-2 bd-highlight">d-xxl-inline</div>
```

- d-*-inline-block

```
<div class="d-inline-block p-2 bd-highlight">
d-inline-block</div>
<div class="d-sm-inline-block p-2 bd-highlight">
d-sm-inline-block</div>
<div class="d-md-inline-block p-2 bd-highlight">
d-md-inline-block</div>
<div class="d-lg-inline-block p-2 bd-highlight">
d-lg-inline-block</div>
<div class="d-xl-inline-block p-2 bd-highlight">
d-xl-inline-block</div>
<div class="d-xxl-inline-block p-2 bd-highlight">
d-xxl-inline-block</div>
```

- d-*-block

```
<span class="d-block p-2 bd-highlight">d-block
</span>
<span class="d-sm-block p-2 bd-highlight">
d-sm-block</span>
<span class="d-md-block p-2 bd-highlight">
d-md-block</span>
<span class="d-lg-block p-2 bd-highlight">
d-lg-block</span>
<span class="d-xl-block p-2 bd-highlight">
d-xl-block</span>
<span class="d-xxl-block p-2 bd-highlight">
d-xxl-block</span>
```

- d-*-grid

```
<span class="d-grid p-2 bd-highlight">d-grid</span>
<span class="d-sm-grid p-2 bd-highlight">
d-sm-grid</span>
<span class="d-md-grid p-2 bd-highlight">
d-md-grid</span>
<span class="d-lg-grid p-2 bd-highlight">
d-lg-grid</span>
```

```
<span class="d-xl-grid p-2 bd-highlight">
d-xl-grid</span>
<span class="d-xxl-grid p-2 bd-highlight">
d-xxl-grid</span>
```

- d-*-table

```
<span class="d-table p-2 bd-highlight">d-table
</span>
<span class="d-sm-table p-2 bd-highlight">
d-sm-table</span>
<span class="d-md-table p-2 bd-highlight">
d-md-table</span>
<span class="d-lg-table p-2 bd-highlight">
d-lg-table</span>
<span class="d-xl-table p-2 bd-highlight">
d-xl-table</span>
<span class="d-xxl-table p-2 bd-highlight">
d-xxl-table</span>
```

- d-*-table-cell

```
<div class="d-table-cell p-2 bd-highlight">
d-table-cell</div>
<div class="d-sm-table-cell p-2 bd-highlight">
d-sm-table-cell</div>
<div class="d-md-table-cell p-2 bd-highlight">
d-md-table-cell</div>
<div class="d-lg-table-cell p-2 bd-highlight">
d-lg-table-cell</div>
<div class="d-xl-table-cell p-2 bd-highlight">
d-xl-table-cell</div>
<div class="d-xxl-table-cell p-2 bd-highlight">
d-xxl-table-cell</div>
```

- d-*-table-row

```
<span class="d-table-row p-2 bd-highlight">
d-table-row</span>
<span class="d-sm-table-row p-2 bd-highlight">
d-sm-table-row</span>
<span class="d-md-table-row p-2 bd-highlight">
d-md-table-row</span>
<span class="d-lg-table-row p-2 bd-highlight">
d-lg-table-row</span>
```

```
<span class="d-xl-table-row p-2 bd-highlight">
d-xl-table-row</span>
<span class="d-xxl-table-row p-2 bd-highlight">
d-xxl-table-row</span>
```

- d-*-flex

```
<span class="d-flex p-2 bd-highlight">
d-flex</span>
<span class="d-sm-flex p-2 bd-highlight">
d-sm-flex</span>
<span class="d-md-flex p-2 bd-highlight">
d-md-flex</span>
<span class="d-lg-flex p-2 bd-highlight">
d-lg-flex</span>
<span class="d-xl-flex p-2 bd-highlight">
d-xl-flex</span>
<span class="d-xxl-flex p-2 bd-highlight">
d-xxl-flex</span>
```

- d-*-inline-flex

```
<div class="d-inline-flex p-2 bd-highlight">
d-inline-flex</div>
<div class="d-sm-inline-flex p-2 bd-highlight">
d-sm-inline-flex</div>
<div class="d-md-inline-flex p-2 bd-highlight">
d-md-inline-flex</div>
<div class="d-lg-inline-flex p-2 bd-highlight">
d-lg-inline-flex</div>
<div class="d-xl-inline-flex p-2 bd-highlight">
d-xl-inline-flex</div>
<div class="d-xxl-inline-flex p-2 bd-highlight">
d-xxl-inline-flex</div>
```

- d-print-{display}

```
<div class="d-print-none p-2 bd-highlight">
d-print-none</div>
<div class="d-print-inline p-2 bd-highlight">
d-print-inline</div>
<div class="d-print-inline-block p-2 bd-highlight">
d-print-inline-block</div>
<div class="d-print-block p-2 bd-highlight">
d-print-block</div>
```

```
<div class="d-print-grid p-2 bd-highlight">
d-print-grid</div>
<div class="d-print-table p-2 bd-highlight">
d-print-table</div>
<div class="d-print-table-row p-2 bd-highlight">
d-print-table-row</div>
<div class="d-print-table-cell p-2 bd-highlight">
d-print-table-cell</div>
<div class="d-print-flex p-2 bd-highlight">
d-print-flex</div>
<div class="d-print-inline-flex p-2 bd-highlight">
d-print-inline-flex</div>
```

## Utility: Misc

Used to set utility for miscellaneous properties.

- user-select-{option}

```
<p class="user-select-all">Paragraph Selection done
entirely when clicked by the user.</p>
<p class="user-select-auto">This paragraph has
default select behavior.</p>
<p class="user-select-none">This paragraph will not
be selectable when clicked by the user.</p>
```

- pe-{option}

```
<p><a href="#" class="pe-none" tabindex="-1" aria-
disabled="true">This link</a> can not be clicked.</p>
<p><a href="#" class="pe-auto">This link</a> can be
clicked (this is default behavior).</p>
<p class="pe-none"><a href="#" tabindex="-1" aria-
disabled="true">This link</a> can not be clicked
because the <code>pointer-events</code> property is
inherited from its parent. However, <a href="#"
class="pe-auto">this link</a> has a <code>pe-auto
</code> class and can be clicked.</p>
```

- overflow-{option}

```
<div class="d-sm-flex d-md-block d-xxl-flex">
  <div class="overflow-auto p-3 mb-3 me-sm-3
bg-light" style="max-width: 260px; max-height:
100px;">
```

```
    This is an example using <code>.overflow-auto
</code> on an element with set width and height
dimensions. By
    design, this content will vertically scroll.
    </div>
    <div class="overflow-hidden p-3 mb-3 me-sm-3
bg-light" style="max-width: 260px; max-height:
100px;">
    This is an example of using <code>.overflow-
hidden</code> on an element with set width and
height dimensions.
    </div>
</div>
<div class="d-sm-flex d-md-block d-xxl-flex">
    <div class="overflow-visible p-3 mb-3 me-sm-3
bg-light" style="max-width: 260px; max-height:
100px;">
    <!-- New -->
    This is an example of using <code>.overflow-
visible</code> on an element with set width and
height dimensions.
    </div>
    <div class="overflow-scroll p-3 bg-light"
style="max-width: 260px; max-height: 100px;">
    <!-- New -->
    This is an example of using <code>.overflow-
scroll</code> on an element with set width and
height dimensions.
    </div>
</div>
```

- shadow / shadow-{option}

```
<div class="shadow-none p-3 mb-5 bg-light
rounded">No shadow</div>
<div class="shadow-sm p-3 mb-5 bg-white
rounded">Small shadow</div>
<div class="shadow p-3 mb-5 bg-white
rounded">Regular shadow</div>
<div class="shadow-lg p-3 mb-5 bg-white
rounded">Larger shadow</div>
```

- w-{option}

```
<div class="w-25 p-3" style="background-color:
#eee;">Width 25%</div>
```

```
<div class="w-50 p-3" style="background-color:
#eee;">Width 50%</div>
<div class="w-75 p-3" style="background-color:
#eee;">Width 75%</div>
<div class="w-100 p-3" style="background-color:
#eee;">Width 100%</div>
<div class="w-auto p-3" style="background-color:
#eee;">Width auto</div>
```

- h-{option}

```
<div style="height: 100px; background-color:
rgba(255,0,0,0.1);">
  <div class="h-25 d-inline-block" style="width:
120px; background-color: rgba(0,0,255,.1)">Height
25%</div>
  <div class="h-50 d-inline-block" style="width:
120px; background-color: rgba(0,0,255,.1)">Height
50%</div>
  <div class="h-75 d-inline-block" style="width:
120px; background-color: rgba(0,0,255,.1)">Height
75%</div>
  <div class="h-100 d-inline-block" style="width:
120px; background-color: rgba(0,0,255,.1)">Height
100%</div>
  <div class="h-auto d-inline-block" style="width:
120px; background-color: rgba(0,0,255,.1)">Height
auto</div>
</div>
```

- mw-100

```
<img src="assets/images/bs-images/img-2x1.png"
class="mw-100" alt="Max-width-100">
```

- mh-100

```
<div style="height: 100px; background-color:
rgba(255,0,0,.1);">
  <div class="mh-100" style="width: 100px; height:
200px; background-color: rgba(0,0,255,.1);">
Max-height 100%</div>
</div>
```

- viewport

```
<div class="min-vw-100 bg-light mb-3">Min-width
100vw</div>
```

```
<div class="min-vh-100 bg-light mb-3">Min-height
100vh</div>
<div class="vw-100 bg-light mb-3">Width 100vw</div>
<div class="vh-100 bg-light">Height 100vh</div>
```

- visible

```
<div class="visible">...</div>
```

- invisible

```
<div class="invisible">...</div>
```

## Utility: Position

Used to quickly configure the position of an element.

- float-*-{option}

```
<!-- float can be used for responsive cases with
the help of .float-{sm|md|lg|xl|xxl}-{start|end|
none} class -->
<div class="float-start">Float start on all
viewport sizes</div><br>
<div class="float-end">Float end on all viewport
sizes</div><br>
<div class="float-none">Don't float on all viewport
sizes</div>
```

- position-{option}

```
<div class="position-static">position-static</div>
<div class="position-relative">position-relative</div>
<div class="position-absolute">position-absolute</div>
<div class="position-fixed">position-fixed</div>
<div class="position-sticky">position-sticky</div>
```

- {direction}-{position}

```
<div class="position-relative">
  <div class="position-absolute top-0 start-0"></div>
  <div class="position-absolute top-0 end-0"></div>
  <div class="position-absolute top-50 start-50"></div>
  <div class="position-absolute bottom-50 end-50">
</div>
  <div class="position-absolute bottom-0 start-0">
</div>
  <div class="position-absolute bottom-0 end-0"></div>
</div>
```

- translate-middle

```
<div class="position-relative">
  <div class="position-absolute top-0 start-0
translate-middle"></div>
  <div class="position-absolute top-0 start-50
translate-middle"></div>
  <div class="position-absolute top-0 start-100
translate-middle"></div>
  <div class="position-absolute top-50 start-0
translate-middle"></div>
  <div class="position-absolute top-50 start-50
translate-middle"></div>
  <div class="position-absolute top-50 start-100
translate-middle"></div>
  <div class="position-absolute top-100 start-0
translate-middle"></div>
  <div class="position-absolute top-100 start-50
translate-middle"></div>
  <div class="position-absolute top-100 start-100
translate-middle"></div>
</div>
```

- translate-middle-{direction}

```
<div class="position-relative">
  <div class="position-absolute top-0 start-0"></div>
  <div class="position-absolute top-0 start-50
translate-middle-x"></div>
  <div class="position-absolute top-0 end-0"></div>
  <div class="position-absolute top-50 start-0
translate-middle-y"></div>
  <div class="position-absolute top-50 start-50
translate-middle"></div>
  <div class="position-absolute top-50 end-0
translate-middle-y"></div>
  <div class="position-absolute bottom-0 start-0">
</div>
  <div class="position-absolute bottom-0 start-50
translate-middle-x"></div>
  <div class="position-absolute bottom-0 end-0"></div>
</div>
```

- align-{option}

```
<span class="align-baseline">baseline</span>
<span class="align-top">top</span>
<span class="align-middle">middle</span>
<span class="align-bottom">bottom</span>
<span class="align-text-top">text-top</span>
<span class="align-text-bottom">text-bottom</span>
```

## Utility: Spacing

Used to modify an element's appearance by using responsive margin, padding, and gap utility classes.

- m-*-{option}

```
<!-- Margin can be used for responsive cases with
the help of .m-{sm|md|lg|xl|xxl}-{0|1|2|3|4|5|auto}
class -->
<div class="d-flex flex-wrap align-items-start">
  <div class="m-0 bd-highlight d-inline-
block">.m-0</div>
  <div class="m-1 bd-highlight d-inline-
block">.m-1</div>
  <div class="m-2 bd-highlight d-inline-
block">.m-2</div>
  <div class="m-3 bd-highlight d-inline-
block">.m-3</div>
  <div class="m-4 bd-highlight d-inline-
block">.m-4</div>
  <div class="m-5 bd-highlight d-inline-
block">.m-5</div>
  <div class="m-auto bd-highlight d-inline-
block">.m-auto</div>
</div>
```

- mt-*-{option}

```
<!-- Margin on top can be used for responsive cases
with the help of .mt-{sm|md|lg|xl|xxl}-
{0|1|2|3|4|5|auto} class -->
<div class="d-flex flex-wrap align-items-start">
  <div class="mt-0 bd-highlight d-inline-block">.
mt-0</div>
  <div class="mt-1 bd-highlight d-inline-block">.
mt-1</div>
```

```
  <div class="mt-2 bd-highlight d-inline-block">.
mt-2</div>
  <div class="mt-3 bd-highlight d-inline-block">.
mt-3</div>
  <div class="mt-4 bd-highlight d-inline-block">.
mt-4</div>
  <div class="mt-5 bd-highlight d-inline-block">.
mt-5</div>
  <div class="mt-auto bd-highlight d-inline-block">.
mt-auto</div>
</div>
```

- me-*-{option}

```
<!-- Margin on right can be used for responsive
cases with the help of .me-{sm|md|lg|xl|xxl}-
{0|1|2|3|4|5|auto} class -->
<div class="d-flex flex-wrap align-items-start">
  <div class="me-0 bd-highlight d-inline-block">.
me-0</div>
  <div class="me-1 bd-highlight d-inline-block">.
me-1</div>
  <div class="me-2 bd-highlight d-inline-block">.
me-2</div>
  <div class="me-3 bd-highlight d-inline-block">.
me-3</div>
  <div class="me-4 bd-highlight d-inline-block">.
me-4</div>
  <div class="me-5 bd-highlight d-inline-block">.
me-5</div>
  <div class="me-auto bd-highlight d-inline-block">.
me-auto</div>
</div>
```

- mb-*-{option}

```
<!-- Margin on bottom can be used for responsive
cases with the help of .mb-{sm|md|lg|xl|xxl}-
{0|1|2|3|4|5|auto} class -->
<div class="mb-0 bd-highlight">.mb-0</div>
<div class="mb-1 bd-highlight">.mb-1</div>
<div class="mb-2 bd-highlight">.mb-2</div>
<div class="mb-3 bd-highlight">.mb-3</div>
<div class="mb-4 bd-highlight">.mb-4</div>
```

```
<div class="mb-5 bd-highlight">.mb-5</div>
<div class="mb-auto bd-highlight">.mb-auto</div>
```

- ms-*-{option}

```
<!-- Margin on left can be used for responsive
cases with the help of .ms-{sm|md|lg|xl|xxl}-
{0|1|2|3|4|5|auto} class -->
<div class="d-flex flex-wrap align-items-start">
  <div class="ms-0 bd-highlight d-inline-block">.
ms-0</div>
  <div class="ms-1 bd-highlight d-inline-block">.
ms-1</div>
  <div class="ms-2 bd-highlight d-inline-block">.
ms-2</div>
  <div class="ms-3 bd-highlight d-inline-block">.
ms-3</div>
  <div class="ms-4 bd-highlight d-inline-block">.
ms-4</div>
  <div class="ms-5 bd-highlight d-inline-block">.
ms-5</div>
  <div class="ms-auto bd-highlight d-inline-block">.
ms-auto</div>
</div>
```

- mx-*-{option}

```
<!-- Margin on right and left can be used for
responsive cases with the help of
.mx-{sm|md|lg|xl|xxl}-{0|1|2|3|4|5|auto} class -->
<div class="d-flex flex-wrap align-items-start">
  <div class="mx-0 bd-highlight d-inline-block">.
mx-0</div>
  <div class="mx-1 bd-highlight d-inline-block">.
mx-1</div>
  <div class="mx-2 bd-highlight d-inline-block">.
mx-2</div>
  <div class="mx-3 bd-highlight d-inline-block">.
mx-3</div>
  <div class="mx-4 bd-highlight d-inline-block">.
mx-4</div>
  <div class="mx-5 bd-highlight d-inline-block">.
mx-5</div>
  <div class="mx-auto bd-highlight d-inline-block">.
mx-auto</div>
</div>
```

- my-\*-{option}

```
<!-- Margin on top and bottom can be used for
responsive cases with the help of
.my-{sm|md|lg|xl|xxl}-{0|1|2|3|4|5|auto} class -->
<div class="d-flex flex-wrap align-items-start">
  <div class="my-0 bd-highlight d-inline-block">.
my-0</div>
  <div class="my-1 bd-highlight d-inline-block">.
my-1</div>
  <div class="my-2 bd-highlight d-inline-block">.
my-2</div>
  <div class="my-3 bd-highlight d-inline-block">.
my-3</div>
  <div class="my-4 bd-highlight d-inline-block">.
my-4</div>
  <div class="my-5 bd-highlight d-inline-block">.
my-5</div>
  <div class="my-auto bd-highlight d-inline-block">.
my-auto</div>
</div>
```

- p-\*-{option}

```
<!-- Padding can be used for responsive cases with the
help of .p-{sm|md|lg|xl|xxl}-{0|1|2|3|4|5} class -->
<div class="d-flex flex-wrap align-items-start">
  <div class="p-0 me-1 bd-highlight d-inline-
block">.p-0</div>
  <div class="p-1 me-1 bd-highlight d-inline-
block">.p-1</div>
  <div class="p-2 me-1 bd-highlight d-inline-
block">.p-2</div>
  <div class="p-3 me-1 bd-highlight d-inline-
block">.p-3</div>
  <div class="p-4 me-1 bd-highlight d-inline-
block">.p-4</div>
  <div class="p-5 bd-highlight d-inline-
block">.p-5</div>
</div>
```

- pt-\*-{option}

```
<!-- Padding on top can be used for responsive
cases with the help of
.pt-{sm|md|lg|xl|xxl}-{0|1|2|3|4|5} class -->
```

```
<div class="d-flex flex-wrap align-items-start">
  <div class="pt-0 me-1 bd-highlight d-inline-
block">.pt-0</div>
  <div class="pt-1 me-1 bd-highlight d-inline-
block">.pt-1</div>
  <div class="pt-2 me-1 bd-highlight d-inline-
block">.pt-2</div>
  <div class="pt-3 me-1 bd-highlight d-inline-
block">.pt-3</div>
  <div class="pt-4 me-1 bd-highlight d-inline-
block">.pt-4</div>
  <div class="pt-5 bd-highlight d-inline-block">.
pt-5</div>
</div>
```

- pe-*-{option}

```
<!-- Padding on right can be used for responsive
cases with the help of
.pe-{sm|md|lg|xl|xxl}-{0|1|2|3|4|5} class -->
<div class="d-flex flex-wrap align-items-start">
  <div class="pe-0 me-1 bd-highlight d-inline-
block">.pe-0</div>
  <div class="pe-1 me-1 bd-highlight d-inline-
block">.pe-1</div>
  <div class="pe-2 me-1 bd-highlight d-inline-
block">.pe-2</div>
  <div class="pe-3 me-1 bd-highlight d-inline-
block">.pe-3</div>
  <div class="pe-4 me-1 bd-highlight d-inline-
block">.pe-4</div>
  <div class="pe-5 bd-highlight d-inline-block">.
pe-5</div>
</div>
```

- pb-*-{option}

```
<!-- Padding on bottom can be used for responsive
cases with the help of
.pb-{sm|md|lg|xl|xxl}-{0|1|2|3|4|5} class -->
<div class="d-flex flex-wrap align-items-start">
  <div class="pb-0 me-1 bd-highlight d-inline-
block">.pb-0</div>
  <div class="pb-1 me-1 bd-highlight d-inline-
block">.pb-1</div>
```

```
  <div class="pb-2 me-1 bd-highlight d-inline-
block">.pb-2</div>
  <div class="pb-3 me-1 bd-highlight d-inline-
block">.pb-3</div>
  <div class="pb-4 me-1 bd-highlight d-inline-
block">.pb-4</div>
  <div class="pb-5 bd-highlight d-inline-block">.
pb-5</div>
</div>
```

- ps-*-{option}

```
<!-- Padding on left can be used for responsive
cases with the help of
.ps-{sm|md|lg|xl|xxl}-{0|1|2|3|4|5} class -->
<div class="d-flex flex-wrap align-items-start">
  <div class="ps-0 me-1 bd-highlight d-inline-
block">.ps-0</div>
  <div class="ps-1 me-1 bd-highlight d-inline-
block">.ps-1</div>
  <div class="ps-2 me-1 bd-highlight d-inline-
block">.ps-2</div>
  <div class="ps-3 me-1 bd-highlight d-inline-
block">.ps-3</div>
  <div class="ps-4 me-1 bd-highlight d-inline-
block">.ps-4</div>
  <div class="ps-5 bd-highlight d-inline-block">.
ps-5</div>
</div>
```

- px-*-{option}

```
<!-- Padding on right and left can be used for
responsive cases with the help of
.px-{sm|md|lg|xl|xxl}-{0|1|2|3|4|5} class -->
<div class="d-flex flex-wrap align-items-start">
  <div class="px-0 me-1 bd-highlight d-inline-
block">.px-0</div>
  <div class="px-1 me-1 bd-highlight d-inline-
block">.px-1</div>
  <div class="px-2 me-1 bd-highlight d-inline-
block">.px-2</div>
  <div class="px-3 me-1 bd-highlight d-inline-
block">.px-3</div>
  <div class="px-4 me-1 bd-highlight d-inline-
block">.px-4</div>
```

```
    <div class="px-5 bd-highlight d-inline-block">.
px-5</div>
</div>
```

- py-*-{option}

```
<!-- Padding on top and bottom can be used for
responsive cases with the help of
.py-{sm|md|lg|xl|xxl}-{0|1|2|3|4|5} class -->
<div class="d-flex flex-wrap align-items-start">
    <div class="py-0 me-1 bd-highlight d-inline-
block">.py-0</div>
    <div class="py-1 me-1 bd-highlight d-inline-
block">.py-1</div>
    <div class="py-2 me-1 bd-highlight d-inline-
block">.py-2</div>
    <div class="py-3 me-1 bd-highlight d-inline-
block">.py-3</div>
    <div class="py-4 me-1 bd-highlight d-inline-
block">.py-4</div>
    <div class="py-5 bd-highlight d-inline-block">.
py-5</div>
</div>
```

- m{direction}-*-n{size}

```
<!-- Negative margins are disabled by default, but
can be enabled in Sass by setting $enable-negative-
margins: true.
This class can be used as .m{t|e|b|s|x|y}-{sm|md|lg
|xl|xxl}-n{0|1|2|3|4|5} -->
<div class="d-flex flex-wrap align-items-start">
    <div class="m-n0 bd-highlight d-inline-
block">Spaced Div</div>
    <div class="mt-n1 bd-highlight d-inline-
block">Spaced Div</div>
    <div class="me-n2 bd-highlight d-inline-
block">Spaced Div</div>
    <div class="mb-n3 bd-highlight d-inline-
block">Spaced Div</div>
    <div class="ms-n4 bd-highlight d-inline-
block">Spaced Div</div>
    <div class="mx-n5 bd-highlight d-inline-
block">Spaced Div</div>
```

```
<div class="my-md-n3 bd-highlight d-inline-
block">Spaced Div</div>
</div>
```

- gap-*-{size}

```
<!-- Gap can be used for responsive cases with the
help of .dap-{sm|md|lg|xl|xxl}-{0|1|2|3|4|5} class -->
<div class="d-grid gap-3">
  <div class="p-2 bg-light border">Grid item 1</div>
  <div class="p-2 bg-light border">Grid item 2</div>
  <div class="p-2 bg-light border">Grid item 3</div>
</div>
```

## Utility: Text

Used to control alignment, wrapping, weight, and more by using these text utilities.

- text-*-start

```
<!-- text-start can be used for responsive cases with
the help of .text-{sm|md|lg|xl|xxl}-start class -->
<p class="text-start">Start aligned text on all
viewport sizes.</p>
<p class="text-sm-start">Start aligned text on
viewports sized SM (small) or wider.</p>
<p class="text-md-start">Start aligned text on
viewports sized MD (medium) or wider.</p>
<p class="text-lg-start">Start aligned text on
viewports sized LG (large) or wider.</p>
<p class="text-xl-start">Start aligned text on
viewports sized XL (extra-large) or wider.</p>
<p class="text-xxl-start">Start aligned text on
viewports sized XXL (extra-extra-large) or wider.</p>
```

- text-*-center

```
<!-- text-center can be used for responsive cases
with the help of .text-{sm|md|lg|xl|xxl}-center
class -->
<p class="text-center">Center aligned text on all
viewport sizes.</p>
<p class="text-sm-center">Center aligned text on
viewports sized SM (small) or wider.</p>
```

```
<p class="text-md-center">Center aligned text on
viewports sized MD (medium) or wider.</p>
<p class="text-lg-center">Center aligned text on
viewports sized LG (large) or wider.</p>
<p class="text-xl-center">Center aligned text on
viewports sized XL (extra-large) or wider.</p>
<p class="text-xxl-center">Center aligned text on
viewports sized XXL (extra-extra-large) or wider.</p>
```

- text-*-end

```
<!-- text-end can be used for responsive cases with
the help of .text-{sm|md|lg|xl|xxl}-end class -->
<p class="text-end">End aligned text on all
viewport sizes.</p>
<p class="text-sm-end">End aligned text on
viewports sized SM (small) or wider.</p>
<p class="text-md-end">End aligned text on
viewports sized MD (medium) or wider.</p>
<p class="text-lg-end">End aligned text on
viewports sized LG (large) or wider.</p>
<p class="text-xl-end">End aligned text on
viewports sized XL (extra-large) or wider.</p>
<p class="text-xxl-end">End aligned text on viewports
sized XXL (extra-extra-large) or wider.</p>
```

- text-wrap

```
<div class="badge bg-secondary text-wrap"
style="width: 6rem;">
  This text should wrap.
</div>
```

- text-nowrap

```
<div class="text-nowrap bd-highlight" style="width:
8rem;">
  This text should overflow the parent.
</div>
```

- text-break

```
<p class="text-break">
    mmmmmmmmmmmmmmmmmmmmmmmmmmmmmmmmmmmmmmmmmmmmmmmmmmmmmmmmmmmmmmmmmmmmmmmmmmmm
mmmmmmmmmmmmmmmmmmmmmmmmmmmmmmmmmmmmmmmmmmmmmmmmmmmmmmmmmmmmmmmmmmmmmmm</p>
```

- text-{option}

```
<p class="text-lowercase">Lowercased text.</p>
<p class="text-uppercase">Uppercased text.</p>
<p class="text-capitalize">CapiTaliZed text.</p>
```

- fs-{size}

```
<p class="fs-1">.fs-1 text</p>
<p class="fs-2">.fs-2 text</p>
<p class="fs-3">.fs-3 text</p>
<p class="fs-4">.fs-4 text</p>
<p class="fs-5">.fs-5 text</p>
<p class="fs-6">.fs-6 text</p>
```

- fw-{weight}

```
<p class="fw-bold">Bold text.</p>
<p class="fw-bolder">Bolder weight text (relative
to the parent element).</p>
<p class="fw-normal">Normal weight text.</p>
<p class="fw-light">Light weight text.</p>
<p class="fw-lighter">Lighter weight text (relative
to the parent element).</p>
```

- fst-{style}

```
<p class="fst-italic">Italic text.</p>
<p class="fst-normal">Text with normal font style</p>
<!-- New -->
```

- lh-{style}

```
<p class="lh-1">Vivamus sagittis lacus vel augue
laoreet rutrum faucibus dolor auctor. Donec sed odio
dui. Cras mattis
  pannenkoek purus sit amet . Praesent cursus magna,
vel scelerisque nisl consectetur et. Nullam id
  dolor id nibh vehicula ut id elit. Cras mattis
purus sit amet fermentum.</p>
<p class="lh-sm">Vivamus sagittis vel augue laoreet
rutrum faucibus dolor auctor. Donec sed odio dui.
Cras mattis
  pannenkoek purus sit amet fermentum. Praesent
cursus magna, vel scelerisque nisl consectetur et.
Nullam id
```

dolor id nibh vehicula ut id elit. Cras mattis
consectetur sit amet fermentum.</p>
<p class="lh-base">Vivamus sagittis lacus vel augue
laoreet rutrum faucibus dolor auctor. Donec sed odio
dui. Cras
  mattis pannenkoek purus sit amet fermentum. cursus
magna, vel nisl consectetur et.
  Nullam id dolor id nibh ultricies vehicula ut id
elit. Cras mattis consectetur purus sit
fermentum.</p>
<p class="lh-lg">Vivamus lacus vel augue laoreet
rutrum faucibus dolor auctor. Donec sed odio dui.
Cras mattis
  pannenkoek purus sit amet . Praesent commodo
cursus magna, vel scelerisque nisl consectetur et.
Nullam id
  dolor id ultricies vehicula ut id elit. Cras
mattis consectetur sit amet fermentum.</p>

- font-monospace

<p class="font-monospace">This is in monospace</p>

- text-reset

<p class="text-muted">

## CHAPTER 9

# Cheat Sheet 2

```
Muted text with a <a href="#" class="text-reset">
reset link</a>.
</p>
```

- text-decoration-{option}

```
<p class="text-decoration-underline">This text has
a line underneath it.</p><!-- New -->
<p class="text-decoration-line-through">This text
has a line going through it.</p><!-- New -->
<a href="#" class="text-decoration-none">This link
has its text decoration removed</a>
```

## UTILITY: OPACITY

Used to control the opacity of elements.

- opacity-{value}

```
<div class="opacity-100 p-2 m-1 bg-primary text-
light fw-bold rounded">100%</div>
<div class="opacity-75 p-2 m-1 bg-primary text-
light fw-bold rounded">75%</div>
<div class="opacity-50 p-2 m-1 bg-primary text-
light fw-bold rounded">50%</div>
<div class="opacity-25 p-2 m-1 bg-primary text-
light fw-bold rounded">25%</div>
```

DOI: 10.1201/9781003309383-9

- bg-opacity-{value}

```
<div class="bg-success p-2 text-white">This is
default success background</div>
<div class="bg-success p-2 text-white bg-opacity-
75">This is 75% opacity success background</div>
<div class="bg-success p-2 text-dark bg-opacity-
50">This is 50% opacity success background</div>
<div class="bg-success p-2 text-dark bg-opacity-
25">This is 25% opacity success background</div>
<div class="bg-success p-2 text-dark bg-opacity-
10">This is 10% opacity success background</div>
```

- text-opacity-{value}

```
<div class="text-primary">This is default primary
text</div>
<div class="text-primary text-opacity-75">This is
75% opacity primary text</div>
<div class="text-primary text-opacity-50">This is
50% opacity primary text</div>
<div class="text-primary text-opacity-25">This is
25% opacity primary text</div>
```

## BOOTSTRAP KEY COMPONENTS

### Alerts

Alert is a user message that is mostly used to display a message to the user based on a prior user action.

- alert-primary

```
<div class="alert alert-primary" role="alert">
  A simple primary alert—check it out!
</div>
```

- alert-secondary

```
<div class="alert alert-secondary" role="alert">
  A simple secondary alert—check it out!
</div>
```

- alert-success

```
<div class="alert alert-success" role="alert">
  A simple success alert—check it out!
</div>
```

- alert-danger

```
<div class="alert alert-danger" role="alert">
A simple danger alert—check it out!
</div>
```

- alert-warning

```
<div class="alert alert-warning" role="alert">
  A simple warning alert—check it out!
</div>
```

- alert-info

```
<div class="alert alert-info" role="alert">
  A simple info alert—check it out!
</div>
```

- alert-light

```
<div class="alert alert-light" role="alert">
  A simple light alert—check it out!
</div>
```

- alert-dark

```
<div class="alert alert-dark" role="alert">
  A simple dark alert—check it out!
</div>
```

- alert-link

Used to add a link in the alert class

```
<div class="alert alert-primary" role="alert">
  A simple primary alert with <a href="#"
class="alert-link">an example link</a>. Give it a
click if you like.
</div>
```

- alert-dismissible

Can be used with any other alert color class like info, danger, success, etc. for styling.

```
<div class="alert alert-warning alert-dismissible
fade show" role="alert">
```

```
<strong>Holy guacamole!</strong> You should check
in on some of those fields below.
   <button type="button" class="btn-close" data-bs-
dismiss="alert" aria-label="Close"></button>
</div>
```

- alert-heading

Can be used with any other alert color class like info, danger, success, etc. for styling.

```
<div class="alert alert-success" role="alert">
   <h4 class="alert-heading">Well done!</h4>
   <p>Aww yeah, you successfully read this important
alert message. This example text is going to run a
bit longer so
     that you can see how spacing within an alert
works with this kind of content.</p>
   <hr>
   <p class="mb-0">Whenever you need to, be sure to
use margin utilities to keep things nice and
tidy.</p>
</div>
```

## Badges

Badges are used to display extra information next to a category button, or any other element. Badges will also scale to match the size of the immediate parent element. You can also use badges as part of a button or a link and use it as a counter.

- badge

Used to add a badge of the same size as the parent element by using em units or a similar font size relative to the parent.

```
<h1>Example heading <span class="badge
bg-secondary">New</span></h1>
<h2>Example heading <span class="badge
bg-secondary">New</span></h2>
<h3>Example heading <span class="badge
bg-secondary">New</span></h3>
<h4>Example heading <span class="badge
bg-secondary">New</span></h4>
<h5>Example heading <span class="badge
bg-secondary">New</span></h5>
<h6>Example heading <span class="badge
bg-secondary">New</span></h6>
```

- Notification badge

Can be used next to a button as a counter.

```
<button type="button" class="btn btn-primary">
  Notifications <span class="badge bg-secondary">4
</span>
</button>
```

- Pill badge

Used to make badges more rounded and with a larger border radius.

```
<span class="badge rounded-pill
bg-primary">Primary</span>
<span class="badge rounded-pill
bg-secondary">Secondary</span>
<span class="badge rounded-pill
bg-success">Success</span>
<span class="badge rounded-pill bg-danger">Danger
</span>
<span class="badge rounded-pill bg-warning text-
dark">Warning</span>
<span class="badge rounded-pill bg-info text-
dark">Info</span>
<span class="badge rounded-pill bg-light text-
dark">Light</span>
<span class="badge rounded-pill bg-dark">Dark
</span>
```

- badge-primary

```
<span class="badge bg-primary">Primary</span>
```

- badge-secondary

```
<span class="badge bg-secondary">Secondary</span>
```

- badge-success

```
<span class="badge bg-success">Success</span>
```

- badge-danger

```
<span class="badge bg-danger">Danger</span>
```

- badge-warning

```
<span class="badge bg-warning text-dark">Warning
</span>
```

- badge-info

```
<span class="badge bg-info text-dark">Info</span>
```

- badge-light

```
<span class="badge bg-light text-dark">Light</span>
```

- badge-dark

```
<span class="badge bg-dark">Dark</span>
```

## Breadcrumb

Used to indicate the location of the current page along with its navigational hierarchy.

- breadcrumb

```
<nav aria-label="breadcrumb">
  <ol class="breadcrumb">
    <li class="breadcrumb-item active"
aria-current="page">Home</li>
  </ol>
</nav>
<nav aria-label="breadcrumb">
  <ol class="breadcrumb">
    <li class="breadcrumb-item"><a href="#">Home
</a></li>
    <li class="breadcrumb-item active" aria-
current="page">Library</li>
  </ol>
</nav>
<nav aria-label="breadcrumb">
  <ol class="breadcrumb">
    <li class="breadcrumb-item"><a href="#">Home
</a></li>
    <li class="breadcrumb-item"><a
href="#">Library</a></li>
    <li class="breadcrumb-item active" aria-
current="page">Data</li>
  </ol>
</nav>
```

- breadcrumb-divider

```
<nav style="--bs-breadcrumb-divider: '>';"
aria-label="breadcrumb">
```

```
<ol class="breadcrumb">
  <li class="breadcrumb-item"><a href="#">Home
</a></li>
  <li class="breadcrumb-item active"
aria-current="page">Library</li>
  </ol>
</nav>
```

## Button

- btn-primary

```
<button type="button" class="btn btn-
primary">Primary</button>
```

- btn-secondary

```
<button type="button" class="btn btn-
secondary">Secondary</button>
```

- btn-success

```
<button type="button" class="btn btn-
success">Success</button>
```

- btn-danger

```
<button type="button" class="btn btn-
danger">Danger</button>
```

- btn-warning

```
<button type="button" class="btn btn-
warning">Warning</button>
```

- btn-info

```
<button type="button" class="btn btn-info">Info
</button>
```

- btn-light

```
<button type="button" class="btn btn-light">Light
</button>
```

- btn-dark

```
<button type="button" class="btn btn-dark">Dark
</button>
```

- btn-link

```
<button type="button" class="btn btn-link">Link
</button>
```

- btn-outline-primary

```
<button type="button" class="btn btn-outline-
primary">Primary</button>
```

- btn-outline-secondary

```
<button type="button" class="btn btn-outline-sec
ondary">Secondary</button>
```

- btn-outline-success

```
<button type="button" class="btn btn-outline-
success">Success</button>
```

- btn-outline-danger

```
<button type="button" class="btn btn-outline-
danger">Danger</button>
```

- btn-outline-warning

```
<button type="button" class="btn btn-outline-
warning">Warning</button>
```

- btn-outline-info

```
<button type="button" class="btn btn-outline-
info">Info</button>
```

- btn-outline-light

```
<button type="button" class="btn btn-outline-
light">Light</button>
```

- btn-outline-dark

```
<button type="button" class="btn btn-outline-
dark">Dark</button>
```

- btn-lg

```
<button type="button" class="btn btn-primary btn-
lg">Large button</button>
<button type="button" class="btn btn-secondary
btn-lg">Large button</button>
```

- btn-sm

```
<button type="button" class="btn btn-primary btn-
sm">Small button</button>
<button type="button" class="btn btn-secondary
btn-sm">Small button</button>
```

- Block Buttons

```
<div class="d-grid gap-2">
  <button class="btn btn-primary"
type="button">Button</button>
  <button class="btn btn-primary"
type="button">Button</button>
</div>
```

- btn-close

```
<button type="button" class="btn-close" aria-
label="Close"></button>
```

- btn-close-white

```
<button type="button" class="btn-close btn-close-
white" aria-label="Close"></button>
```

## Button Plugin

- single button toggle

```
<button type="button" class="btn btn-outline-
primary" data-bs-toggle="button"
autocomplete="off">Toggle button</button>
```

- btn-group with checkbox

```
<div class="btn-group" role="group" aria-
label="Basic checkbox toggle button group">
  <input type="checkbox" class="btn-check"
id="btnCheck1" autocomplete="off">
  <label class="btn btn-outline-primary"
for="btnCheck1">Checkbox 1</label>
<input type="checkbox" class="btn-check"
id="btnCheck2" autocomplete="off">
  <label class="btn btn-outline-primary"
for="btnCheck2">Checkbox 2</label>
  <input type="checkbox" class="btn-check"
id="btnCheck3" autocomplete="off">
```

```
<label class="btn btn-outline-primary"
for="btnCheck3">Checkbox 3</label>
</div>
```

- btn-group with radio

```
<div class="btn-group" role="group" aria-
label="Basic radio toggle button group">
  <input type="radio" class="btn-check"
name="btnGroupRadio" id="btnRadio1"
autocomplete="off" checked="">
  <label class="btn btn-outline-primary"
for="btnRadio1">Radio 1</label>
  <input type="radio" class="btn-check"
name="btnGroupRadio" id="btnRadio2"
autocomplete="off">
  <label class="btn btn-outline-primary"
for="btnRadio2">Radio 2</label>
  <input type="radio" class="btn-check"
name="btnGroupRadio" id="btnRadio3"
autocomplete="off">
  <label class="btn btn-outline-primary"
for="btnRadio3">Radio 3</label>
</div>
```

## Button Group

Used to display a group of similar sized buttons without having to code them separately.

- btn-group

```
<div class="btn-group" role="group" aria-
label="Basic example">
  <button type="button" class="btn btn-
primary">Left</button>
  <button type="button" class="btn btn-
primary">Middle</button>
  <button type="button" class="btn btn-
primary">Right</button>
</div>
```

- btn-group (Nested)

```
<div class="btn-group" role="group" aria-
label="Button group with nested dropdown">
```

```
  <button type="button" class="btn btn-primary">1
</button>
  <button type="button" class="btn btn-primary">2
</button>
  <div class="btn-group" role="group">
    <button id="btnGroupDrop1" type="button"
class="btn btn-primary dropdown-toggle"
data-bs-toggle="dropdown"
    aria-expanded="false">
    Dropdown
    </button>
    <ul class="dropdown-menu"
aria-labelledby="btnGroupDrop1">
      <li><a class="dropdown-item" href="#">Dropdown
link</a></li>
      <li><a class="dropdown-item" href="#">Dropdown
link</a></li>
    </ul>
  </div>
</div>
```

• btn-group with links

```
<div class="btn-group">
  <a href="#" class="btn btn-primary active" aria-
current="page">Active link</a>
  <a href="#" class="btn btn-primary">Link</a>
  <a href="#" class="btn btn-primary">Link</a>
</div>
```

• outlined btn-group

```
<div class="btn-group" role="group" aria-
label="Basic outlined button group">
  <button type="button" class="btn btn-outline-
primary">Left</button>
  <button type="button" class="btn btn-outline-
primary">Middle</button>
  <button type="button" class="btn btn-outline-
primary">Right</button>
</div>
```

• btn-toolbar

```
<div class="btn-toolbar" role="toolbar" aria-
label="Toolbar with button groups">
```

```
  <div class="btn-group me-2" role="group"
aria-label="First group">
    <button type="button" class="btn btn-
primary">1</button>
    <button type="button" class="btn btn-
primary">2</button>
    <button type="button" class="btn btn-
primary">3</button>
    <button type="button" class="btn btn-
primary">4</button>
  </div>
  <div class="btn-group me-2" role="group" aria-
label="Second group">
    <button type="button" class="btn btn-
secondary">5</button>
    <button type="button" class="btn btn-
secondary">6</button>
    <button type="button" class="btn btn-
secondary">7</button>
  </div>
  <div class="btn-group" role="group" aria-
label="Third group">
    <button type="button" class="btn btn-info">
8</button>
  </div>
</div>
```

- btn-group-lg

```
<div class="btn-group btn-group-lg" role="group"
aria-label="Large button group">
  <button type="button" class="btn btn-
primary">Left</button>
  <button type="button" class="btn btn-
primary">Middle</button>
  <button type="button" class="btn btn-
primary">Right</button>
</div>
```

- btn-group-sm

```
<div class="btn-group btn-group-sm" role="group"
aria-label="Small button group">
  <button type="button" class="btn
btn-primary">Left</button>
```

```
   <button type="button" class="btn btn-
primary">Middle</button>
   <button type="button" class="btn btn-
primary">Right</button>
</div>
```

- btn-group-vertical

```
<div class="btn-group-vertical" role="group" aria-
label="Vertical button group">
   <button type="button" class="btn btn-
primary">Button</button>
   <button type="button" class="btn btn-
primary">Button</button>
   <button type="button" class="btn btn-
primary">Button</button>
</div>
```

## Cards

Cards are content containers similar to a business card that have a padding around the content. There are various ways to choose from like header, content, footer, etc.

- card

```
<div class="card">
  <div class="card-header">
    Featured
  </div>
  <div class="card-body">
    <h5 class="card-title">Special title treatment</h5>
    <p class="card-text">As a natural lead-in to
extra content, the supporting text below.</p>
    <a href="#" class="btn btn-primary">Go
somewhere</a>
  </div>
  <div class="card-footer text-muted">
    2 days ago
  </div>
</div>
```

- card-body

```
<div class="card">
  <div class="card-body">
```

```
      This text inside a card body.
    </div>
</div>
```

- titles, text, links

```
<div class="card">
  <div class="card-body">
    <h5 class="card-title">Card title</h5>
    <h6 class="card-subtitle mb-2 text-muted">Card
subtitle</h6>
    <p class="card-text">Some simple example text to
go along with the card title and make up the
majority of the card's content.
      content.</p>
    <a href="#" class="card-link">Card link</a>
    <a href="#" class="card-link">Another link</a>
  </div>
</div>
```

- list-group

```
<div class="card">
  <ul class="list-group list-group-flush">
    <li class="list-group-item">Cras justo odio</li>
    <li class="list-group-item">Dapibus ac facilisis
in</li>
    <li class="list-group-item">Vestibulum at eros</li>
  </ul>
</div>
```

- card-header

```
<div class="card">
  <div class="card-header">
    Featured
  </div>
  <div class="card-body">
    <h5 class="card-title">Special title treatment
</h5>
    <p class="card-text">With helping text below as
additional content.</p>
    <a href="#" class="btn btn-primary">Go
somewhere</a>
  </div>
</div>
```

- card-footer

```
<div class="card">
  <div class="card-body">
    <h5 class="card-title">Special title treatment
</h5>
    <p class="card-text">With helping text below as
additional content..</p>
    <a href="#" class="btn btn-primary">Go
somewhere</a>
  </div>
  <div class="card-footer text-muted">
    2 days ago
  </div>
</div>
```

- navigation in card

```
<!-- Tabs or Pills can be used in a card with the
help of .nav-{tabs|pills} and .card-header-
{tabs|pills} classes -->
<div class="card">
  <div class="card-header">
    <ul class="nav nav-tabs card-header-tabs"
id="myTab" role="tablist">
      <li class="nav-item" role="presentation">
        <a class="nav-link active" id="home-tab"
data-bs-toggle="tab" href="#home" role="tab"
          aria-controls="home" aria-
selected="true">Home</a>
      </li>
      <li class="nav-item" role="presentation">
        <a class="nav-link" id="profile-tab" data-bs-
toggle="tab" href="#profile" role="tab"
          aria-controls="profile" aria-
selected="false">Profile</a>
      </li>
      <li class="nav-item">
        <a class="nav-link disabled" id="disabled-
tab" data-bs-toggle="tab" href="#disabled"
role="tab"
          aria-controls="disabled" tabindex="-1"
aria-disabled="true">Disabled</a>
      </li>
    </ul>
```

```
    </div>
    <div class="card-body">
      <div class="tab-content" id="myTabContent">
        <div class="tab-pane fade show active"
id="home" role="tabpanel" aria-labelledby="home-
tab">Lorem ipsum
          dolor sit amet consectetur adipisicing elit.
Eligendi alias praesentium illo omnis adipisci ipsa
          suscipit rerum quidem doloribus magnam?</div>
        <div class="tab-pane fade" id="profile"
role="tabpanel" aria-labelledby="profile-tab">Lorem
ipsum dolor sit
          amet consectetur adipisicing elit. Iure,
asperiores provident ea eaque quis omnis adipisci in
          exercitationem necessitatibus dolorem.</div>
        <div class="tab-pane fade" id="disabled"
role="tabpanel" aria-labelledby="disabled-
tab">Lorem, ipsum dolor
          sit amet consectetur adipisicing elit.
Suscipit rem accusamus officia quia eos ducimus
consequuntur!
          Impedit aliquid vero suscipit.</div>
      </div>
    </div>
</div>
```

- card-img-top

```
<div class="card">
  <img src="assets/images/bs-images/img-2x1.png"
class="card-img-top" alt="card-img-top">
  <div class="card-body">
    <h5 class="card-title">Card title</h5>
    <p class="card-text">This is a wider card with
supporting text below as a natural lead-in to
additional content.
      This content is a little bit longer.</p>
    <p class="card-text"><small class="text-
muted">Last updated 3 mins ago</small></p>
  </div>
</div>
```

- card-img-bottom

```
<div class="card">
  <div class="card-body">
    <h5 class="card-title">Card title</h5>
    <p class="card-text">This is a wider card with
supporting text below as a natural lead-in to
additional content.
      This content is a little bit longer.</p>
    <p class="card-text"><small class="text-
muted">Last updated 3 mins ago</small></p>
  </div>
  <img src="assets/images/bs-images/img-2x1.png"
class="card-img-bottom" alt="card-img-bottom">
</div>
```

- card-img-overlay

```
<div class="card bg-dark text-dark">
  <img src="assets/images/bs-images/img-2x1.png"
class="card-img" alt="card-img-overlay">
  <div class="card-img-overlay">
    <h5 class="card-title">Card title</h5>
    <p class="card-text">This is a wider card with
supporting text below as a natural lead-in to
additional content.
    </p>
    <p class="card-text">Last updated 3 mins ago</p>
  </div>
</div>
```

- horizontal card

```
<div class="card">
  <div class="row g-0">
    <div class="col-5 col-sm-4">
      <img src="assets/images/bs-images/img-3x4.png"
class="img-fluid w-100"
alt="card-horizontal-image">
    </div>
    <div class="col-7 col-sm-8">
      <div class="card-body">
        <h5 class="card-title">Card title</h5>
```

```
        <p class="card-text">This is a wider card
with supporting text below as a natural lead-in to
additional
        content.</p>
        <p class="card-text"><small class="text-
muted">Last updated 3 mins ago</small></p>
      </div>
    </div>
  </div>
</div>
```

- bg-{color}

It is used to change the background color of the card based on the color code of Bootstrap.

1. Primary

```
<div class="card text-white bg-primary mb-3"
style="max-width: 18rem;">
  <div class="card-header">Header</div>
  <div class="card-body">
    <h5 class="card-title">Primary card title</h5>
    <p class="card-text">Some example text to build
on the card title and make up the bulk of the card's
      content.</p>
  </div>
</div>
```

2. Secondary

```
<div class="card text-white bg-secondary mb-3"
style="max-width: 18rem;">
  <div class="card-header">Header</div>
  <div class="card-body">
    <h5 class="card-title">Secondary card title</h5>
    <p class="card-text">Some quick example text to
build on the card title and make up the bulk of the
card's
      content.</p>
  </div>
</div>
```

### 3. Success

```
<div class="card text-white bg-success mb-3"
style="max-width: 18rem;">
  <div class="card-header">Header</div>
  <div class="card-body">
    <h5 class="card-title">Success card title</h5>
    <p class="card-text">Some quick example text to
build on the card title and make up the bulk of the
card's
      content.</p>
  </div>
</div>
```

### 4. Danger

```
<div class="card text-white bg-danger mb-3"
style="max-width: 18rem;">
  <div class="card-header">Header</div>
  <div class="card-body">
    <h5 class="card-title">Danger card title</h5>
    <p class="card-text">Some quick example text to
build on the card title and make up the bulk of the
card's
      content.</p>
  </div>
</div>
```

### 5. Warning

```
<div class="card text-dark bg-warning mb-3"
style="max-width: 18rem;">
  <div class="card-header">Header</div>
  <div class="card-body">
    <h5 class="card-title">Warning card title</h5>
    <p class="card-text">Some quick example text to
build on the card title and make up the bulk of the
card's
      content.</p>
  </div>
</div>
```

## 6. Info

```
<div class="card text-dark bg-info mb-3"
style="max-width: 18rem;">
  <div class="card-header">Header</div>
  <div class="card-body">
    <h5 class="card-title">Info card title</h5>
    <p class="card-text">Some quick example text to
build on the card title and make up the bulk of the
card's
      content.</p>
  </div>
</div>
```

## 7. Light

```
<div class="card text-dark bg-light mb-3"
style="max-width: 18rem;">
  <div class="card-header">Header</div>
  <div class="card-body">
    <h5 class="card-title">Light card title</h5>
    <p class="card-text">Some quick example text to
build on the card title and make up the bulk of the
card's
      content.</p>
  </div>
</div>
```

## 8. Dark

```
<div class="card text-white bg-dark mb-3"
style="max-width: 18rem;">
  <div class="card-header">Header</div>
  <div class="card-body">
    <h5 class="card-title">Dark card title</h5>
    <p class="card-text">Some quick example text to
build on the card title and make up the bulk of the
card's
      content.</p>
  </div>
</div>
```

- border-{color}

Used to change the border color of the card based on the color code of Bootstrap.

### 1. Primary

```
div class="card border-primary mb-3" style="max-
width: 18rem;">
  <div class="card-header">Header</div>
  <div class="card-body text-primary">
    <h5 class="card-title">Primary card title</h5>
    <p class="card-text">Some quick example text to
build on the card title and make up the bulk of the
card's
      content.</p>
  </div>
</div>
```

### 2. Secondary

```
<div class="card border-secondary mb-3" style="max-
width: 18rem;">
  <div class="card-header">Header</div>
  <div class="card-body text-secondary">
    <h5 class="card-title">Secondary card title</h5>
    <p class="card-text">Some quick example text to
build on the card title and make up the bulk of the
card's
      content.</p>
  </div>
</div>
```

### 3. Success

```
<div class="card border-success mb-3" style="max-
width: 18rem;">
  <div class="card-header">Header</div>
  <div class="card-body text-success">
    <h5 class="card-title">Success card title</h5>
    <p class="card-text">Some quick example text to
build on the card title and make up the bulk of the
card's
```

```
      content.</p>
  </div>
</div>
```

## 4. Danger

```
<div class="card border-danger mb-3" style="max-
width: 18rem;">
  <div class="card-header">Header</div>
  <div class="card-body text-danger">
    <h5 class="card-title">Danger card title</h5>
    <p class="card-text">Some quick example text to
build on the card title and make up the bulk of the
card's
      content.</p>
  </div>
</div>
```

## 5. Warning

```
<div class="card border-warning mb-3" style="max-
width: 18rem;">
  <div class="card-header">Header</div>
  <div class="card-body">
    <h5 class="card-title">Warning card title</h5>
    <p class="card-text">Some quick example text to
build on the card title and make up the bulk of the
card's
      content.</p>
  </div>
</div>
```

## 6. Info

```
<div class="card border-info mb-3" style="max-
width: 18rem;">
  <div class="card-header">Header</div>
  <div class="card-body">
    <h5 class="card-title">Info card title</h5>
    <p class="card-text">Some quick example text to
build on the card title and make up the bulk of the
card's
```

```
        content.</p>
   </div>
</div>
```

## 7. Light

```
<div class="card border-light mb-3" style="max-
width: 18rem;">
   <div class="card-header">Header</div>
   <div class="card-body">
      <h5 class="card-title">Light card title</h5>
      <p class="card-text">Some quick example text to
build on the card title and make up the bulk of the
card's
         content.</p>
   </div>
</div>
```

## 8. Dark

```
<div class="card border-dark mb-3" style="max-
width: 18rem;">
   <div class="card-header">Header</div>
   <div class="card-body text-dark">
      <h5 class="card-title">Dark card title</h5>
      <p class="card-text">Some quick example text to
build on the card title and make up the bulk of the
card's
         content.</p>
   </div>
</div>
```

- text-{color}

Used to change the text color for the card text based on the color code of Bootstrap.

## 1. Primary

```
<div class="card border-primary text-primary
bg-light">
   <div class="card-header border-primary">Header
</div>
```

```
  <div class="card-body">
    <h5 class="card-title">Primary card title</h5>
    <p class="card-text">Some quick example text to
build on the card title and make up the bulk of the
card's
      content.</p>
  </div>
</div>
```

## 2. Secondary

```
<div class="card border-primary text-secondary
bg-light">
  <div class="card-header border-primary">Header</div>
  <div class="card-body">
    <h5 class="card-title">Secondary card title</h5>
    <p class="card-text">Some quick example text to
build on the card title and make up the bulk of the
card's
      content.</p>
  </div>
</div>
```

## 3. Success

```
<div class="card border-primary text-success
bg-light">
  <div class="card-header border-primary">Header</div>
  <div class="card-body">
    <h5 class="card-title">Success card title</h5>
    <p class="card-text">Some quick example text to
build on the card title and make up the bulk of the
card's
      content.</p>
  </div>
</div>
```

## 4. Danger

```
<div class="card border-primary text-danger
bg-light">
  <div class="card-header border-primary">Header</div>
  <div class="card-body">
```

```
    <h5 class="card-title">Danger card title</h5>
    <p class="card-text">Some quick example text to
build on the card title and make up the bulk of the
card's
      content.</p>
  </div>
</div>
```

## 5. Warning

```
<div class="card border-primary text-warning
bg-light">
  <div class="card-header border-primary">Header</div>
  <div class="card-body">
    <h5 class="card-title">Warning card title</h5>
    <p class="card-text">Some quick example text to
build on the card title and make up the bulk of the
card's
      content.</p>
  </div>
</div>
```

## 6. Info

```
<div class="card border-primary text-info
bg-light">
  <div class="card-header border-primary">Header</div>
  <div class="card-body">
    <h5 class="card-title">Info card title</h5>
    <p class="card-text">Some quick example text to
build on the card title and make up the bulk of the
card's
      content.</p>
  </div>
</div>
```

## 7. Light

```
<div class="card border-primary text-light bg-dark">
  <div class="card-header border-primary">Header</div>
  <div class="card-body">
    <h5 class="card-title">Light card title</h5>
```

```
    <p class="card-text">Some quick example text to
build on the card title and make up the bulk of the
card's
      content.</p>
  </div>
</div>
```

8. Dark

```
<div class="card border-primary text-dark
bg-light">
  <div class="card-header border-primary">Header
</div>
  <div class="card-body">
    <h5 class="card-title">Dark card title</h5>
    <p class="card-text">Some quick example text to
build on the card title and make up the bulk of the
card's
      content.</p>
  </div>
</div>
```

• bg-transparent

```
<div class="card">
  <div class="card-header bg-transparent">Header
</div>
  <div class="card-body">
    <h5 class="card-title">Card title</h5>
    <p class="card-text">Some quick example text to
build on the card title and make up the bulk of the
card's
      content.</p>
  </div>
  <div class="card-footer bg-transparent">Footer
</div>
</div>
```

• card-group

```
<div class="card-group">
  <div class="card">
    <img src="assets/images/bs-images/img-2x1.png"
class="card-img-top" alt="card-group-image">
```

```html
    <div class="card-body">
      <h5 class="card-title">Card title</h5>
      <p class="card-text">This is a wider card with
supporting text below as a natural lead-in to
additional
        content. This content is a little bit
longer.</p>
    </div>
    <div class="card-footer">
      <small class="text-muted">Last updated 3 mins
ago</small>
    </div>
  </div>
  <div class="card">
    <img src="assets/images/bs-images/img-2x1.png"
class="card-img-top" alt="card-group-image">
    <div class="card-body">
      <h5 class="card-title">Card title</h5>
      <p class="card-text">This card has supporting
text below as a natural lead-in to additional
content.</p>
    </div>
    <div class="card-footer">
      <small class="text-muted">Last updated 3 mins
ago</small>
    </div>
  </div>
  <div class="card">
    <img src="assets/images/bs-images/img-2x1.png"
class="card-img-top" alt="card-group-image">
    <div class="card-body">
      <h5 class="card-title">Card title</h5>
      <p class="card-text">This is a wider card with
text below as a natural lead-in to additional
        content. This card has even longer than the
first to show that equal height action.</p>
    </div>
    <div class="card-footer">
      <small class="text-muted">Last updated 3 mins
ago</small>
    </div>
  </div>
</div>
```

- grid cards

```
<div class="row row-cols-1 row-cols-sm-2 g-3">
  <div class="col">
    <div class="card">
      <img src="assets/images/bs-images/img-2x1.png"
class="card-img-top" alt="card-grid-image">
      <div class="card-body">
        <h5 class="card-title">Card title</h5>
        <p class="card-text">This is a longer card
with supporting text below as a natural lead-in to
additional
          content. This content is a little bit
longer.</p>
      </div>
    </div>
  </div>
  <div class="col">
    <div class="card">
      <img src="assets/images/bs-images/img-2x1.png"
class="card-img-top" alt="card-grid-image">
      <div class="card-body">
        <h5 class="card-title">Card title</h5>
        <p class="card-text">This is a longer card
with supporting text below as a natural lead-in to
additional
          content. This content is a little bit
longer.</p>
      </div>
    </div>
  </div>
  <div class="col">
    <div class="card">
      <img src="assets/images/bs-images/img-2x1.png"
class="card-img-top" alt="card-grid-image">
      <div class="card-body">
        <h5 class="card-title">Card title</h5>
        <p class="card-text">This is a longer card
with supporting text below as a natural lead-in to
additional
          content.</p>
      </div>
```

```
          </div>
        </div>
        <div class="col">
          <div class="card">
            <img src="assets/images/bs-images/img-2x1.png"
class="card-img-top" alt="card-grid-image">
            <div class="card-body">
              <h5 class="card-title">Card title</h5>
              <p class="card-text">This is a longer card
with supporting text below as a natural lead-in to
additional
              content. This content is a little bit
longer.</p>
            </div>
          </div>
        </div>
      </div>
```

## Carousel

Used to set up a slideshow that cycles through a series of slides, text, or images. It is built using CSS 3D and a little bit of JavaScript. It also has support for previous and next controls.

- carousel (slides only)

```
<div id="carouselExampleSlidesOnly" class="carousel
slide" data-bs-ride="carousel">
  <div class="carousel-inner">
    <div class="carousel-item active">
      <img src="..." class="d-block w-100"
alt="...">
    </div>
    <div class="carousel-item">
      <img src="..." class="d-block w-100"
alt="...">
    </div>
    <div class="carousel-item">
      <img src="..." class="d-block w-100"
alt="...">
    </div>
  </div>
</div>
```

- carousel with controls

```
<div id="carouselExampleControls" class="carousel
slide" data-bs-ride="carousel">
  <div class="carousel-inner">
    <div class="carousel-item active">
      <img src="..." class="d-block w-100"
alt="...">
    </div>
    <div class="carousel-item">
      <img src="..." class="d-block w-100"
alt="...">
    </div>
    <div class="carousel-item">
      <img src="..." class="d-block w-100"
alt="...">
    </div>
  </div>
  <button class="carousel-control-prev"
type="button" data-bs-target="#carouselExampleCon
trols" data-bs-slide="prev">
    <span class="carousel-control-prev-icon" aria-
hidden="true"></span>
    <span class="visually-hidden">Previous</span>
  </button>
  <button class="carousel-control-next"
type="button" data-bs-target="#carouselExampleCon
trols" data-bs-slide="next">
    <span class="carousel-control-next-icon" aria-
hidden="true"></span>
    <span class="visually-hidden">Next</span>
  </button>
</div>
```

- carousel-indicators

```
<div id="carouselExampleIndicators" class="carousel
slide" data-bs-ride="carousel">
  <div class="carousel-indicators">
    <button type="button" data-bs-target="#carousel
ExampleIndicators" data-bs-slide-to="0"
class="active"
    aria-current="true" aria-label="Slide 1">
  </button>
```

```
    <button type="button" data-bs-target="#carousel
ExampleIndicators" data-bs-slide-to="1"
      aria-label="Slide 2"></button>
    <button type="button" data-bs-target="#carousel
ExampleIndicators" data-bs-slide-to="2"
      aria-label="Slide 3"></button>
  </div>
  <div class="carousel-inner">
    <div class="carousel-item active">
      <img src="..." class="d-block w-100"
alt="...">
    </div>
    <div class="carousel-item">
      <img src="..." class="d-block w-100"
alt="...">
    </div>
    <div class="carousel-item">
      <img src="..." class="d-block w-100"
alt="...">
    </div>
  </div>
  <button class="carousel-control-prev"
type="button" data-bs-target="#carouselExampleInd
icators"
    data-bs-slide="prev">
    <span class="carousel-control-prev-icon" aria-
hidden="true"></span>
    <span class="visually-hidden">Previous</span>
  </button>
  <button class="carousel-control-next"
type="button" data-bs-target="#carouselExampleInd
icators"
    data-bs-slide="next">
    <span class="carousel-control-next-icon" aria-
hidden="true"></span>
    <span class="visually-hidden">Next</span>
  </button>
</div>
```

- carousel-caption

```
<div id="carouselExampleCaptions" class="carousel
slide" data-bs-ride="carousel">
```

```
<div class="carousel-indicators">
  <button type="button" data-bs-target="#carousel
ExampleCaptions" data-bs-slide-to="0" class="active"
    aria-current="true" aria-label="Slide 1"></
button>
  <button type="button" data-bs-target="#carousel
ExampleCaptions" data-bs-slide-to="1"
    aria-label="Slide 2"></button>
  <button type="button" data-bs-target="#carousel
ExampleCaptions" data-bs-slide-to="2"
    aria-label="Slide 3"></button>
</div>
<div class="carousel-inner">
  <div class="carousel-item active">
    <img src="..." class="d-block w-100"
alt="...">
    <div class="carousel-caption d-none
d-md-block">
      <h5>First slide label</h5>
      <p>Some representative placeholder content
for the first slide.</p>
    </div>
  </div>
  <div class="carousel-item">
    <img src="..." class="d-block w-100"
alt="...">
    <div class="carousel-caption d-none
d-md-block">
      <h5>Second slide label</h5>
      <p>Some representative placeholder content
for the second slide.</p>
    </div>
  </div>
  <div class="carousel-item">
    <img src="..." class="d-block w-100"
alt="...">
    <div class="carousel-caption d-none
d-md-block">
      <h5>Third slide label</h5>
      <p>Some representative placeholder content
for the third slide.</p>
    </div>
```

```
    </div>
  </div>
  <button class="carousel-control-prev"
type="button" data-bs-target="#carouselExampleCap
tions" data-bs-slide="prev">
    <span class="carousel-control-prev-icon" aria-
hidden="true"></span>
    <span class="visually-hidden">Previous</span>
  </button>
  <button class="carousel-control-next"
type="button" data-bs-target="#carouselExampleCap
tions" data-bs-slide="next">
    <span class="carousel-control-next-icon" aria-
hidden="true"></span>
    <span class="visually-hidden">Next</span>
  </button>
</div>
```

- carousel-fade

```
<div id="carouselExampleFade" class="carousel slide
carousel-fade" data-bs-ride="carousel">
  <div class="carousel-inner">
    <div class="carousel-item active">
      <img src="..." class="d-block w-100"
alt="...">
    </div>
    <div class="carousel-item">
      <img src="..." class="d-block w-100"
alt="...">
    </div>
    <div class="carousel-item">
      <img src="..." class="d-block w-100"
alt="...">
    </div>
  </div>
  <button class="carousel-control-prev"
type="button" data-bs-target="#carouselExampleFade"
data-bs-slide="prev">
    <span class="carousel-control-prev-icon" aria-
hidden="true"></span>
    <span class="visually-hidden">Previous</span>
  </button>
```

```
    <button class="carousel-control-next"
type="button" data-bs-target="#carouselExampleFade"
data-bs-slide="next">
    <span class="carousel-control-next-icon" aria-
hidden="true"></span>
    <span class="visually-hidden">Next</span>
    </button>
</div>
```

- carousel with intervals

```
<div id="carouselExampleInterval" class="carousel
slide" data-bs-ride="carousel">
  <div class="carousel-inner">
    <div class="carousel-item active"
data-bs-interval="10000">
      <img src="..." class="d-block w-100"
alt="...">
    </div>
    <div class="carousel-item"
data-bs-interval="2000">
      <img src="..." class="d-block w-100"
alt="...">
    </div>
    <div class="carousel-item">
      <img src="..." class="d-block w-100"
alt="...">
    </div>
  </div>
  <button class="carousel-control-prev"
type="button" data-bs-target="#carouselExampleInt
erval" data-bs-slide="prev">
    <span class="carousel-control-prev-icon" aria-
hidden="true"></span>
    <span class="visually-hidden">Previous</span>
  </button>
  <button class="carousel-control-next"
type="button" data-bs-target="#carouselExampleInt
erval" data-bs-slide="next">
    <span class="carousel-control-next-icon" aria-
hidden="true"></span>
    <span class="visually-hidden">Next</span>
  </button>
</div>
```

- carousel-dark

```
<div id="carouselExampleDark" class="carousel
carousel-dark slide" data-bs-ride="carousel">
  <div class="carousel-indicators">
    <button type="button" data-bs-
target="#carouselExampleDark" data-bs-slide-to="0"
class="active"
      aria-current="true" aria-label="Slide 1">
</button>
    <button type="button" data-bs-
target="#carouselExampleDark" data-bs-slide-to="1"
aria-label="Slide 2"></button>
    <button type="button" data-bs-
target="#carouselExampleDark" data-bs-slide-to="2"
aria-label="Slide 3"></button>
  </div>
  <div class="carousel-inner">
    <div class="carousel-item active"
data-bs-interval="10000">
      <img src="..." class="d-block w-100"
alt="...">
      <div class="carousel-caption d-none
d-md-block">
        <h5>First slide label</h5>
        <p>Some representative placeholder content
for the first slide.</p>
      </div>
    </div>
    <div class="carousel-item"
data-bs-interval="2000">
      <img src="..." class="d-block w-100"
alt="...">
      <div class="carousel-caption d-none
d-md-block">
        <h5>Second slide label</h5>
        <p>Some representative placeholder content
for the second slide.</p>
      </div>
    </div>
    <div class="carousel-item">
      <img src="..." class="d-block w-100" alt="...">
```

```
    <div class="carousel-caption d-none
d-md-block">
        <h5>Third slide label</h5>
        <p>Some representative placeholder content
for the third slide.</p>
      </div>
    </div>
  </div>
  <button class="carousel-control-prev"
type="button" data-bs-target="#carouselExampleDark"
data-bs-slide="prev">
    <span class="carousel-control-prev-icon" aria-
hidden="true"></span>
    <span class="visually-hidden">Previous</span>
  </button>
  <button class="carousel-control-next"
type="button" data-bs-target="#carouselExampleDark"
data-bs-slide="next">
    <span class="carousel-control-next-icon"
aria-hidden="true"></span>
    <span class="visually-hidden">Next</span>
  </button>
</div>
```

## Collapse

Collapse is a JavaScript plugin that is used to show and hide content. Usually a button or anchor is used as a trigger as they are mapped to specific elements that you can toggle.

- Collapse

```
<p>
  <a class="btn btn-primary" data-bs-
toggle="collapse" href="#collapseExample"
role="button" aria-expanded="false"
    aria-controls="collapseExample">
    Link with href
  </a>
  <button class="btn btn-primary" type="button"
data-bs-toggle="collapse"
data-bs-target="#collapseExample"
    aria-expanded="false"
aria-controls="collapseExample">
```

```
    Button with data-bs-target
  </button>
</p>
<div class="collapse" id="collapseExample">
  <div class="card card-body">
    Some placeholder content for the collapse
component. The panel is hidden by default but
revealed when the user
    activates the relevant trigger.
  </div>
</div>
```

- multi-collapse

```
<p>
  <a class="btn btn-primary" data-bs-
toggle="collapse" href="#multiCollapseExample1"
role="button"
    aria-expanded="false" aria-controls="multiColla
pseExample1">Toggle first element</a>
  <button class="btn btn-primary" type="button"
data-bs-toggle="collapse" data-bs-target="#multiColl
apseExample2"
    aria-expanded="false" aria-controls="multiColla
pseExample2">Toggle second element</button>
  <button class="btn btn-primary" type="button"
data-bs-toggle="collapse" data-bs-target=".
multi-collapse"
    aria-expanded="false" aria-
controls="multiCollapseExample1
multiCollapseExample2">Toggle both elements</button>
</p>
<div class="row">
  <div class="col">
    <div class="collapse multi-collapse"
id="multiCollapseExample1">
      <div class="card card-body">
      Some placeholder content for first collapse
component of multi-collapse example. This panel is
      hidden by default but revealed when the
activates the relevant trigger.
      </div>
    </div>
  </div>
```

```
<div class="col">
  <div class="collapse multi-collapse"
id="multiCollapseExample2">
    <div class="card card-body">
      Some placeholder content for the second
collapse component of multi-collapse example. The
panel is
      hidden by default but revealed when user
activates the relevant trigger.
    </div>
  </div>
</div>
</div>
```

- collapse-horizontal

```
<p>
  <button class="btn btn-primary" type="button"
data-bs-toggle="collapse"
data-bs-target="#collapseWidthExample"
    aria-controls="collapseWidthExample">
    Toggle width collapse
  </button>
</p>
<div style="min-height: 120px;">
  <div class="collapse collapse-horizontal"
id="collapseWidthExample">
    <div class="card card-body" style="width:
300px;">
      This is some placeholder content for a
horizontal collapse. It is hidden by default and
shown when triggered.
    </div>
  </div>
</div>
```

Accordion

An accordion displays collapsible behavior to cards. To create an open accordion, use the .open class with the .accordion class. The .accordion class should always be used as a wrapper.

- Accordion

```
<div class="accordion" id="accordionExample">
  <div class="accordion-item">
```

```
    <h2 class="accordion-header" id="headingOne">
        <button class="accordion-button" type="button"
data-bs-toggle="collapse"
data-bs-target="#collapseOne"
        aria-expanded="true"
aria-controls="collapseOne">
          Accordion Item #1
        </button>
    </h2>
    <div id="collapseOne" class="accordion-collapse
collapse show" aria-labelledby="headingOne"
        data-bs-parent="#accordionExample">
        <div class="accordion-body">
          <strong>This is the first item's accordion
body.</strong>Displays automatically, until wrap
          the plugin adds the appropriate classes that
we use to style each element. These classes control
everything
          appearance, and display and hide with CSS
changes. You can fix any of this with
          Custom CSS or our default dynamics skip. It
is also worth noting that almost any HTML can go
          within <code>.accordion-body</code>, though
the transition does limit overflow.
        </div>
      </div>
    </div>
    <div class="accordion-item">
      <h2 class="accordion-header" id="headingTwo">
        <button class="accordion-button collapsed"
type="button" data-bs-toggle="collapse"
        data-bs-target="#collapseTwo" aria-
expanded="false" aria-controls="collapseTwo">
          Accordion Item #2
        </button>
      </h2>
      <div id="collapseTwo" class="accordion-collapse
collapse" aria-labelledby="headingTwo"
        data-bs-parent="#accordionExample">
        <div class="accordion-body">
          <strong>Displays automatically, until wrap
          the plugin adds the appropriate classes that
we use to style each element. These classes control
everything
```

appearance, and display and hide with CSS
changes. You can fix any of this with
        Custom CSS or our default dynamics skip. It
is also worth noting that almost any HTML can go
        within <code>.accordion-body</code>, though
the transition does limit overflow.
        </div>
      </div>
    </div>
    <div class="accordion-item">
      <h2 class="accordion-header" id="headingThree">
        <button class="accordion-button collapsed"
type="button" data-bs-toggle="collapse"
        data-bs-target="#collapseThree" aria-
expanded="false" aria-controls="collapseThree">
        Accordion Item #3
        </button>
      </h2>
      <div id="collapseThree" class="accordion-
collapse collapse" aria-labelledby="headingThree"
        data-bs-parent="#accordionExample">
        <div class="accordion-body">
        <strong>Displays automatically, until wrap
        the plugin adds the appropriate classes that
we use to style each element. These classes control
everything
        appearance, and display and hide with CSS
changes. You can fix any of this with
        Custom CSS or our default dynamics skip. It
is also worth noting that almost any HTML can go
        within <code>.accordion-body</code>, though
the transition does limit overflow.
        </div>
      </div>
    </div>
</div>

- accordion-flush

<div class="accordion accordion-flush"
id="accordionFlushExample">
  <div class="accordion-item">
    <h2 class="accordion-header"
id="flush-headingOne">

```
    <button class="accordion-button collapsed"
type="button" data-bs-toggle="collapse"
    data-bs-target="#flush-collapseOne" aria-
expanded="false" aria-controls="flush-collapseOne">
    Accordion Item #1
    </button>
  </h2>
  <div id="flush-collapseOne" class="accordion-
collapse collapse"
aria-labelledby="flush-headingOne"
    data-bs-parent="#accordionFlushExample">
    <div class="accordion-body">Placeholder
content for this accordion, which is intended to
demonstrate the
      <code>.accordion-flush</code> class. This is
the first item's accordion body.</div>
  </div>
</div>
<div class="accordion-item">
  <h2 class="accordion-header"
id="flush-headingTwo">
    <button class="accordion-button collapsed"
type="button" data-bs-toggle="collapse"
    data-bs-target="#flush-collapseTwo" aria-
expanded="false" aria-controls="flush-collapseTwo">
    Accordion Item #2
    </button>
  </h2>
  <div id="flush-collapseTwo" class="accordion-
collapse collapse"
aria-labelledby="flush-headingTwo"
    data-bs-parent="#accordionFlushExample">
    <div class="accordion-body">Placeholder
content for this accordion, which is intended to
demonstrate the
      <code>.accordion-flush</code> class. This is
the second item's accordion body. Let's imagine this
being
      filled with some actual content.</div>
  </div>
</div>
<div class="accordion-item">
  <h2 class="accordion-header" id="flush-headingThree">
```

```
      <button class="accordion-button collapsed"
type="button" data-bs-toggle="collapse"
        data-bs-target="#flush-collapseThree" aria-
expanded="false"
aria-controls="flush-collapseThree">
        Accordion Item #3
      </button>
    </h2>
    <div id="flush-collapseThree" class="accordion-
collapse collapse"
aria-labelledby="flush-headingThree"
        data-bs-parent="#accordionFlushExample">
        <div class="accordion-body">Placeholder
content for this accordion, which is intended to
demonstrate the
        <code>.accordion-flush</code>class. This is
the accordion body of the third object. Nothing is
too exciting
        which happens here in terms of content, but
just to fill the space to look, at least in the
beginning
        view, more representation of how this will
look in the real world app.</div>
    </div>
  </div>
</div>
```

## Dropdowns

Used to create contextual overlays for displaying lists of user links. It is an easy option for creating menus as well. Dropdowns are built using Popper .js, a third-party library, so make sure you include popper.min.js before Bootstrap's own JavaScript. Or you can use bootstrap.bundle.min.js as they both contain Popper and JavaScript.

- Dropdown

```
<div class="dropdown">
  <button class="btn btn-primary dropdown-toggle"
type="button" id="dropdownMenuButton"
data-bs-toggle="dropdown"
    aria-expanded="false">
  Dropdown button
  </button>
```

```
    <ul class="dropdown-menu" aria-labelledby="dropdow
nMenuButton">
        <li><a class="dropdown-item" href="#">Action
</a></li>
        <li><a class="dropdown-item" href="#">Another
action</a></li>
        <li><a class="dropdown-item" href="#">Something
else here</a></li>
    </ul>
</div>
```

- dropdown-toggle-split

```
<div class="btn-group">
    <button type="button" class="btn btn-
primary">Split Button</button>
    <button type="button" class="btn btn-primary
dropdown-toggle dropdown-toggle-split"
data-bs-toggle="dropdown"
        aria-expanded="false">
        <span class="visually-hidden">Toggle Dropdown
</span>
    </button>
    <ul class="dropdown-menu">
        <li><a class="dropdown-item" href="#">Action
</a></li>
        <li><a class="dropdown-item" href="#">Another
action</a></li>
        <li><a class="dropdown-item" href="#">Something
else here</a></li>
    </ul>
</div>
```

- dropdown-menu-dark

```
<div class="dropdown">
    <button class="btn btn-primary dropdown-toggle"
type="button" id="dropdownMenuDark"
data-bs-toggle="dropdown"
        aria-expanded="false">
    Dropdown Menu Dark
    </button>
    <ul class="dropdown-menu dropdown-menu-dark" aria-
labelledby="dropdownMenuDark">
```

```
    <li><a class="dropdown-item" href="#">Action
</a></li>
    <li><a class="dropdown-item" href="#">Another
action</a></li>
    <li><a class="dropdown-item" href="#">Something
else here</a></li>
  </ul>
</div>
```

- Dropup

```
<div class="btn-group dropup">
  <button type="button" class="btn btn-primary
dropdown-toggle" data-bs-toggle="dropdown"
aria-expanded="false">
    Dropup
  </button>
  <ul class="dropdown-menu">
    <li><a class="dropdown-item" href="#">Action
</a></li>
    <li><a class="dropdown-item" href="#">Another
action</a></li>
    <li><a class="dropdown-item" href="#">Something
else here</a></li>
  </ul>
</div>
```

- dropup (split)

```
<div class="btn-group dropup">
  <button type="button" class="btn btn-primary">
    Split dropup
  </button>
  <button type="button" class="btn btn-primary
dropdown-toggle dropdown-toggle-split"
data-bs-toggle="dropdown"
    aria-expanded="false">
    <span class="visually-hidden">Toggle Dropdown
</span>
  </button>
  <ul class="dropdown-menu">
    <li><a class="dropdown-item" href="#">Action
</a></li>
```

```
   <li><a class="dropdown-item" href="#">Another
action</a></li>
   <li><a class="dropdown-item" href="#">Something
else here</a></li>
  </ul>
</div>
```

• dropend

```
<div class="btn-group dropend">
  <button type="button" class="btn btn-primary
dropdown-toggle" data-bs-toggle="dropdown"
aria-expanded="false">
    Dropend
  </button>
  <ul class="dropdown-menu">
    <li><a class="dropdown-item" href="#">Action
</a></li>
    <li><a class="dropdown-item" href="#">Another
action</a></li>
    <li><a class="dropdown-item" href="#">Something
else here</a></li>
  </ul>
</div>
```

• dropstart

```
<div class="btn-group dropstart">
  <button type="button" class="btn btn-primary
dropdown-toggle" data-bs-toggle="dropdown"
aria-expanded="false">
    Dropstart
  </button>
  <ul class="dropdown-menu">
    <li><a class="dropdown-item" href="#">Action
</a></li>
    <li><a class="dropdown-item" href="#">Another
action</a></li>
    <li><a class="dropdown-item" href="#">Something
else here</a></li>
  </ul>
</div>
```

- dropdown-item-text

```
<div class="btn-group">
  <button type="button" class="btn btn-primary
dropdown-toggle" data-bs-toggle="dropdown"
aria-expanded="false">
    Dropdown item text
  </button>
  <ul class="dropdown-menu">
    <li><span class="dropdown-item-text">Dropdown
item text</span></li>
    <li><a class="dropdown-item" href="#">Action
</a></li>
    <li><a class="dropdown-item" href="#">Another
action</a></li>
    <li><a class="dropdown-item" href="#">Something
else here</a></li>
  </ul>
</div>
```

- active dropdown-item

```
<div class="btn-group">
  <button type="button" class="btn btn-primary
dropdown-toggle" data-bs-toggle="dropdown"
aria-expanded="false">
    Dropdown
  </button>
  <ul class="dropdown-menu">
    <li><a class="dropdown-item" href="#">Regular
link</a></li>
    <li><a class="dropdown-item active" href="#"
aria-current="true">Active link</a></li>
    <li><a class="dropdown-item" href="#">Another
link</a></li>
  </ul>
</div>
```

## CHAPTER 10

# Cheat Sheet 3

## CODE SNIPPETS

- disabled dropdown-item

```
<div class="btn-group">
  <button type="button" class="btn btn-primary
dropdown-toggle" data-bs-toggle="dropdown"
aria-expanded="false">
    Dropdown
  </button>
  <ul class="dropdown-menu">
    <li><a class="dropdown-item" href="#">Regular
link</a></li>
    <li><a class="dropdown-item disabled" href="#"
tabindex="-1" aria-disabled="true">Disabled link
</a></li>
    <li><a class="dropdown-item" href="#">Another
link</a></li>
  </ul>
</div>
```

- dropdown-menu-end

```
<div class="btn-group">
  <button type="button" class="btn btn-primary
dropdown-toggle" data-bs-toggle="dropdown"
aria-expanded="false">
    Right-aligned dropdown-menu
  </button>
```

DOI: 10.1201/9781003309383-10

```
<ul class="dropdown-menu dropdown-menu-end">
  <li><a class="dropdown-item" href="#">Action
</a></li>
    <li><a class="dropdown-item" href="#">Another
action</a></li>
    <li><a class="dropdown-item" href="#">Something
else here</a></li>
  </ul>
</div>
```

- dropdown-menu-*-{direction}

```
<!-- Right or left aligned dropdown menu can be use
at different breakpoints with the help of .dropdown-
menu-*-{end|start} class -->
<div class="btn-group">
  <button type="button" class="btn btn-primary
dropdown-toggle" data-bs-toggle="dropdown"
aria-expanded="false">
    Dropdown
  </button>
  <ul class="dropdown-menu dropdown-menu-sm-end
dropdown-menu-xl-start">
    <li><a class="dropdown-item" href="#">Action
</a></li>
    <li><a class="dropdown-item" href="#">Another
action</a></li>
    <li><a class="dropdown-item" href="#">Something
else here</a></li>
  </ul>
</div>
```

- dropdown-header

```
<div class="btn-group">
  <button type="button" class="btn btn-primary
dropdown-toggle" data-bs-toggle="dropdown"
aria-expanded="false">
    Dropdown
  </button>
  <ul class="dropdown-menu">
    <li>
      <h6 class="dropdown-header">Dropdown header
</h6>
    </li>
```

```
   <li><a class="dropdown-item" href="#">Action
</a></li>
   <li><a class="dropdown-item" href="#">Another
action</a></li>
   <li><a class="dropdown-item" href="#">Something
else here</a></li>
  </ul>
</div>
```

- dropdown-divider

```
<div class="btn-group">
  <button type="button" class="btn btn-primary
dropdown-toggle" data-bs-toggle="dropdown"
aria-expanded="false">
   Dropdown
  </button>
  <ul class="dropdown-menu">
   <li><a class="dropdown-item" href="#">Action
</a></li>
   <li><a class="dropdown-item" href="#">Another
action</a></li>
   <li><a class="dropdown-item" href="#">Something
else here</a></li>
   <li>
     <hr class="dropdown-divider">
   </li>
   <li><a class="dropdown-item" href="#">Separated
link</a></li>
  </ul>
</div>
```

- dropdown-reference

```
<div class="btn-group">
  <button type="button" class="btn btn-
primary">Reference</button>
  <button type="button" class="btn btn-primary
dropdown-toggle dropdown-toggle-split"
id="dropdownMenuReference"
   data-bs-toggle="dropdown" aria-expanded="false"
data-bs-reference="parent">
   <span class="visually-hidden">Toggle Dropdown
</span>
```

```
  </button>
  <ul class="dropdown-menu" aria-labelledby="dropdow
nMenuReference">
    <li><a class="dropdown-item" href="#">Action
</a></li>
    <li><a class="dropdown-item" href="#">Another
action</a></li>
    <li><a class="dropdown-item" href="#">Something
else here</a></li>
  </ul>
</div>
```

## IMAGES

- img-fluid

```
<img src="assets/images/bs-images/img-2x1.png"
class="img-fluid" alt="img-fluid">
```

- img-thumbnail

```
<img src="assets/images/bs-images/img-2x2.png"
class="img-thumbnail" alt="img-thumbnail">
```

## FIGURES

- figures

```
<figure class="figure">
  <img src="assets/images/bs-images/img-4x3.png"
class="figure-img img-fluid rounded"
alt="figure-img">
  <figcaption class="figure-caption">A caption for
above image.</figcaption>
</figure>
```

## TABLES

- table

```
<table class="table">
  <thead>
    <tr>
      <th scope="col">#</th>
      <th scope="col">First</th>
      <th scope="col">Last</th>
      <th scope="col">Handle</th>
```

```
    </tr>
  </thead>
  <tbody>
    <tr>
      <th scope="row">1</th>
      <td>Mark</td>
      <td>Otto</td>
      <td>@mdo</td>
    </tr>
    <tr>
      <th scope="row">2</th>
      <td>Jacob</td>
      <td>Thornton</td>
      <td>@fat</td>
    </tr>
    <tr>
      <th scope="row">3</th>
      <td colspan="2">Larry the Bird</td>
      <td>@twitter</td>
    </tr>
  </tbody>
</table>
```

- table-{color}

```
<!-- .table-{color} can be use with .table, thead,
tbody, tr, th and td -->
<table class="table">
  <thead>
    <tr>
      <th scope="col">Class</th>
      <th scope="col">Heading</th>
      <th scope="col">Heading</th>
    </tr>
  </thead>
  <tbody>
    <tr>
      <th scope="row">Default</th>
      <td>Cell</td>
      <td>Cell</td>
    </tr>
    <tr class="table-primary">
      <th scope="row">.table-primary</th>
```

```
      <td>Cell</td>
      <td>Cell</td>
    </tr>
    <tr class="table-secondary">
      <th scope="row">.table-secondary</th>
      <td>Cell</td>
      <td>Cell</td>
    </tr>
    <tr class="table-success">
      <th scope="row">.table-success</th>
      <td>Cell</td>
      <td>Cell</td>
    </tr>
    <tr class="table-danger">
      <th scope="row">.table-danger</th>
      <td>Cell</td>
      <td>Cell</td>
    </tr>
    <tr class="table-warning">
      <th scope="row">.table-warning</th>
      <td>Cell</td>
      <td>Cell</td>
    </tr>
    <tr class="table-info">
      <th scope="row">.table-info</th>
      <td>Cell</td>
      <td>Cell</td>
    </tr>
    <tr class="table-light">
      <th scope="row">.table-light</th>
      <td>Cell</td>
      <td>Cell</td>
    </tr>
    <tr class="table-dark">
      <th scope="row">.table-dark</th>
      <td>Cell</td>
      <td>Cell</td>
    </tr>
  </tbody>
</table>
```

- table-striped

```
<table class="table table-striped">
  <thead>
    <tr>
      <th scope="col">#</th>
      <th scope="col">First</th>
      <th scope="col">Last</th>
      <th scope="col">Handle</th>
    </tr>
  </thead>
  <tbody>
    <tr>
      <th scope="row">1</th>
      <td>Mark</td>
      <td>Otto</td>
      <td>@mdo</td>
    </tr>
    <tr>
      <th scope="row">2</th>
      <td>Jacob</td>
      <td>Thornton</td>
      <td>@fat</td>
    </tr>
    <tr>
      <th scope="row">3</th>
      <td colspan="2">Larry the Bird</td>
      <td>@twitter</td>
    </tr>
  </tbody>
</table>
```

- table-hover

```
<table class="table table-hover">
  <thead>
    <tr>
      <th scope="col">#</th>
      <th scope="col">First</th>
      <th scope="col">Last</th>
      <th scope="col">Handle</th>
    </tr>
  </thead>
```

```
<tbody>
  <tr>
    <th scope="row">1</th>
    <td>Mark</td>
    <td>Otto</td>
    <td>@mdo</td>
  </tr>
  <tr>
    <th scope="row">2</th>
    <td>Jacob</td>
    <td>Thornton</td>
    <td>@fat</td>
  </tr>
  <tr>
    <th scope="row">3</th>
    <td colspan="2">Larry the Bird</td>
    <td>@twitter</td>
  </tr>
</tbody>
</table>
```

• table-active

```
<table class="table">
  <thead>
    <tr>
      <th scope="col">#</th>
      <th scope="col">First</th>
      <th scope="col">Last</th>
      <th scope="col">Handle</th>
    </tr>
  </thead>
  <tbody>
    <tr class="table-active">
      <th scope="row">1</th>
      <td>Mark</td>
      <td>Otto</td>
      <td>@mdo</td>
    </tr>
    <tr>
      <th scope="row">2</th>
      <td>Jacob</td>
      <td>Thornton</td>
```

```
      <td>@fat</td>
    </tr>
    <tr>
      <th scope="row">3</th>
      <td colspan="2" class="table-active">Larry the
Bird</td>
      <td>@twitter</td>
    </tr>
  </tbody>
</table>
```

- table-bordered

```
<table class="table table-bordered">
  <thead>
    <tr>
      <th scope="col">#</th>
      <th scope="col">First</th>
      <th scope="col">Last</th>
      <th scope="col">Handle</th>
    </tr>
  </thead>
  <tbody>
    <tr>
      <th scope="row">1</th>
      <td>Mark</td>
      <td>Otto</td>
      <td>@mdo</td>
    </tr>
    <tr>
      <th scope="row">2</th>
      <td>Jacob</td>
      <td>Thornton</td>
      <td>@fat</td>
    </tr>
    <tr>
      <th scope="row">3</th>
      <td colspan="2">Larry the Bird</td>
      <td>@twitter</td>
    </tr>
  </tbody>
</table>
```

- table-borderless

```
<table class="table table-borderless">
  <thead>
    <tr>
      <th scope="col">#</th>
      <th scope="col">First</th>
      <th scope="col">Last</th>
      <th scope="col">Handle</th>
    </tr>
  </thead>
  <tbody>
    <tr>
      <th scope="row">1</th>
      <td>Mark</td>
      <td>Otto</td>
      <td>@mdo</td>
    </tr>
    <tr>
      <th scope="row">2</th>
      <td>Jacob</td>
      <td>Thornton</td>
      <td>@fat</td>
    </tr>
    <tr>
      <th scope="row">3</th>
      <td colspan="2">Larry the Bird</td>
      <td>@twitter</td>
    </tr>
  </tbody>
</table>
```

- table-sm

```
<table class="table table-sm">
  <thead>
    <tr>
      <th scope="col">#</th>
      <th scope="col">First</th>
      <th scope="col">Last</th>
      <th scope="col">Handle</th>
    </tr>
  </thead>
```

```
  <tbody>
    <tr>
      <th scope="row">1</th>
      <td>Mark</td>
      <td>Otto</td>
      <td>@mdo</td>
    </tr>
    <tr>
      <th scope="row">2</th>
      <td>Jacob</td>
      <td>Thornton</td>
      <td>@fat</td>
    </tr>
    <tr>
      <th scope="row">3</th>
      <td colspan="2">Larry the Bird</td>
      <td>@twitter</td>
    </tr>
  </tbody>
</table>
```

- caption-top

```
<table class="table caption-top">
  <caption>List of users</caption>
  <thead>
    <tr>
      <th scope="col">#</th>
      <th scope="col">First</th>
      <th scope="col">Last</th>
      <th scope="col">Handle</th>
    </tr>
  </thead>
  <tbody>
    <tr>
      <th scope="row">1</th>
      <td>Mark</td>
      <td>Otto</td>
      <td>@mdo</td>
    </tr>
    <tr>
      <th scope="row">2</th>
      <td>Jacob</td>
```

```
        <td>Thornton</td>
        <td>@fat</td>
      </tr>
      <tr>
        <th scope="row">3</th>
        <td colspan="2">Larry the Bird</td>
        <td>@twitter</td>
      </tr>
          </tbody>
</table>
```

- table-responsive

```
<div class="table-responsive">
  <table class="table">
    <thead>
      <tr>
        <th scope="col">#</th>
        <th scope="col">Heading</th>
        <th scope="col">Heading</th>
        <th scope="col">Heading</th>
        <th scope="col">Heading</th>
        <th scope="col">Heading</th>
        <th scope="col">Heading</th>
        <th scope="col">Heading</th>
        <th scope="col">Heading</th>
        <th scope="col">Heading</th>
      </tr>
    </thead>
    <tbody>
      <tr>
        <th scope="row">1</th>
        <td>Cell</td>
        <td>Cell</td>
        <td>Cell</td>
        <td>Cell</td>
        <td>Cell</td>
        <td>Cell</td>
        <td>Cell</td>
        <td>Cell</td>
        <td>Cell</td>
      </tr>
      <tr>
```

```
      <th scope="row">2</th>
      <td>Cell</td>
      <td>Cell</td>
      <td>Cell</td>
      <td>Cell</td>
      <td>Cell</td>
      <td>Cell</td>
      <td>Cell</td>
      <td>Cell</td>
      <td>Cell</td>
    </tr>
    <tr>
      <th scope="row">3</th>
      <td>Cell</td>
      <td>Cell</td>
      <td>Cell</td>
      <td>Cell</td>
      <td>Cell</td>
      <td>Cell</td>
      <td>Cell</td>
      <td>Cell</td>
      <td>Cell</td>
    </tr>
  </tbody>
  </table>
</div>
```

- table-responsive-*

Value of * can be { sm | md | lg | xl | xxl }

```
<div class="table-responsive-xl">
  <table class="table">
    <thead>
      <tr>
        <th scope="col">#</th>
        <th scope="col">Heading</th>
        <th scope="col">Heading</th>
        <th scope="col">Heading</th>
        <th scope="col">Heading</th>
        <th scope="col">Heading</th>
        <th scope="col">Heading</th>
        <th scope="col">Heading</th>
        <th scope="col">Heading</th>
```

```
          <th scope="col">Heading</th>
        </tr>
      </thead>
      <tbody>
        <tr>
          <th scope="row">1</th>
          <td>Cell</td>
          <td>Cell</td>
          <td>Cell</td>
          <td>Cell</td>
          <td>Cell</td>
          <td>Cell</td>
          <td>Cell</td>
          <td>Cell</td>
          <td>Cell</td>
        </tr>
        <tr>
          <th scope="row">2</th>
          <td>Cell</td>
          <td>Cell</td>
          <td>Cell</td>
          <td>Cell</td>
          <td>Cell</td>
          <td>Cell</td>
          <td>Cell</td>
          <td>Cell</td>
          <td>Cell</td>
        </tr>
        <tr>
          <th scope="row">3</th>
          <td>Cell</td>
          <td>Cell</td>
          <td>Cell</td>
          <td>Cell</td>
          <td>Cell</td>
          <td>Cell</td>
          <td>Cell</td>
          <td>Cell</td>
        </tr>
      </tbody>
    </table>
  </div>
```

## INPUT GROUP

Used for extending form controls by adding text, buttons, or button group.

- input-group (left side)

```
<div class="input-group">
  <span class="input-group-text" id="input-group-
left-example">@</span>
  <input type="text" class="form-control"
placeholder="Username" aria-label="Username"
    aria-describedby="input-group-left">
</div>
```

- input-group (right side)

```
<div class="input-group">
  <input type="text" class="form-control"
placeholder="Username" aria-label="Username"
    aria-describedby="input-group-right">
  <span class="input-group-text" id="input-group-
right-example">@</span>
</div>
```

- input-group (both sides)

```
<div class="input-group">
  <span class="input-group-text">$</span>
  <input type="text" class="form-control" aria-
label="Amount (to the nearest dollar)">
  <span class="input-group-text">.00</span>
</div>
```

- input-group-lg

```
<div class="input-group input-group-lg">
  <span class="input-group-text" id="input-group-lg-
example">Large</span>
  <input type="text" class="form-control" aria-
label="Large input group"
aria-describedby="input-group-lg">
</div>
```

- input-group-sm

```
<div class="input-group input-group-sm">
  <span class="input-group-text" id="input-group-sm-
example">Small</span>
```

```
  <input type="text" class="form-control" aria-
label="Small input group"
aria-describedby="input-group-sm">
</div>
```

- input-group with checkbox

```
<div class="input-group">
  <div class="input-group-text">
    <input class="form-check-input" type="checkbox"
value="" aria-label="Checkbox for following text
input">
  </div>
  <input type="text" class="form-control"
aria-label="Text input with checkbox">
</div>
```

- input-group with radio

```
<div class="input-group">
  <div class="input-group-text">
    <input class="form-check-input" type="radio"
value="" aria-label="Radio for following text
input">
  </div>
  <input type="text" class="form-control"
aria-label="Text input with radio">
</div>
```

- input-group with button

```
<div class="input-group mb-2">
  <button type="button" class="btn btn-outline-
secondary" id="input-group-button-left">Button
</button>
  <input type="text" class="form-control"
placeholder="Username" aria-label="Username"
    aria-describedby="input-group-button-left">
</div>
<div class="input-group">
  <input type="text" class="form-control"
placeholder="Username" aria-label="Username"
    aria-describedby="input-group-button-right">
  <button type="button" class="btn btn-outline-
secondary" id="input-group-button-right">Button</button>
</div>
```

- input-group with dropdown

```
<div class="input-group mb-2">
  <button class="btn btn-outline-secondary dropdown-
toggle" type="button" data-bs-toggle="dropdown"
    aria-expanded="false">Dropdown</button>
  <ul class="dropdown-menu">
    <li><a class="dropdown-item" href="#">Action
</a></li>
    <li><a class="dropdown-item" href="#">Another
action</a></li>
    <li><a class="dropdown-item" href="#">Something
else here</a></li>
    <li>
      <hr class="dropdown-divider">
    </li>
    <li><a class="dropdown-item" href="#">Separated
link</a></li>
  </ul>
  <input type="text" class="form-control" aria-
label="Text input with dropdown button">
</div>
<div class="input-group">
  <input type="text" class="form-control" aria-
label="Text input with segmented dropdown button">
  <button type="button" class="btn btn-outline-
secondary">Action</button>
  <button type="button" class="btn btn-outline-
secondary dropdown-toggle dropdown-toggle-split"
    data-bs-toggle="dropdown" aria-expanded="false">
    <span class="visually-hidden">Toggle Dropdown
</span>
  </button>
  <ul class="dropdown-menu dropdown-menu-end">
    <li><a class="dropdown-item" href="#">Action
</a></li>
    <li><a class="dropdown-item" href="#">Another
action</a></li>
    <li><a class="dropdown-item" href="#">Something
else here</a></li>
    <li>
      <hr class="dropdown-divider">
    </li>
```

```
    <li><a class="dropdown-item" href="#">Separated
link</a></li>
  </ul>
</div>
```

## FORMS

Used for form controls and styling forms with custom styles, sizing, etc.

- form-control

```
<input type="text" class="form-control"
placeholder="Default Input">
```

- form-label

```
<label for="formControlInput" class="form-
label">Email address</label>
<input type="email" class="form-control"
id="formControlInput" placeholder="name@example.
com">
```

- form-control-lg

```
<input class="form-control form-control-lg"
type="text" placeholder=".form-control-lg" aria-
label=".form-control-lg">
```

- form-control-sm

```
<input class="form-control form-control-sm"
type="text" placeholder=".form-control-sm" aria-
label=".form-control-sm">
```

- form-control-plaintext

```
<label for="staticInput" class="form-label">Email
</label>
<input type="text" readonly="" class="form-
control-plaintext" id="staticInput" value="email
@example.com">
```

- file input

```
<label for="formFile" class="form-label">Default
file input</label>
<input class="form-control" type="file"
id="formFile">
```

- form-control-color

```
<label for="colorInput" class="form-label">Color
picker</label>
<input type="color" class="form-control form-
control-color" id="colorInput" value="#563d7c"
title="Choose your color">
```

- form-select

```
<select class="form-select" aria-label="Default
select">
  <option selected="">Open this select menu
</option>
  <option value="1">One</option>
  <option value="2">Two</option>
  <option value="3">Three</option>
</select>
```

- form-select-lg

```
<select class="form-select form-select-lg"
aria-label="Large select">
  <option selected="">Open this select menu
</option>
  <option value="1">One</option>
  <option value="2">Two</option>
  <option value="3">Three</option>
</select>
```

- form-select-sm

```
<select class="form-select form-select-sm"
aria-label="Small select">
  <option selected="">Open this select menu
</option>
  <option value="1">One</option>
  <option value="2">Two</option>
  <option value="3">Three</option>
</select>
```

- form-check (checkbox)

```
<div class="form-check">
  <input class="form-check-input" type="checkbox"
value="" id="formCheckDefault">
```

```
  <label class="form-check-label"
for="formCheckDefault">Default checkbox</label>
</div>
<div class="form-check">
  <input class="form-check-input" type="checkbox"
value="" id="formCheckChecked" checked="">
  <label class="form-check-label"
for="formCheckChecked">Checked checkbox</label>
</div>
```

- form- check-inline (checkbox)

```
<div class="form-check form-check-inline">
  <input class="form-check-input" type="checkbox"
value="" id="inlineCheckDefault">
  <label class="form-check-label" for="inlineCheckDe
fault">Default checkbox</label>
</div>
<div class="form-check form-check-inline">
  <input class="form-check-input" type="checkbox"
value="" id="inlineCheckChecked" checked="">
  <label class="form-check-label" for="inlineCheckCh
ecked">Checked checkbox</label>
</div>
```

- form-check (radio)

```
<div class="form-check">
  <input class="form-check-input" type="radio"
name="radioDefault" id="formRadioDefault">
  <label class="form-check-label"
for="formRadioDefault">Default radio</label>
</div>
<div class="form-check">
  <input class="form-check-input" type="radio"
name="radioDefault" id="formRadioChecked"
checked="">
  <label class="form-check-label"
for="formRadioChecked">Default checked radio
</label>
</div>
```

- form-check-inline (radio)

```
<div class="form-check form-check-inline">
  <input class="form-check-input" type="radio"
name="radioInline" id="inlineRadioDefault">
```

```
<label class="form-check-label" for="inlineRadioDe
fault">Default radio</label>
</div>
<div class="form-check form-check-inline">
  <input class="form-check-input" type="radio"
name="radioInline" id="inlineRadioChecked"
checked="">
  <label class="form-check-label" for="inlineRadioCh
ecked">Default checked radio</label>
</div>
```

- form-switch

```
<div class="form-check form-switch">
  <input class="form-check-input" type="checkbox"
id="formSwitchCheckDefault">
  <label class="form-check-label" for="formSwitchChe
ckDefault">Default switch checkbox input</label>
</div>
<div class="form-check form-switch">
  <input class="form-check-input" type="checkbox"
id="formSwitchCheckChecked" checked="">
  <label class="form-check-label" for="formSwitchChe
ckChecked">Checked switch checkbox input</label>
</div>
```

- form-range

```
<label for="formRange" class="form-label">Example
range</label>
<input type="range" class="form-range" min="0"
max="5" step="0.5" id="formRange">
```

## FLOATING LABELS

Used to create form labels that float over the input fields.

- form-floating

```
<div class="form-floating mb-3">
  <input type="email" class="form-control"
id="floatingInput" placeholder="name@example.com">
  <label for="floatingInput">Email address</label>
</div>
<div class="form-floating">
  <input type="password" class="form-control"
id="floatingPassword" placeholder="Password">
```

```
  <label for="floatingPassword">Password</label>
</div>
```

- form-floating with textarea

```
<div class="form-floating">
  <textarea class="form-control" placeholder="Leave
a comment here" id="floatingTextarea"
    style="height: 100px"></textarea>
  <label for="floatingTextarea">Comments</label>
</div>
```

- form-floating with select

```
<div class="form-floating">
  <select class="form-select" id="floatingSelect"
aria-label="Floating label select example">
    <option selected="">Open this select menu
</option>
    <option value="1">One</option>
    <option value="2">Two</option>
    <option value="3">Three</option>
  </select>
  <label for="floatingSelect">Works with selects
</label>
</div>
```

## FORM LAYOUT

Used to give the form some structure.

- horizontal form

```
<form>
  <div class="row mb-3">
    <label for="inputEmail3" class="col-sm-2
col-form-label">Email</label>
    <div class="col-sm-10">
      <input type="email" class="form-control"
id="inputEmail3">
    </div>
  </div>
  <div class="row mb-3">
    <label for="inputPassword3" class="col-sm-2
col-form-label">Password</label>
    <div class="col-sm-10">
```

```
        <input type="password" class="form-control"
id="inputPassword3">
    </div>
  </div>
  <fieldset class="row mb-3">
    <legend class="col-form-label col-sm-2
pt-0">Radios</legend>
    <div class="col-sm-10">
      <div class="form-check">
        <input class="form-check-input" type="radio"
name="gridRadios" id="gridRadios1" value="option1"
        checked="">
        <label class="form-check-label"
for="gridRadios1">
          First radio
        </label>
      </div>
      <div class="form-check">
        <input class="form-check-input" type="radio"
name="gridRadios" id="gridRadios2" value="option2">
        <label class="form-check-label"
for="gridRadios2">
          Second radio
        </label>
      </div>
      <div class="form-check disabled">
        <input class="form-check-input" type="radio"
name="gridRadios" id="gridRadios3" value="option3"
        disabled="">
        <label class="form-check-label"
for="gridRadios3">
          Third disabled radio
        </label>
      </div>
    </div>
  </fieldset>
  <div class="row mb-3">
    <div class="col-sm-10 offset-sm-2">
      <div class="form-check">
        <input class="form-check-input"
type="checkbox" id="gridCheck1">
        <label class="form-check-label"
for="gridCheck1">
```

```
      Example checkbox
    </label>
  </div>
 </div>
</div>
<button type="submit" class="btn btn-primary">
Sign in</button>
</form>
```

• col-form-label-{size}

```
<!-- Different sized labels for horizontal form can
be used with the help of .col-form-label-{sm|lg}
class -->
<div class="row mb-3">
 <label for="colFormLabelLg" class="col-sm-2
col-form-label col-form-label-lg">Email</label>
 <div class="col-sm-10">
   <input type="email" class="form-control form-
control-lg" id="colFormLabelLg"
placeholder="col-form-label-lg">
 </div>
</div>
<div class="row mb-3">
 <label for="colFormLabel" class="col-sm-2
col-form-label">Email</label>
 <div class="col-sm-10">
   <input type="email" class="form-control"
id="colFormLabel" placeholder="col-form-label">
 </div>
</div>
<div class="row">
 <label for="colFormLabelSm" class="col-sm-2
col-form-label col-form-label-sm">Email</label>
 <div class="col-sm-10">
   <input type="email" class="form-control
form-control-sm" id="colFormLabelSm"
placeholder="col-form-label-sm">
 </div>
</div>
```

## FORM VALIDATION

- valid-feedback

```
<!-- Note: A custom script is used to activate
validation:
var forms = document.querySelectorAll('.needs-valida
tion')
Array.prototype.slice.call(forms)
 .forEach(function (form) {
  form.addEventListener('submit', function (event) {
   if (!form.checkValidity()) {
    event.preventDefault()
    event.stopPropagation()
   }
   form.classList.add('was-validated')
  }, false)
 })
-->
<form class="row g-3 needs-validation"
novalidate="">
  <div class="col-md-4">
    <label for="validationCustom01" class="form-
label">First name</label>
    <input type="text" class="form-control"
id="validationCustom01" value="Mark" required="">
    <div class="valid-feedback">
      Looks good!
    </div>
  </div>
  <div class="col-md-4">
    <label for="validationCustom02" class="form-
label">Last name</label>
    <input type="text" class="form-control"
id="validationCustom02" value="Otto" required="">
    <div class="valid-feedback">
      Looks good!
    </div>
  </div>
```

```
<div class="col-md-4">
  <label for="validationCustomUsername"
class="form-label">Username</label>
    <div class="input-group has-validation">
      <span class="input-group-text"
id="inputGroupPrepend">@</span>
      <input type="text" class="form-control"
id="validationCustomUsername" aria-describedby=
"inputGroupPrepend"
        required="">
      <div class="invalid-feedback">
        Please choose a username.
      </div>
    </div>
  </div>
  <div class="col-md-6">
    <label for="validationCustom03"
class="form-label">City</label>
    <input type="text" class="form-control"
id="validationCustom03" required="">
    <div class="invalid-feedback">
      Please provide a valid city.
    </div>
  </div>
  <div class="col-md-3">
    <label for="validationCustom04"
class="form-label">State</label>
    <select class="form-select"
id="validationCustom04" required="">
      <option selected="" disabled=""
value="">Choose...</option>
      <option>Option 1</option>
      <option>Option 2</option>
      <option>Option 3</option>
    </select>
    <div class="invalid-feedback">
      Please select a valid state.
    </div>
  </div>
  <div class="col-md-3">
    <label for="validationCustom05"
class="form-label">Zip</label>
```

```
  <input type="text" class="form-control"
id="validationCustom05" required="">
    <div class="invalid-feedback">
      Please provide a valid zip.
    </div>
  </div>
  <div class="col-12">
    <div class="form-check">
      <input class="form-check-input" type="checkbox"
value="" id="invalidCheck" required="">
      <label class="form-check-label"
for="invalidCheck">
        Agree to terms and conditions
      </label>
      <div class="invalid-feedback">
        You must agree before submitting.
      </div>
    </div>
  </div>
  <div class="col-12">
    <button class="btn btn-primary"
type="submit">Submit form</button>
  </div>
</form>
```

- valid-tooltip

```
<!-- Note: A custom script is used to activate
validation:
var forms = document.querySelectorAll('.needs-valida
tion')
Array.prototype.slice.call(forms)
 .forEach(function (form) {
  form.addEventListener('submit', function (event) {
   if (!form.checkValidity()) {
    event.preventDefault()
    event.stopPropagation()
   }
   form.classList.add('was-validated')
  }, false)
 })
-->
<form class="row g-3 needs-validation"
novalidate="">
```

```
<div class="col-md-4 position-relative">
  <label for="validationTooltip01" class="form-
label">First name</label>
  <input type="text" class="form-control"
id="validationTooltip01" value="Mark" required="">
  <div class="valid-tooltip">
   Looks good!
  </div>
</div>
<div class="col-md-4 position-relative">
  <label for="validationTooltip02" class="form-
label">Last name</label>
  <input type="text" class="form-control"
id="validationTooltip02" value="Otto" required="">
  <div class="valid-tooltip">
   Looks good!
  </div>
</div>
<div class="col-md-4 position-relative">
  <label for="validationTooltipUsername"
class="form-label">Username</label>
  <div class="input-group has-validation">
    <span class="input-group-text" id="validationT
ooltipUsernamePrepend">@</span>
    <input type="text" class="form-control"
id="validationTooltipUsername"
      aria-describedby="validationTooltipUserna
mePrepend" required="">
    <div class="invalid-tooltip">
      Please choose a unique and valid username.
    </div>
  </div>
</div>
<div class="col-md-6 position-relative">
  <label for="validationTooltip03" class="form-
label">City</label>
  <input type="text" class="form-control"
id="validationTooltip03" required="">
  <div class="invalid-tooltip">
   Please provide a valid city.
  </div>
</div>
<div class="col-md-3 position-relative">
```

```
    <label for="validationTooltip04"
class="form-label">State</label>
    <select class="form-select"
id="validationTooltip04" required="">
      <option selected="" disabled=""
value="">Choose...</option>
      <option>...</option>
    </select>
    <div class="invalid-tooltip">
      Please select a valid state.
    </div>
  </div>
  <div class="col-md-3 position-relative">
    <label for="validationTooltip05"
class="form-label">Zip</label>
    <input type="text" class="form-control"
id="validationTooltip05" required="">
    <div class="invalid-tooltip">
      Please provide a valid zip.
    </div>
  </div>
  <div class="col-12">
    <button class="btn btn-primary"
type="submit">Submit form</button>
  </div>
</form>
```

## LIST GROUP

Used for displaying a series of content

- list-group

```
<ul class="list-group">
  <li class="list-group-item">Cras justo odio</li>
  <li class="list-group-item">Morbi leo risus</li>
  <li class="list-group-item">Porta ac consectetur
ac</li>
  <li class="list-group-item">Vestibulum at eros</li>
</ul>
```

- list-group-item active

```
<ul class="list-group">
  <li class="list-group-item active"
aria-current="true">Cras justo odio</li>
```

```
  <li class="list-group-item">Morbi leo risus</li>
  <li class="list-group-item">Porta ac consectetur
ac</li>
  <li class="list-group-item">Vestibulum at eros
</li>
</ul>
```

- list-group-item disabled

```
<ul class="list-group">
  <li class="list-group-item disabled" aria-
disabled="true">Cras justo odio</li>
  <li class="list-group-item">Morbi leo risus</li>
  <li class="list-group-item">Porta ac consectetur
ac</li>
  <li class="list-group-item">Vestibulum at eros
</li>
</ul>
```

- list-group-flush

```
<ul class="list-group list-group-flush">
  <li class="list-group-item">Cras justo odio</li>
  <li class="list-group-item">Morbi leo risus</li>
  <li class="list-group-item">Porta ac consectetur
ac</li>
  <li class="list-group-item">Vestibulum at eros
</li>
</ul>
```

- list-group-numbered

```
<ul class="list-group list-group-numbered">
  <li class="list-group-item">Cras justo odio</li>
  <li class="list-group-item">Morbi leo risus</li>
  <li class="list-group-item">Porta ac consectetur
ac</li>
  <li class="list-group-item">Vestibulum at eros
</li>
</ul>
```

- list-group-horizontal

```
<ul class="list-group list-group-horizontal">
  <li class="list-group-item">Cras justo odio</li>
  <li class="list-group-item">Morbi leo risus</li>
```

```
    <li class="list-group-item">Vestibulum at eros
</li>
</ul>
```

- list-group-horizontal-*

```
<ul class="list-group list-group-horizontal-md">
  <li class="list-group-item">Cras justo odio</li>
  <li class="list-group-item">Morbi leo risus</li>
  <li class="list-group-item">Vestibulum at eros
</li>
</ul>
```

- list-group-item-{color}

```
<ul class="list-group">
  <li class="list-group-item">Dapibus ac facilisis
in</li>
  <li class="list-group-item list-group-item-
primary">A simple primary list group item</li>
  <li class="list-group-item list-group-item-
secondary">A simple secondary list group item</li>
  <li class="list-group-item list-group-item-
success">A simple success list group item</li>
  <li class="list-group-item list-group-item-
danger">A simple danger list group item</li>
  <li class="list-group-item list-group-item-
warning">A simple warning list group item</li>
  <li class="list-group-item list-group-item-info">
A simple info list group item</li>
  <li class="list-group-item list-group-item-
light">A simple light list group item</li>
  <li class="list-group-item list-group-item-dark">
A simple dark list group item</li>
</ul>
```

- list-group-item-action

```
<ul class="list-group">
  <li class="list-group-item list-group-item-
action">Cras justo odio</li>
  <li class="list-group-item list-group-item-
action">Morbi leo risus</li>
  <li class="list-group-item list-group-item-
action">Porta ac consectetur ac</li>
```

```
  <li class="list-group-item list-group-item-
action">Vestibulum at eros</li>
</ul>
```

• custom content

```
<div class="list-group">
  <a href="#" class="list-group-item list-group-
item-action active" aria-current="true">
    <div class="d-flex w-100
justify-content-between">
      <h5 class="mb-1">List group item heading</h5>
      <small>3 days ago</small>
    </div>
    <p class="mb-1">Donec id elit non mi porta at
eget metus. Maecenas diam eget risus varius blandit.
    </p>
    <small>Donec id elit non mi porta.</small>
  </a>
  <a href="#" class="list-group-item
list-group-item-action">
    <div class="d-flex w-100
justify-content-between">
      <h5 class="mb-1">List group item heading</h5>
      <small class="text-muted">3 days ago</small>
    </div>
    <p class="mb-1">Donec id elit non mi gravida at
eget metus. Maecenas sed eget risus varius blandit.
    </p>
    <small class="text-muted">Donec id elit mi
porta.</small>
  </a>
  <a href="#" class="list-group-item
list-group-item-action">
    <div class="d-flex w-100
justify-content-between">
      <h5 class="mb-1">List group item heading</h5>
      <small class="text-muted">3 days ago</small>
    </div>
    <p class="mb-1">Donec elit non mi porta at eget
metus. Maecenas sed diam eget risus blandit.
    </p>
```

```
  <small class="text-muted">Donec elit non mi
porta.</small>
  </a>
</div>
```

- list-group with checkbox

```
<div class="list-group">
  <label class="list-group-item">
    <input class="form-check-input me-1"
type="checkbox">
    Cras justo odio
  </label>
  <label class="list-group-item">
    <input class="form-check-input me-1"
type="checkbox">
    Dapibus ac facilisis in
  </label>
  <label class="list-group-item">
    <input class="form-check-input me-1"
type="checkbox">
    Morbi leo risus
  </label>
  <label class="list-group-item">
    <input class="form-check-input me-1"
type="checkbox">
    Porta ac consectetur ac
  </label>
  <label class="list-group-item">
    <input class="form-check-input me-1"
type="checkbox">
    Vestibulum at eros
  </label>
</div>
```

- list-group with radio

```
<div class="list-group">
  <label class="list-group-item">
    <input class="form-check-input me-1"
type="radio">
    Cras justo odio
  </label>
  <label class="list-group-item">
```

```
    <input class="form-check-input me-1"
type="radio">
    Dapibus ac facilisis in
  </label>
  <label class="list-group-item">
    <input class="form-check-input me-1"
type="radio">
    Morbi leo risus
  </label>
  <label class="list-group-item">
    <input class="form-check-input me-1"
type="radio">
    Porta ac consectetur ac
  </label>
  <label class="list-group-item">
    <input class="form-check-input me-1"
type="radio">
    Vestibulum at eros
  </label>
</div>
```

- JavaScript behavior

```
<div class="row">
  <div class="col-5 col-lg-4">
    <div class="list-group" id="list-tab"
role="tablist">
      <a class="list-group-item list-group-item-
action active" id="list-home-list"
data-bs-toggle="list"
      href="#list-home" role="tab" aria-
controls="home">Home</a>
      <a class="list-group-item list-group-item-
action" id="list-profile-list" data-bs-toggle="list"
      href="#list-profile" role="tab" aria-
controls="profile">Profile</a>
      <a class="list-group-item list-group-item-
action" id="list-messages-list"
data-bs-toggle="list"
      href="#list-messages" role="tab" aria-control
s="messages">Messages</a>
      <a class="list-group-item list-group-item-
action" id="list-settings-list"
data-bs-toggle="list"
```

```
      href="#list-settings" role="tab" aria-control
s="settings">Settings</a>
    </div>
  </div>
  <div class="col-7 col-lg-8">
    <div class="tab-content"
id="list-nav-tabContent">
      <div class="tab-pane fade show active"
id="list-home" role="tabpanel"
aria-labelledby="list-home-list">Lorem
      ipsum dolor sit amet adipisicing elit. Maxime
consequatur neque laborum, dolores
      nemo magnam perspiciatis aperiam nisi, in
quas sint rem placeat.</div>
      <div class="tab-pane fade" id="list-profile"
role="tabpanel" aria-labelledby="list-profile-list">
Lorem ipsum
      dolor sit, amet consectetur adipisicing elit.
Tempore, omnis fugit consectetur labore error iusto
esse
      repellat vel expedita ad eligendi asperiores
cupiditate molestias consequatur!</div>
      <div class="tab-pane fade" id="list-messages"
role="tabpanel" aria-labelledby="list-messages-list">
Lorem
      ipsum dolor sit amet consectetur adipisicing
elit. Perferendis, quod aliquam esse, iste nostrum
aut,
      aspernatur eaque dolore nulla mollitia vero
ex. Illum, in ipsa!</div>
      <div class="tab-pane fade" id="list-settings"
role="tabpanel" aria-labelledby="list-settings-list">
Lorem
      ipsum dolor, sit amet consectetur elit.
Soluta facilis aspernatur harum , quibusdam
      consectetur voluptatem illum maxime vitae
excepturi praesentium , sint maiores?</div>
    </div>
  </div>
</div>
```

## MODAL

Used to add dialogs for user notifications, lightboxes, or completely custom content.

- Modal

```
<div class="modal" tabindex="-1">
  <div class="modal-dialog">
   <div class="modal-content">
    <div class="modal-header">
     <h5 class="modal-title"
id="modalBasicLabel">Modal title</h5>
     <button type="button" class="btn-close"
aria-label="Close"></button>
    </div>
    <div class="modal-body">...</div>
    <div class="modal-footer">
     <button type="button" class="btn btn-
secondary">Close</button>
     <button type="button" class="btn btn-
primary">Save changes</button>
    </div>
   </div>
  </div>
 </div>
```

- static backdrop

```
<div class="modal" data-bs-backdrop="static"
data-bs-keyboard="false" tabindex="-1">
  <div class="modal-dialog">
    <div class="modal-content">
      <div class="modal-header">
        <h5 class="modal-title" id="modalStaticBackdr
opLabel">Modal title</h5>
        <button type="button" class="btn-close"
aria-label="Close"></button>
      </div>
      <div class="modal-body">...</div>
      <div class="modal-footer">
        <button type="button" class="btn
btn-secondary">Close</button>
        <button type="button" class="btn
btn-primary">Save changes</button>
```

```
        </div>
      </div>
    </div>
</div>
```

- modal-dialog-scrollable

```
<div class="modal" tabindex="-1">
  <div class="modal-dialog modal-dialog-scrollable">
    <div class="modal-content">
      <div class="modal-header">
        <h5 class="modal-title"
id="modalScrollableLabel">Modal title</h5>
        <button type="button" class="btn-close"
aria-label="Close"></button>
      </div>
      <div class="modal-body">
        <p>Lorem ipsum dolor sit amet, adipisicing
elit. Optio numquam, saepe repellat perspiciatis
        rerum magnam, vel molestiae cum beatae
error corporis eum atque eveniet!</p>
        <p>Lorem ipsum dolor sit amet adipisicing
elit. Facere mollitia vero odio quos error dolorem
        numquam, nemo explicabo modi similique!
Eveniet porro exercitationem autem ratione.</p>
      </div>
      <div class="modal-footer">
        <button type="button" class="btn btn-
secondary">Close</button>
        <button type="button" class="btn btn-
primary">Save changes</button>
      </div>
    </div>
  </div>
</div>
```

- modal-dialog-centered

```
<div class="modal" tabindex="-1">
  <div class="modal-dialog modal-dialog-centered">
    <div class="modal-content">
      <div class="modal-header">
        <h5 class="modal-title" id="modalVerticallyCe
nteredLabel">Modal title</h5>
```

```
       <button type="button" class="btn-close"
aria-label="Close"></button>
    </div>
    <div class="modal-body">...</div>
    <div class="modal-footer">
       <button type="button" class="btn btn-
secondary">Close</button>
       <button type="button" class="btn btn-
primary">Save changes</button>
    </div>
  </div>
 </div>
</div>
```

- modal-{size}

```
<!-- Different sized modals can be used with the
help of .modal-{sm|lg|xl} class -->
<div class="modal" tabindex="-1">
  <div class="modal-dialog modal-lg">
    <div class="modal-content">
    <div class="modal-header">
 <h5 class="modal-title" id="modalSizeLabel">
Modal title</h5>
       <button type="button" class="btn-close"
aria-label="Close"></button>
    </div>
    <div class="modal-body">...</div>
    <div class="modal-footer">
       <button type="button" class="btn btn-
secondary">Close</button>
       <button type="button" class="btn btn-
primary">Save changes</button>
    </div>
  </div>
 </div>
</div>
```

- modal-fullscreen

```
<div class="modal" tabindex="-1">
  <div class="modal-dialog modal-fullscreen">
    <div class="modal-content">
    <div class="modal-header">
```

```
    <h5 class="modal-title"
id="modalFullscreenLabel">Modal title</h5>
      <button type="button" class="btn-close"
aria-label="Close"></button>
    </div>
    <div class="modal-body">
      <p>Lorem ipsum dolor sit amet, adipisicing
elit. Optio numquam, repellat perspiciatis
        rerum magnam, sapiente vel cum beatae error
corporis eum atque eveniet!</p>
      <p>Lorem ipsum dolor sit amet adipisicing
elit. Facere mollitia vero odio quos error dolorem
        numquam, nemo explicabo modi similique!
Eveniet porro exercitationem autem ratione.</p>
      <p>Lorem ipsum dolor sit, amet adipisicing
elit. Sint et sunt dolorum, non velit minus
        reprehenderit eaque, vero voluptas
excepturi maxime? Atque explicabo accusantium
facilis.</p>
      <p>Lorem ipsum sit amet consectetur
adipisicing elit. Dolor illo corrupti reiciend amet
        error odio repudiandae doloremque , quasi
eius quis possimus commodi dolorem.</p>
    </div>
    <div class="modal-footer">
      <button type="button" class="btn btn-
secondary">Close</button>
      <button type="button" class="btn btn-
primary">Save changes</button>
    </div>
  </div>
  </div>
</div>
```

- modal-fullscreen-*-down

```
<div class="modal" tabindex="-1">
  <div class="modal-dialog
modal-fullscreen-md-down">
    <div class="modal-content">
      <div class="modal-header">
        <h5 class="modal-title" id="modalFullscreenSi
zeLabel">Modal title</h5>
```

```
        <button type="button" class="btn-close"
aria-label="Close"></button>
      </div>
      <div class="modal-body">...</div>
      <div class="modal-footer">
        <button type="button" class="btn btn-
secondary">Close</button>
        <button type="button" class="btn btn-
primary">Save changes</button>
      </div>
    </div>
  </div>
</div>
```

## NAVBAR

- navbar

```
<nav class="navbar navbar-expand-xl navbar-light
bg-light">
  <div class="container-fluid">
    <a class="navbar-brand" href="#">Navbar</a>
    <button class="navbar-toggler" type="button"
data-bs-toggle="collapse"
data-bs-target="#navbarBasic"
      aria-controls="navbarBasic" aria-
expanded="false" aria-label="Toggle navigation">
      <span class="navbar-toggler-icon"></span>
    </button>
    <div class="collapse navbar-collapse show"
id="navbarBasic">
      <ul class="navbar-nav me-auto mb-2 mb-xl-0">
        <li class="nav-item">
          <a class="nav-link active" aria-
current="page" href="#">Home</a>
        </li>
        <li class="nav-item">
          <a class="nav-link" href="#">Link</a>
        </li>
        <li class="nav-item">
          <a class="nav-link disabled" href="#"
tabindex="-1" aria-disabled="true">Disabled</a>
        </li>
      </ul>
```

```
    <form class="d-flex">
      <input class="form-control me-2"
type="search" placeholder="Search"
aria-label="Search">
      <button class="btn btn-outline-success"
type="submit">Search</button>
    </form>
   </div>
  </div>
</nav>
```

- navbar-brand

```
<nav class="navbar navbar-light bg-light">
  <div class="container-fluid">
    <a class="navbar-brand" href="#">Navbar</a>
  </div>
</nav>
```

- navbar without using list

```
<nav class="navbar navbar-expand-lg navbar-light
bg-light">
  <div class="container-fluid">
    <a class="navbar-brand" href="#">Navbar</a>
    <button class="navbar-toggler" type="button"
data-bs-toggle="collapse"
data-bs-target="#navbarNavAltMarkup"
    aria-controls="navbarNavAltMarkup" aria-
expanded="false" aria-label="Toggle navigation">
      <span class="navbar-toggler-icon"></span>
    </button>
    <div class="collapse navbar-collapse show"
id="navbarNavAltMarkup">
      <div class="navbar-nav">
        <a class="nav-link active" aria-
current="page" href="#">Home</a>
        <a class="nav-link" href="#">Features</a>
        <a class="nav-link" href="#">Pricing</a>
        <a class="nav-link disabled" href="#"
tabindex="-1" aria-disabled="true">Disabled</a>
      </div>
    </div>
  </div>
</nav>
```

- navbar with dropdown

```
<nav class="navbar navbar-expand-xl navbar-light
bg-light">
  <div class="container-fluid">
    <a class="navbar-brand" href="#">Navbar</a>
    <button class="navbar-toggler" type="button"
data-bs-toggle="collapse"
data-bs-target="#navbarWithDropdown"
    aria-controls="navbarWithDropdown" aria-
expanded="false" aria-label="Toggle navigation">
      <span class="navbar-toggler-icon"></span>
    </button>
    <div class="collapse navbar-collapse show"
id="navbarWithDropdown">
      <ul class="navbar-nav">
        <li class="nav-item">
          <a class="nav-link active" aria-
current="page" href="#">Home</a>
        </li>
        <li class="nav-item">
          <a class="nav-link" href="#">Features</a>
        </li>
        <li class="nav-item">
          <a class="nav-link" href="#">Pricing</a>
        </li>
        <li class="nav-item dropdown">
          <a class="nav-link dropdown-toggle"
href="#" id="navbarDropdownMenuLink" role="button"
          data-bs-toggle="dropdown"
aria-expanded="false">
            Dropdown link
          </a>
          <ul class="dropdown-menu" aria-labelledby
="navbarDropdownMenuLink">
            <li><a class="dropdown-item"
href="#">Action</a></li>
            <li><a class="dropdown-item"
href="#">Another action</a></li>
            <li><a class="dropdown-item"
href="#">Something else here</a></li>
          </ul>
        </li>
```

```
      <li class="nav-item">
        <a class="nav-link disabled" href="#"
tabindex="-1" aria-disabled="true">Disabled</a>
      </li>
    </ul>
  </div>
 </div>
</nav>
```

• navbar-text

```
<nav class="navbar navbar-expand-xl navbar-light
bg-light">
  <div class="container-fluid">
    <a class="navbar-brand" href="#">Navbar</a>
    <button class="navbar-toggler" type="button"
data-bs-toggle="collapse"
data-bs-target="#navbarText"
      aria-controls="navbarText" aria-
expanded="false" aria-label="Toggle navigation">
      <span class="navbar-toggler-icon"></span>
    </button>
    <div class="collapse navbar-collapse show"
id="navbarText">
      <ul class="navbar-nav me-auto mb-2 mb-xl-0">
        <li class="nav-item">
          <a class="nav-link active" aria-
current="page" href="#">Home</a>
        </li>
        <li class="nav-item">
          <a class="nav-link" href="#">Features</a>
        </li>
        <li class="nav-item">
          <a class="nav-link" href="#">Pricing</a>
        </li>
      </ul>
      <span class="navbar-text">
        Navbar text with an inline element
      </span>
    </div>
  </div>
</nav>
```

- navbar-dark

```
<nav class="navbar navbar-expand-xl navbar-dark
bg-dark">
  <div class="container-fluid">
    <a class="navbar-brand" href="#">Navbar</a>
    <button class="navbar-toggler" type="button"
data-bs-toggle="collapse"
data-bs-target="#navbarDark"
    aria-controls="navbarDark" aria-
expanded="false" aria-label="Toggle navigation">
    <span class="navbar-toggler-icon"></span>
    </button>
    <div class="collapse navbar-collapse show"
id="navbarDark">
    <ul class="navbar-nav me-auto mb-2 mb-xl-0">
      <li class="nav-item">
        <a class="nav-link active" aria-
current="page" href="#">Home</a>
      </li>
      <li class="nav-item">
        <a class="nav-link" href="#">Features</a>
      </li>
      <li class="nav-item">
        <a class="nav-link disabled" href="#"
tabindex="-1" aria-disabled="true">Disabled</a>
      </li>
    </ul>
    <form class="d-flex">
      <input class="form-control me-2"
type="search" placeholder="Search"
aria-label="Search">
      <button class="btn btn-outline-light"
type="submit">Search</button>
    </form>
    </div>
  </div>
</nav>
```

- navbar-light

```
<nav class="navbar navbar-expand-xl navbar-light"
style="background-color: #e3f2fd;">
  <div class="container-fluid">
```

```
    <a class="navbar-brand" href="#">Navbar</a>
    <button class="navbar-toggler" type="button"
data-bs-toggle="collapse"
data-bs-target="#navbarLight"
    aria-controls="navbarLight" aria-
expanded="false" aria-label="Toggle navigation">
    <span class="navbar-toggler-icon"></span>
    </button>
    <div class="collapse navbar-collapse show"
id="navbarLight">
    <ul class="navbar-nav me-auto mb-2 mb-xl-0">
      <li class="nav-item">
        <a class="nav-link active" aria-
current="page" href="#">Home</a>
      </li>
      <li class="nav-item">
        <a class="nav-link" href="#">Features</a>
      </li>
      <li class="nav-item">
        <a class="nav-link disabled" href="#"
tabindex="-1" aria-disabled="true">Disabled</a>
      </li>
    </ul>
    <form class="d-flex">
      <input class="form-control me-2"
type="search" placeholder="Search"
aria-label="Search">
      <button class="btn btn-outline-primary"
type="submit">Search</button>
    </form>
   </div>
  </div>
</nav>
```

• fixed-top

```
<nav class="navbar fixed-top navbar-light
bg-light">
  <div class="container-fluid">
   <a class="navbar-brand" href="#">Fixed top</a>
  </div>
</nav>
```

- fixed-bottom

```
<nav class="navbar fixed-bottom navbar-light
bg-light">
  <div class="container-fluid">
    <a class="navbar-brand" href="#">Fixed bottom
</a>
  </div>
</nav>
```

- sticky-top

```
<nav class="navbar sticky-top navbar-light
bg-light">
  <div class="container-fluid">
    <a class="navbar-brand" href="#">Sticky top</a>
  </div>
</nav>
```

- brand in collapse

```
<nav class="navbar navbar-expand-xl navbar-light
bg-light">
  <div class="container-fluid">
    <button class="navbar-toggler" type="button"
data-bs-toggle="collapse"
data-bs-target="#navbarTogglerDemo1"
    aria-controls="navbarTogglerDemo1" aria-
expanded="false" aria-label="Toggle navigation">
    <span class="navbar-toggler-icon"></span>
    </button>
    <div class="collapse navbar-collapse show"
id="navbarTogglerDemo1">
    <a class="navbar-brand" href="#">Hidden
brand</a>
    <ul class="navbar-nav me-auto mb-2 mb-xl-0">
      <li class="nav-item">
        <a class="nav-link active" aria-
current="page" href="#">Home</a>
      </li>
      <li class="nav-item">
        <a class="nav-link" href="#">Link</a>
      </li>
      <li class="nav-item">
```

```
      <a class="nav-link disabled" href="#"
tabindex="-1" aria-disabled="true">Disabled</a>
      </li>
    </ul>
    <form class="d-flex">
      <input class="form-control me-2"
type="search" placeholder="Search"
aria-label="Search">
      <button class="btn btn-outline-success"
type="submit">Search</button>
    </form>
  </div>
  </div>
</nav>
```

- navbar-toggler on right

```
<nav class="navbar navbar-expand-xl navbar-light
bg-light">
  <div class="container-fluid">
    <a class="navbar-brand" href="#">Navbar</a>
    <button class="navbar-toggler" type="button"
data-bs-toggle="collapse"
data-bs-target="#navbarTogglerDemo2"
    aria-controls="navbarTogglerDemo2" aria-
expanded="false" aria-label="Toggle navigation">
      <span class="navbar-toggler-icon"></span>
    </button>
    <div class="collapse navbar-collapse show"
id="navbarTogglerDemo2">
      <ul class="navbar-nav me-auto mb-2 mb-xl-0">
        <li class="nav-item">
          <a class="nav-link active" aria-
current="page" href="#">Home</a>
        </li>
        <li class="nav-item">
          <a class="nav-link" href="#">Link</a>
        </li>
        <li class="nav-item">
          <a class="nav-link disabled" href="#"
tabindex="-1" aria-disabled="true">Disabled</a>
        </li>
      </ul>
```

```
    <form class="d-flex">
      <input class="form-control me-2"
type="search" placeholder="Search"
aria-label="Search">
      <button class="btn btn-outline-success"
type="submit">Search</button>
    </form>
  </div>
 </div>
</nav>
```

- navbar-toggler on left

```
<nav class="navbar navbar-expand-xl navbar-light
bg-light">
 <div class="container-fluid">
  <button class="navbar-toggler" type="button"
data-bs-toggle="collapse"
data-bs-target="#navbarTogglerDemo3"
    aria-controls="navbarTogglerDemo3" aria-
expanded="false" aria-label="Toggle navigation">
    <span class="navbar-toggler-icon"></span>
  </button>
  <a class="navbar-brand" href="#">Navbar</a>
  <div class="collapse navbar-collapse show"
id="navbarTogglerDemo3">
    <ul class="navbar-nav me-auto mb-2 mb-xl-0">
     <li class="nav-item">
      <a class="nav-link active" aria-
current="page" href="#">Home</a>
     </li>
     <li class="nav-item">
      <a class="nav-link" href="#">Link</a>
     </li>
     <li class="nav-item">
      <a class="nav-link disabled" href="#"
tabindex="-1" aria-disabled="true">Disabled</a>
     </li>
    </ul>
    <form class="d-flex">
     <input class="form-control me-2"
type="search" placeholder="Search"
aria-label="Search">
```

```
      <button class="btn btn-outline-success"
type="submit">Search</button>
    </form>
  </div>
 </div>
</nav>
```

## NAVS, TABS, PILLS

Used for Bootstrap's navigation components

- Ul.nav

```
<ul class="nav">
  <li class="nav-item">
    <a class="nav-link active" aria-current="page"
href="#">Active</a>
  </li>
  <li class="nav-item">
    <a class="nav-link" href="#">Link</a>
  </li>
  <li class="nav-item">
    <a class="nav-link" href="#">Link</a>
  </li>
  <li class="nav-item">
    <a class="nav-link disabled" href="#"
tabindex="-1" aria-disabled="true">Disabled</a>
  </li>
</ul>
```

- Nav.nav

```
<nav class="nav">
  <a class="nav-link active" aria-current="page"
href="#">Active</a>
  <a class="nav-link" href="#">Link</a>
  <a class="nav-link" href="#">Link</a>
  <a class="nav-link disabled" href="#"
tabindex="-1" aria-disabled="true">Disabled</a>
</nav>
```

- vertical nav

```
<nav class="nav flex-column">
  <a class="nav-link active" aria-current="page"
href="#">Active</a>
```

```
<a class="nav-link" href="#">Link</a>
<a class="nav-link" href="#">Link</a>
<a class="nav-link disabled" href="#"
tabindex="-1" aria-disabled="true">Disabled</a>
</nav>
```

- nav-tabs

```
<nav class="nav nav-tabs" id="nav-tab"
role="tablist">
<a class="nav-link active" id="nav-home-tab" data-
bs-toggle="tab" href="#nav-home" role="tab"
  aria-controls="nav-home" aria-
selected="true">Home</a>
<a class="nav-link" id="nav-profile-tab" data-bs-
toggle="tab" href="#nav-profile" role="tab"
  aria-controls="nav-profile" aria-
selected="false">Profile</a>
<a class="nav-link disabled" id="nav-disabled-tab"
data-bs-toggle="tab" href="#nav-disabled" role="tab"
  aria-controls="nav-disabled" tabindex="-1" aria-
disabled="true">Disabled</a>
</nav>
<div class="tab-content" id="nav-tabContent">
<div class="tab-pane fade show active" id="nav-
home" role="tabpanel" aria-labelledby="nav-home-
tab">Lorem ipsum
  dolor sit amet consectetur adipisicing elit.
tempore tempora molestiae , voluptate fuga corrupti
  est reiciendis maxime totam dolores, , dolorem
eaque sequi.</div>
<div class="tab-pane fade" id="nav-profile"
role="tabpanel" aria-labelledby="nav-profile-
tab">Lorem ipsum dolor sit
  amet, consectetur adipisicing elit. Magni, sed
soluta necessitatibus aspernatur? Praesentium, odit
  explicabo distinctio dolore officia iure, ut
magnam optio aliquam at similique veritatis.</div>
<div class="tab-pane fade" id="nav-disabled"
role="tabpanel" aria-labelledby="nav-disabled-
tab">Lorem ipsum dolor
  sit amet consectetur, elit. Laudantium minima
repellat incidunt facilis obcaecati blanditiis
```

corrupti ad officia doloribus ullam sapiente
ipsum, a, excepturi voluptatem voluptatibus velit eum
    dignissimos ut, nam tempora? illo itaque
veritatis eligendi fuga, mollitia ratione totam esse
    in.</div>
</div>

- nav-pills

```
<nav class="nav nav-pills" id="pills-tab"
role="tablist">
  <a class="nav-link active" id="pills-home-tab"
data-bs-toggle="pill" href="#pills-home" role="tab"
    aria-controls="pills-home" aria-
selected="true">Home</a>
  <a class="nav-link" id="pills-profile-tab" data-
bs-toggle="pill" href="#pills-profile" role="tab"
    aria-controls="pills-profile" aria-
selected="false">Profile</a>
  <a class="nav-link disabled" id="pills-disabled-
tab" data-bs-toggle="pill" href="#pills-disabled"
role="tab"
    aria-controls="pills-disabled" tabindex="-1"
aria-disabled="true">Disabled</a>
</nav>
<div class="tab-content" id="pills-tabContent">
  <div class="tab-pane fade show active" id="pills-
home" role="tabpanel"
aria-labelledby="pills-home-tab">Lorem
    dolor sit amet consectetur adipisicing elit.
Aliquid tempore tempora molestiae pariatur,
voluptate fuga corrupti
    est maxime totam dolores, voluptates, dolorem
eaque sequi.</div>
  <div class="tab-pane fade" id="pills-profile"
role="tabpanel" aria-labelledby="pills-profile-tab">
Lorem ipsum dolor
    sit amet, consectetur adipisicing elit. Magni,
sed soluta necessitatibus aspernatur? Praesentium,
    odit explicabo dolore adipisci officia iure, ut
magnam optio aliquam at similique veritatis.</div>
  <div class="tab-pane fade" id="pills-disabled"
role="tabpanel" aria-labelledby="pills-disabled-tab">
Lorem ipsum
```

dolor sit amet consectetur, adipisicing elit.
Laudantium minima repellat incidunt obcaecati
blanditiis
    corrupti ad officia doloribus ullam sapiente ,
nemo a, excepturi voluptatem velit eum
    dignissimos ut, tempora? Reiciendis illo itaque
veritatis fuga, mollitia ratione totam veniam esse
    in.</div>
</div>

- nav-fill

```
<nav class="nav nav-pills nav-fill">
  <a class="nav-link active" aria-current="page"
href="#">Active</a>
  <a class="nav-link" href="#">Much longer nav
link</a>
    <a class="nav-link" href="#">Link</a>
    <a class="nav-link disabled" href="#"
tabindex="-1" aria-disabled="true">Disabled</a>
</nav>
```

- nav-justified

```
<nav class="nav nav-pills nav-justified">
  <a class="nav-link active" aria-current="page"
href="#">Active</a>
  <a class="nav-link" href="#">Much longer nav
link</a>
    <a class="nav-link" href="#">Link</a>
    <a class="nav-link disabled" href="#"
tabindex="-1" aria-disabled="true">Disabled</a>
</nav>
```

- nav-tabs with dropdown

```
<ul class="nav nav-tabs">
  <li class="nav-item">
    <a class="nav-link active" aria-current="page"
href="#">Active</a>
  </li>
  <li class="nav-item dropdown">
    <a class="nav-link dropdown-toggle" data-bs-
toggle="dropdown" href="#" role="button"
    aria-expanded="false">Dropdown</a>
```

```
<ul class="dropdown-menu">
  <li><a class="dropdown-item" href="#">Action</a>
</li>
  <li><a class="dropdown-item" href="#">Another
action</a></li>
  <li><a class="dropdown-item"
href="#">Something else here</a></li>
  <li>
    <hr class="dropdown-divider">
  </li>
  <li><a class="dropdown-item"
href="#">Separated link</a></li>
  </ul>
</li>
<li class="nav-item">
  <a class="nav-link" href="#">Link</a>
</li>
<li class="nav-item">
  <a class="nav-link disabled" href="#"
tabindex="-1" aria-disabled="true">Disabled</a>
</li>
</ul>
```

- nav-pills with dropdown

```
<ul class="nav nav-pills">
  <li class="nav-item">
    <a class="nav-link active" aria-current="page"
href="#">Active</a>
  </li>
  <li class="nav-item dropdown">
    <a class="nav-link dropdown-toggle" data-bs-
toggle="dropdown" href="#" role="button"
    aria-expanded="false">Dropdown</a>
    <ul class="dropdown-menu">
      <li><a class="dropdown-item" href="#">Action
</a></li>
      <li><a class="dropdown-item" href="#">Another
action</a></li>
      <li><a class="dropdown-item"
href="#">Something else here</a></li>
      <li>
        <hr class="dropdown-divider">
```

```
    </li>
    <li><a class="dropdown-item"
href="#">Separated link</a></li>
  </ul>
  </li>
  <li class="nav-item">
    <a class="nav-link" href="#">Link</a>
  </li>
  <li class="nav-item">
    <a class="nav-link disabled" href="#"
tabindex="-1" aria-disabled="true">Disabled</a>
  </li>
</ul>
```

- vertical pills

```
<div class="d-flex align-items-start">
  <div class="nav flex-column nav-pills me-3"
id="v-pills-tab" role="tablist"
aria-orientation="vertical">
    <a class="nav-link active" id="v-pills-home-tab"
data-bs-toggle="pill" href="#v-pills-home"
role="tab"
      aria-controls="v-pills-home" aria-
selected="true">Home</a>
    <a class="nav-link" id="v-pills-profile-tab"
data-bs-toggle="pill" href="#v-pills-profile"
role="tab"
      aria-controls="v-pills-profile" aria-
selected="false">Profile</a>
    <a class="nav-link" id="v-pills-messages-tab"
data-bs-toggle="pill" href="#v-pills-messages"
role="tab"
      aria-controls="v-pills-messages"
aria-selected="false">Messages</a>
    <a class="nav-link" id="v-pills-settings-tab"
data-bs-toggle="pill" href="#v-pills-settings"
role="tab"
      aria-controls="v-pills-settings" aria-
selected="false">Settings</a>
  </div>
  <div class="tab-content" id="v-pills-tabContent">
```

```
    <div class="tab-pane fade show active" id="v-
pills-home" role="tabpanel"
aria-labelledby="v-pills-home-tab">
    Lorem ipsum dolor sit, amet adipisicing elit.
Officiis aperiam accusantium facere minus ,
    id cumque sequi ea animi inventore, sunt iste
dicta libero consectetur ab eligendi
    repudiandae.</div>
    <div class="tab-pane fade" id="v-pills-profile"
role="tabpanel" aria-labelledby="v-pills-profile-ta
b">Lorem,
    ipsum dolor sit amet consectetur adipisicing
elit. Id ducimus veniam optio porro impedit amet
odio aliquam
    officia non nobis quisquam soluta , earum
nulla.</div>
    <div class="tab-pane fade" id="v-pills-messages"
role="tabpanel" aria-labelledby="v-pills-messages-t
ab">Lorem
    ipsum, dolor sit amet consectetur adipisicing
elit. Repellat, dolores blanditiis labore sunt
    aperiam adipisci voluptatem minus tempore ,
aspernatur illum temporibus! Rem, quidem? Reiciendis
    ex perferendis nobis.</div>
    <div class="tab-pane fade" id="v-pills-settings"
role="tabpanel" aria-labelledby="v-pills-settings-t
ab">Lorem
    ipsum dolor sit amet consectetur adipisicing
elit. Harum consectetur voluptates inventore
adipisci quaerat
    asperiores ab blanditiis excepturi sunt,
assumenda est ad voluptatum, iste provident?</div>
  </div>
</div>
```

## OFFCANVAS START

- offcanvas-start (default)

```
<div class="offcanvas offcanvas-start"
tabindex="-1" id="offcanvasStart"
aria-labelledby="offcanvasStart">
  <div class="offcanvas-header">
```

```
    <h5 class="offcanvas-title" id="offcanvasStart">
Offcanvas</h5>
    <button type="button" class="btn-close text-
reset" data-bs-dismiss="offcanvas" aria-
label="Close"></button>
  </div>
  <div class="offcanvas-body">
    <p>
    Some text as placeholder. In real life you have
the elements you have chosen. Like, text, images,
lists,
    etc.
    </p>
  </div>
</div>
```

- offcanvas-end

```
<div class="offcanvas offcanvas-end" tabindex="-1"
id="offcanvasEnd" aria-labelledby="offcanvasEndLa
bel">
  <div class="offcanvas-header">
    <h5 class="offcanvas-title" id="offcanvasEndLabe
l">Offcanvas End</h5>
    <button type="button" class="btn-close text-
reset" data-bs-dismiss="offcanvas" aria-
label="Close"></button>
  </div>
  <div class="offcanvas-body">
    <div>
    Some text as placeholder. In real life you have
the elements you have chosen. Like, text, images,
lists,
    etc.
    </div>
  </div>
</div>
```

- offcanvas-top

```
<div class="offcanvas offcanvas-top" tabindex="-1"
id="offcanvasTop" aria-labelledby="offcanvasTopLa
bel">
  <div class="offcanvas-header">
```

```
  <h5 class="offcanvas-title" id="offcanvasTopLabel">
Offcanvas Top</h5>
  <button type="button" class="btn-close
text-reset" data-bs-dismiss="offcanvas"
aria-label="Close"></button>
  </div>
  <div class="offcanvas-body">
    <div>
      Some text as placeholder. In real life you have
the elements you have chosen. Like, text, images,
lists,
      etc.
    </div>
  </div>
</div>
```

- offcanvas-bottom

```
<div class="offcanvas offcanvas-bottom"
tabindex="-1" id="offcanvasBottom"
aria-labelledby="offcanvasBottomLabel">
  <div class="offcanvas-header">
    <h5 class="offcanvas-title" id="offcanvasBottomL
abel">Offcanvas Bottom</h5>
    <button type="button" class="btn-close
text-reset" data-bs-dismiss="offcanvas"
aria-label="Close"></button>
  </div>
  <div class="offcanvas-body">
    <div>
      Some text as placeholder. In real life you have the
elements you have chosen. Like, text, images, lists,
      etc.
    </div>
  </div>
</div>
```

## PLACEHOLDERS

Used to show something is still loading.

- placeholder

```
<p aria-hidden="true">
  <span class="placeholder col-6"></span>
```

```
</p>
<a href="#" class="btn btn-primary disabled
placeholder col-4" aria-hidden="true"></a>
```

- placeholder bg-{color}
```
<span class="placeholder col-12 bg-primary"></span>
```

- placeholder-lg
```
<span class="placeholder col-12 placeholder-lg">
</span>
```

- placeholder-sm
```
<span class="placeholder col-12 placeholder-sm">
</span>
```

- placeholder-xs
```
<span class="placeholder col-12 placeholder-xs">
</span>
```

- placeholder-glow
```
<p class="placeholder-glow">
  <span class="placeholder col-12"></span>
</p>
```

- placeholder-wave
```
<p class="placeholder-wave">
  <span class="placeholder col-12"></span>
</p>
```

## PAGINATION

Used to show that a series of related content exists across multiple pages.

- pagination
```
<nav aria-label="Page navigation">
  <ul class="pagination">
    <li class="page-item">
      <a class="page-link" href="#"
aria-label="Previous">
        <span aria-hidden="true">«</span>
      </a>
    </li>
    <li class="page-item"><a class="page-link"
href="#">1</a></li>
```

```
    <li class="page-item"><a class="page-link"
href="#">2</a></li>
    <li class="page-item"><a class="page-link"
href="#">3</a></li>
    <li class="page-item">
      <a class="page-link" href="#"
aria-label="Next">
        <span aria-hidden="true">»</span>
      </a>
    </li>
  </ul>
</nav>
```

- disabled page-item

```
<nav aria-label="Page navigation">
  <ul class="pagination">
    <li class="page-item disabled">
      <a class="page-link" href="#" tabindex="-1"
aria-disabled="true">Previous</a>
    </li>
    <li class="page-item"><a class="page-link"
href="#">1</a></li>
    <li class="page-item active"
aria-current="page">
      <a class="page-link" href="#">2</a>
    </li>
    <li class="page-item"><a class="page-link"
href="#">3</a></li>
    <li class="page-item">
      <a class="page-link" href="#">Next</a>
    </li>
  </ul>
</nav>
```

- active page-item

```
<nav aria-label="Page navigation">
  <ul class="pagination">
    <li class="page-item disabled">
      <a class="page-link" href="#" tabindex="-1"
aria-disabled="true">Previous</a>
    </li>
    <li class="page-item"><a class="page-link"
href="#">1</a></li>
```

```
    <li class="page-item active"
aria-current="page">
      <a class="page-link" href="#">2</a>
    </li>
    <li class="page-item"><a class="page-link"
href="#">3</a></li>
    <li class="page-item">
      <a class="page-link" href="#">Next</a>
    </li>
  </ul>
</nav>
```

- pagination-lg

```
<nav aria-label="Large page navigation">
  <ul class="pagination pagination-lg">
    <li class="page-item disabled"><span
class="page-link">Previous</span></li>
    <li class="page-item active" aria-
current="page"><a class="page-link" href="#">1
</a></li>
    <li class="page-item"><span class="page-
link">2</span></li>
    <li class="page-item"><a class="page-link"
href="#">3</a></li>
    <li class="page-item"><a class="page-link"
href="#">Next</a></li>
  </ul>
</nav>
```

- pagination-sm

```
<nav aria-label="Small page navigation">
  <ul class="pagination pagination-sm">
    <li class="page-item disabled"><span
class="page-link">Previous</span></li>
    <li class="page-item active" aria-
current="page"><a class="page-link" href="#">1
</a></li>
    <li class="page-item"><span class="page-
link">2</span></li>
    <li class="page-item"><a class="page-link"
href="#">3</a></li>
```

```
    <li class="page-item"><a class="page-link"
href="#">Next</a></li>
    </ul>
</nav>
```

## SCROLLSPY

Used to automatically update Bootstrap navigation components based on scroll position to indicate which link is currently active.

- data-bs-spy

```
<!-- Custom css that makes this example work like
it does: -->
<style type="text/css">
  .scrollspy-example {
    position: relative;
    height: 200px;
    margin-top: .5rem;
    overflow: auto;
  }
</style>
```

## CHAPTER 11

# Cheat Sheet 4

```
<nav id="navbar-scrollspy" class="navbar navbar-
light bg-light px-4">
  <a class="navbar-brand" href="#">Navbar</a>
  <ul class="nav nav-pills">
    <li class="nav-item">
      <a class="nav-link" href="#fat">@fat</a>
    </li>
    <li class="nav-item">
      <a class="nav-link" href="#mdo">@mdo</a>
    </li>
    <li class="nav-item dropdown">
      <a class="nav-link dropdown-toggle" data-bs-
toggle="dropdown" href="#" role="button"
        aria-expanded="false">Dropdown</a>
      <ul class="dropdown-menu dropdown-menu-end">
        <li><a class="dropdown-item"
href="#one">one</a></li>
        <li><a class="dropdown-item"
href="#two">two</a></li>
        <li>
          <hr class="dropdown-divider">
        </li>
        <li><a class="dropdown-item"
href="#three">three</a></li>
      </ul>
    </li>
  </ul>
```

DOI: 10.1201/9781003309383-11

```
</nav>
<div data-bs-spy="scroll" data-bs-target="#navbar-
scrollspy" data-bs-offset="0" tabindex="0"
class="scrollspy-example">
  <h4 id="fat">@fat</h4>
  <p>Lorem ipsum dolor sit consectetur adipisicing
elit. Voluptatem corrupti perspiciatis distinctio,
officia
    ipsam debitis animi hic? Iusto autem est
accusantium quas recusandae consectetur eligendi at
et praesentium
    placeat dignissimos, quasi ipsum neque explicabo
non, maxime nemo reprehenderit corporis doloribus
amet ab omnis
    dolorum, debitis ipsam? Nulla veritatis, fugiat
cum possimus minima reiciendis eos exercitationem
numquam a
    officia sunt voluptatibus. Ducimus et porro non
necessitatibus quae possimus voluptate libero
ratione, iure
    sint! Aspernatur autem saepe doloribus
perferendis eos eaque quo ex. Reiciendis neque
quidem odio, beatae,
    similique eaque iusto voluptatem quae eveniet
unde accusamus iure pariatur consequatur distinctio
qui error?</p>
  <h4 id="mdo">@mdo</h4>
  <p>Lorem ipsum dolor, sit amet adipisicing elit.
Quisquam corporis esse fugiat alias, aut libero
    assumenda saepe neque doloribus ducimus sit
pariatur repudiandae sequi sed dolore culpa vero
itaque! Iure quos
    rerum odit, ducimus culpa quidem nisi voluptas
possimus accusantium iusto, harum hic vel? Unde
illum, odit
    repellendus impedit magni dolores. Minus sunt
laboriosam quisquam eligendi cumque aliquam quas
pariatur minima
    ut ea odio ipsum accusamus amet nostrum,
consectetur ullam deleniti esse debitis repellat
harum nemo illum
    saepe. Molestias autem inventore libero nam
aliquam molestiae, aliquid temporibus magnam quod
iste ut
```

```
    laudantium, adipisci illo enim mollitia
cupiditate reiciendis veniam pariatur.</p>
   <h4 id="one">one</h4>
   <p>Lorem ipsum dolor sit amet adipisicing elit.
Voluptates rem quidem ea exercitationem adipisci non a
   quaerat ducimus reprehenderit officiis ad
aliquid laborum tempora repellendus cupiditate,
perferendis officia
   inventore unde temporibus. Assumenda iste
maiores vitae ea quibusdam omnis vero porro
doloremque. Dolore officia
   cumque ad consectetur harum asperiores, expedita
sit dolores dolorum laboriosam laudantium dolor
repellendus,
   tempora, aliquam omnis quis itaque totam laborum
quaerat. Iure tempora ab vero. Doloribus maxime
distinctio
   dignissimos alias est error incidunt
repudiandae. Tenetur incidunt cupiditate dolore,
odio possimus ab
   voluptatem minima! Odit non culpa ad fugit ab.
Accusamus dicta beatae rem, obcaecati corrupti aut
quaerat!</p>
   <h4 id="two">two</h4>
   <p>Lorem ipsum dolor sit, consectetur adipisicing
elit. Quod asperiores unde illo labore, neque rerum.
   Dignissimos cum voluptatum expedita recusandae
ullam suscipit ipsam in perferendis porro error
autem nulla
   consequuntur delectus ipsa sint magnam voluptate
asperiores excepturi dolor, nisi perspiciatis?
Consequatur
   doloremque laudantium facere quae impedit nemo
deleniti in delectus recusandae enim neque officia
molestiae
   voluptatibus sed ad, maxime ratione? Fugit
reprehenderit iusto voluptates, facilis, impedit
delectus quis eum
   praesentium, expedita qui hic fuga neque nobis.
Et ad necessitatibus illum blanditiis suscipit
excepturi nobis
   autem ipsam nulla laboriosam quasi fugiat
aliquid quas dolorem, fugit accusantium eaque ex
neque atque ea!</p>
```

```html
<h4 id="three">three</h4>
<p>Lorem ipsum dolor sit consectetur adipisicing
elit. Fugit eum quod autem temporibus, voluptatem
doloribus
    optio alias deleniti aperiam architecto sit rem
accusamus voluptas eius facilis! Aperiam, vitae
laboriosam ullam
    doloremque iure ut ipsam blanditiis aliquid non
sunt quae voluptatem hic nisi cum. Nulla, incidunt
harum
    perferendis provident ad odit perspiciatis quis
accusamus maiores nam saepe at necessitatibus
temporibus
    corrupti in voluptas, aut fugit quod rerum est
minima esse iste! Mollitia modi officia temporibus
repellat
    praesentium reiciendis quam officiis magnam
perspiciatis nulla nobis tenetur nesciunt
reprehenderit autem
    deserunt animi sed a quae, earum quasi! Expedita
nisi nemo accusamus nesciunt ipsum!</p>
</div>
```

- nested data-bs-spy

```html
<!-- Custom css that makes this example work like
it does: -->
<style type="text/css">
  .scrollspy-example-2 {
    position: relative;
    height: 350px;
    overflow: auto;
  }
</style>
<div class="row">
  <div class="col-4">
    <nav id="nested-navbar-scrollspy" class="navbar
navbar-light bg-light flex-column">
      <a class="navbar-brand" href="#">Navbar</a>
      <nav class="nav nav-pills flex-column">
        <a class="nav-link" href="#item-1">Item 1</a>
        <nav class="nav nav-pills flex-column">
          <a class="nav-link ms-3 my-1" href=
"#item-1-1">Item 1-1</a>
```

```
        <a class="nav-link ms-3 my-1" href="#item-
1-2">Item 1-2</a>
        </nav>
        <a class="nav-link" href="#item-2">Item 2</a>
        <a class="nav-link" href="#item-3">Item 3</a>
        <nav class="nav nav-pills flex-column">
            <a class="nav-link ms-3 my-1" href="#item-
3-1">Item 3-1</a>
            <a class="nav-link ms-3 my-1" href="#item-
3-2">Item 3-2</a>
        </nav>
      </nav>
    </nav>
  </div>
  <div class="col-8">
    <div data-bs-spy="scroll" data-bs-target="#nes
ted-navbar-scrollspy" data-bs-offset="0"
tabindex="0"
        class="scrollspy-example-2">
      <h4 id="item-1">Item 1</h4>
      <p>Lorem ipsum dolor , amet consectetur
adipisicing elit. Consequuntur assumenda voluptates
minima natus,
        consequatur dolor porro. Facilis dolorem
dolor necessitatibus architecto hic iste porro
consectetur
        officia rem velit voluptates expedita, in
quia ab nesciunt magnam. Aut cum repellat laudantium
eligendi.
        Debitis quis, ex mollitia consequuntur maxime
deleniti atque beatae omnis iste excepturi iusto
inventore
        tenetur autem ipsum placeat vero modi neque
quibusdam architecto id? Placeat soluta, enim, vero
        blanditiis iusto ad aperiam hic a atque
delectus impedit, in repellat molestiae nulla libero
sit? Iste
        corrupti quisquam cumque eveniet iure error
voluptatum quasi incidunt, maiores quam blanditiis
repellat,
        in sint neque.</p>
      <h5 id="item-1-1">Item 1-1</h5>
```

```
    <p>Lorem ipsum dolor amet consectetur,
adipisicing elit. Recusandae, nihil sed id nostrum
possimus iste
    commodi! Necessitatibus, magni, est
cupiditate animi voluptas sequi sapiente dolor ullam
voluptatem
    assumenda tempore. Natus necessitatibus
aliquid, reiciendis assumenda officiis doloribus nam
eaque. Eum
    magni eos odio vel cum magnam, tenetur iusto
esse illum voluptate possimus, dolorem quos alias,
suscipit
    porro at ratione quasi repellendus facilis
dolor eligendi a! Maxime, aliquam earum, suscipit
labore
    sint, repellat minus doloremque rerum beatae
ratione quas fugiat iste eum veritatis quod modi
quae quasi
    adipisci ullam nobis nam? Quae, asperiores.
Cumque architecto doloremque blanditiis quas ad aut
    temporibus eum.</p>
    <h5 id="item-1-2">Item 1-2</h5>
    <p>Lorem ipsum dolor amet consectetur,
adipisicing elit. Dolores distinctio earum qui eius
ducimus ab
    ratione culpa aspernatur error repellendus!
Possimus facere aliquam architecto, quam tenetur
nemo,
    magnam aut quidem laborum quae vel, totam
libero? Quos in aperiam consequatur provident
nesciunt
    pariatur ipsa, illo nemo aut fuga porro,
architecto maiores. Cupiditate, qui tempore. Vero
porro
    delectus assumenda quia neque tempora unde
debitis voluptates fuga? Reprehenderit neque iure id
    voluptate quam deserunt officiis minima,
eligendi accusamus labore porro, sapiente
repudiandae debitis
    beatae est non quia culpa incidunt excepturi
praesentium distinctio voluptas iste! Enim, autem porro
    quod cum similique ab at hic.</p>
```

```
    <h4 id="item-2">Item 2</h4>
    <p>Lorem ipsum dolor amet consectetur,
adipisicing elit. Quisquam, quo. Odio veniam dicta
fugiat nobis
        sed suscipit quos eos quaerat molestiae atque
rem distinctio sit consectetur nemo quia
reprehenderit
        nesciunt exercitationem harum ipsum aliquam,
alias necessitatibus eum ullam! Sit quibusdam,
fugiat quos
        sapiente pariatur ipsam ipsum esse nostrum
voluptatem, ipsa neque, cumque a aspernatur. Eveniet
itaque
        dicta, saepe explicabo dignissimos corrupti
ab ipsa quod minus repellendus obcaecati id,
consectetur
        distinctio fugiat sequi nulla numquam magnam
voluptatum veniam? Aut praesentium omnis asperiores
iure
        tenetur mollitia repudiandae excepturi
sapiente voluptatem exercitationem, voluptate
dolorum? Omnis
        eveniet natus, nemo vel aliquam vitae
dignissimos. Sapiente!</p>
    <h4 id="item-3">Item 3</h4>
    <p>Lorem ipsum dolor amet consectetur
adipisicing elit. Molestias, architecto consequuntur
voluptatem
        voluptatum debitis quidem ipsum! Vel repellat
aspernatur quod delectus? Assumenda iusto beatae
pariatur
        tenetur aliquam veritatis modi unde
repudiandae voluptates laudantium perferendis maxime
necessitatibus
        inventore rem earum quasi dolor dolore
sapiente nemo cum voluptate, ut quibusdam culpa
facilis!
        Reprehenderit accusantium neque ipsum autem!
Officia impedit libero aspernatur placeat atque a eos,
        aperiam aut incidunt fugit cum minus quasi
numquam dolor eius adipisci earum sunt iste quos
distinctio
```

mollitia sint id optio vel? Et nesciunt
expedita ad nemo tempora provident doloremque.
Voluptatibus iste
    ad, autem eligendi saepe blanditiis aut!</p>
    <h5 id="item-3-1">Item 3-1</h5>
    <p>Lorem ipsum dolor amet consectetur
adipisicing elit. Similique tempore culpa
voluptatibus nostrum ut
    nulla mollitia. Nisi dignissimos unde
adipisci dolorum suscipit nesciunt maxime ducimus
iusto et quos
    modi provident nihil, magni commodi facilis,
omnis at, error eius. Labore, ipsam! Perspiciatis
molestiae
    rem ipsam consequuntur voluptatibus quia non
consectetur, enim, nisi eum impedit? Eligendi minima
iste
    minus perspiciatis quo enim, dignissimos
culpa reiciendis optio nisi, corporis aliquam iusto
corrupti
    laborum. Expedita, eum quibusdam explicabo,
harum perferendis optio placeat perspiciatis earum
delectus
    animi, beatae corporis fugit repudiandae
dicta voluptate iste. Tenetur aspernatur quaerat ab
impedit
    dignissimos reiciendis atque iure pariatur
earum!</p>
    <h5 id="item-3-2">Item 3-2</h5>
    <p>Lorem ipsum dolor amet, consectetur
adipisicing elit. Iusto numquam quidem, fugit
accusantium magnam
    quod tenetur et libero aliquam quibusdam
corporis minus. Unde illum nisi labore omnis numquam
esse
    impedit minima facere quam doloribus illo
suscipit deleniti commodi facilis perspiciatis quasi
animi
    dolore libero, sequi reprehenderit doloremque
accusantium magnam aut. Vel quaerat voluptatibus ab
    consectetur blanditiis facilis repellendus
voluptatum consequatur beatae illum ratione pariatur
mollitia

deleniti quisquam expedita ea doloremque
sint, dignissimos quo commodi sed. Earum omnis
blanditiis
     officiis odit magnam quo facere voluptate
aliquam ut dignissimos dolore sequi, voluptas quod
corrupti
     sed doloribus porro quaerat, fugit
accusantium reprehenderit fugiat!</p>
   </div>
  </div>
</div>

## PROGRESS

Used to feature custom progress bars.

- progress

```
<div class="progress">
  <div class="progress-bar" role="progressbar"
style="width: 35%" aria-valuenow="35"
aria-valuemin="0"
    aria-valuemax="100">
  </div>
</div>
```

- progress-bar

```
<div class="progress">
  <div class="progress-bar" role="progressbar"
style="width: 35%" aria-valuenow="35"
aria-valuemin="0"
    aria-valuemax="100"></div>
</div>
```

- progress with label

```
<div class="progress">
  <div class="progress-bar" role="progressbar"
style="width: 35%" aria-valuenow="35"
aria-valuemin="0"
    aria-valuemax="100">35%</div>
</div>
```

- progress with height

```
<div class="progress" style="height: 4px;">
```

```
<div class="progress-bar" role="progressbar"
style="width: 35%" aria-valuenow="35" aria-valuemin="0"
   aria-valuemax="100"></div>
</div>
```

- progress-bar bg-{color}

```
<div class="progress">
  <div class="progress-bar bg-danger"
role="progressbar" style="width: 35%"
aria-valuenow="35" aria-valuemin="0"
   aria-valuemax="100"></div>
</div>
```

- multiple progress-bar

```
<div class="progress">
  <div class="progress-bar bg-success"
role="progressbar" style="width: 30%"
aria-valuenow="30" aria-valuemin="0"
   aria-valuemax="100"></div>
  <div class="progress-bar bg-warning"
role="progressbar" style="width: 15%"
aria-valuenow="15" aria-valuemin="0"
   aria-valuemax="100"></div>
  <div class="progress-bar bg-danger"
role="progressbar" style="width: 25%"
aria-valuenow="25" aria-valuemin="0"
   aria-valuemax="100"></div>
</div>
```

- progress-bar-striped

```
<div class="progress">
  <div class="progress-bar progress-bar-striped"
role="progressbar" style="width: 55%" aria-
valuenow="55" aria-valuemin="0" aria-
valuemax="100"></div>
 </div>
```

- progress-bar-striped bg-{color}

```
<div class="progress">
  <div class="progress-bar progress-bar-striped
bg-success" role="progressbar" style="width: 55%"
aria-valuenow="55" aria-valuemin="0" aria-
valuemax="100"></div>
 </div>
```

- progress-bar-animated

```
<div class="progress">
  <div class="progress-bar progress-bar-striped
progress-bar-animated" role="progressbar"
style="width: 55%" aria-valuenow="55" aria-
valuemin="0" aria-valuemax="100"></div>
  </div>
```

- progress-bar-animated bg-{color}

```
<div class="progress">
  <div class="progress-bar bg-secondary progress-
bar-striped progress-bar-animated"
role="progressbar" style="width: 55%" aria-
valuenow="55" aria-valuemin="0" aria-
valuemax="100"></div>
  </div>
```

## POPOVERS

Used to add popover.

- Popover on right

```
<!-- Note: A custom script used to activate
popovers:
var popoverTriggerList = [].slice.call(document.qu
erySelectorAll('[data-bs-toggle="popover"]'))
var popoverList = popoverTriggerList.map(function
(popoverTriggerEl) {
 return new bootstrap.Popover(popoverTriggerEl)
})
-->
<button type="button" class="btn btn-primary" data-
bs-container="body" data-bs-toggle="popover"
  data-bs-placement="right" data-bs-content="Vivamus
sagittis lacus vel laoreet rutrum faucibus."
  data-bs-original-title="" title="">
  Popover on right
</button>
```

- Popover on top

```
<!-- Note: A custom script used to activate
popovers:
var popoverTriggerList = [].slice.call(document.qu
erySelectorAll('[data-bs-toggle="popover"]'))
```

```
var popoverList = popoverTriggerList.map(function
(popoverTriggerEl) {
 return new bootstrap.Popover(popoverTriggerEl)
})
-->
<button type="button" class="btn btn-primary" data-
bs-container="body" data-bs-toggle="popover"
data-bs-placement="top"
  data-bs-content="Vivamus sagittis lacus vel
laoreet rutrum faucibus." data-bs-original-title=""
title="">
  Popover on top
</button>
```

- Popover on bottom

```
<!-- Note: A custom script used to activate
popovers:
var popoverTriggerList = [].slice.call(document.qu
erySelectorAll('[data-bs-toggle="popover"]'))
var popoverList = popoverTriggerList.map(function
(popoverTriggerEl) {
 return new bootstrap.Popover(popoverTriggerEl)
})
-->
<button type="button" class="btn btn-primary" data-
bs-container="body" data-bs-toggle="popover"
  data-bs-placement="bottom" data-bs-
content="Vivamus sagittis vel augue laoreet rutrum
faucibus."
  data-bs-original-title="" title="">
  Popover on bottom
</button>
```

- Popover on left

```
<!-- Note: A custom script used to activate
popovers:
var popoverTriggerList = [].slice.call(document.qu
erySelectorAll('[data-bs-toggle="popover"]'))
var popoverList = popoverTriggerList.map(function
(popoverTriggerEl) {
 return new bootstrap.Popover(popoverTriggerEl)
})
-->
```

```
<button type="button" class="btn btn-primary" data-
bs-container="body" data-bs-toggle="popover"
data-bs-placement="left"
  data-bs-content="Vivamus sagittis lacus vel
laoreet rutrum faucibus." data-bs-original-title=""
title="">
  Popover on left
</button>
```

- Dismissible popover

```
<!-- Note: A custom script used to activate
popovers:
var popoverTriggerList = [].slice.call(document.qu
erySelectorAll('[data-bs-toggle="popover"]'))
var popoverList = popoverTriggerList.map(function
(popoverTriggerEl) {
 return new bootstrap.Popover(popoverTriggerEl)
})
-->
<a tabindex="0" class="btn btn-primary"
role="button" data-bs-toggle="popover" data-bs-
trigger="focus" title=""
  data-bs-content="And here's some amazing content.
It's very engaging. Right?"
  data-bs-original-title="Dismissible
popover">Dismissible popover</a>
```

## TOASTS

Used to send push notifications to your visitors with an easily customizable alert message.

- toast

```
<!-- Note: A custom script used to activate toasts:
var toastElList = [].slice.call(document.querySe
lectorAll('.toast'))
var toastList = toastElList.map(function (toastEl) {
 return new bootstrap.Toast(toastEl, {
  autohide: false
 }).show()
})
-->
<div class="toast toast-demo fade show" role="alert"
aria-live="assertive" aria-atomic="true">
```

```
  <div class="toast-header">
    <strong class="me-auto">Bootstrap</strong>
    <small>11 mins ago</small>
    <button type="button" class="btn-close" data-bs-
dismiss="toast" aria-label="Close"></button>
  </div>
  <div class="toast-body">
    Hello, world! This is a toast message.
  </div>
</div>
```

- toast with button

```
<!-- Note: A custom script used to activate toasts:
var toastElList = [].slice.call(document.querySe
lectorAll('.toast'))
var toastList = toastElList.map(function (toastEl) {
 return new bootstrap.Toast(toastEl, {
  autohide: false
 }).show()
})
-->
<div class="toast toast-demo fade show"
role="alert" aria-live="assertive"
aria-atomic="true">
  <div class="toast-body">
    Hello, world! This is a toast message.
    <div class="mt-2 pt-2 border-top">
      <button type="button" class="btn btn-primary
btn-sm">Take action</button>
      <button type="button" class="btn btn-secondary
btn-sm" data-bs-dismiss="toast">Close</button>
    </div>
  </div>
</div>
```

- toast bg-{color} text-{color}

```
<!-- Note: A custom script is used to activate
toasts:
var toastElList = [].slice.call(document.querySe
lectorAll('.toast'))
var toastList = toastElList.map(function (toastEl) {
 return new bootstrap.Toast(toastEl, {
  autohide: false
```

```
     }).show()
  })
  -->
<div class="toast toast-demo d-flex align-items-
center text-white bg-primary border-0 fade show"
role="alert"
  aria-live="assertive" aria-atomic="true">
  <div class="toast-body">
    Hello, world! This is a toast message.
  </div>
  <button type="button" class="btn-close btn-close-
white ms-auto me-2" data-bs-dismiss="toast"
    aria-label="Close"></button>
</div>
```

## SPINNERS

It is used to indicate the loading state of a component.

- spinner-border

```
<div class="spinner-border" role="status">
  <span class="visually-hidden">Loading...</span>
</div>
```

- spinner-border text-{color}

```
<div class="spinner-border text-primary"
role="status">
  <span class="visually-hidden">Loading...</span>
</div>
```

- spinner-border-sm

```
<div class="spinner-border spinner-border-sm"
role="status">
  <span class="visually-hidden">Loading...</span>
</div>
```

- spinner-grow

```
<div class="spinner-grow" role="status">
  <span class="visually-hidden">Loading...</span>
</div>
```

- spinner-grow text-{color}

```
<div class="spinner-grow text-primary" role="status">
```

```
    <span class="visually-hidden">Loading...</span>
</div>
```

- spinner-grow-sm

```
<div class="spinner-grow spinner-grow-sm"
role="status">
    <span class="visually-hidden">Loading...</span>
</div>
```

## TOOLTIPS

Used to add tooltips.

- tooltip on top

```
<!-- Note: A custom script used to activate
tooltips:
var tooltipTriggerList = [].slice.call(document.qu
erySelectorAll('[data-bs-toggle="tooltip"]'))
var tooltipList = tooltipTriggerList.map(function
(tooltipTriggerEl) {
 return new bootstrap.Tooltip(tooltipTriggerEl)
})
-->
<button type="button" class="btn btn-primary" data-
bs-toggle="tooltip" data-bs-placement="top" title=""
  data-bs-original-title="Tooltip on top">
  Tooltip on top
</button>
```

- tooltip on right

```
<!-- Note: A custom script used to activate
tooltips:
var tooltipTriggerList = [].slice.call(document.qu
erySelectorAll('[data-bs-toggle="tooltip"]'))
var tooltipList = tooltipTriggerList.map(function
(tooltipTriggerEl) {
 return new bootstrap.Tooltip(tooltipTriggerEl)
})
-->
<button type="button" class="btn btn-primary" data-bs-
toggle="tooltip" data-bs-placement="right" title=""
  data-bs-original-title="Tooltip on right">
  Tooltip on right
</button>
```

- tooltip on bottom

```
<!-- Note: A custom script used to activate
tooltips:
var tooltipTriggerList = [].slice.call(document.qu
erySelectorAll('[data-bs-toggle="tooltip"]'))
var tooltipList = tooltipTriggerList.map(function
(tooltipTriggerEl) {
 return new bootstrap.Tooltip(tooltipTriggerEl)
})
-->
<button type="button" class="btn btn-primary" data-
bs-toggle="tooltip" data-bs-placement="bottom"
title=""
 data-bs-original-title="Tooltip on bottom">
 Tooltip on bottom
</button>
```

- tooltip on left

```
<!-- Note: A custom script is used to activate
tooltips:
var tooltipTriggerList = [].slice.call(document.qu
erySelectorAll('[data-bs-toggle="tooltip"]'))
var tooltipList = tooltipTriggerList.map(function
(tooltipTriggerEl) {
 return new bootstrap.Tooltip(tooltipTriggerEl)
})
-->
<button type="button" class="btn btn-primary" data-
bs-toggle="tooltip" data-bs-placement="left" title=""
 data-bs-original-title="Tooltip on left">
 Tooltip on left
</button>
```

- tooltip with HTML

```
<!-- Note: A custom script is used to activate
tooltips:
var tooltipTriggerList = [].slice.call(document.qu
erySelectorAll('[data-bs-toggle="tooltip"]'))
var tooltipList = tooltipTriggerList.map(function
(tooltipTriggerEl) {
 return new bootstrap.Tooltip(tooltipTriggerEl)
})
-->
```

```
<button type="button" class="btn btn-primary" data-
bs-toggle="tooltip" data-bs-html="true" title=""
  data-bs-original-title="<em>Tooltip</em> with HTML">
  Tooltip with HTML
</button>
```

## HELPERS

- clearfix

```
<div class="clearfix">...</div>
```

- link-{color}

```
<a href="#" class="link-primary">Primary link</a>
```

- ratio-{ratio}

```
<!-- Different radio can be used with the help of
.ratio-{1x1|4x3|16x9|21x9} class -->
<div class="ratio ratio-16x9 mb-3">
  <iframe src="https://www.youtube.com/embed/
zpOULjyy-n8?rel=0" title="YouTube_video"
allowfullscreen=""></iframe>
</div>
<!-- To have a custom ratio, use the following: -->
<div class="ratio" style="--aspect-ratio: 30%;">
  <iframe src="https://www.youtube.com/embed/
zpOULjyy-n8?rel=0" title="YouTube_video"
allowfullscreen=""></iframe>
</div>
```

- fixed-top

```
<div class="fixed-top bd-highlight">Fixed top</div>
```

- fixed-bottom

```
<div class="fixed-bottom bd-highlight">Fixed
bottom</div>
```

- sticky-top

```
<div class="sticky-top bd-highlight">Sticky top</div>
```

- sticky-*-top
```
<div class="sticky-md-top bd-highlight">Sticky
top</div>
```

- visually hidden

```
<h2 class="visually-hidden">Title for screen
readers</h2>
```

- visually-hidden-focusable

```
<a class="visually-hidden-focusable"
href="#content">Skip to main content</a>
```

- stretched-link

```
<!-- .stretched-link class will work properly only
if it's parent element gets position: relative; or
some transform property -->
<div class="card">
  <img src="assets/images/bs-images/img-2x1.png"
class="card-img-top" alt="card-img-top">
  <div class="card-body">
    <h5 class="card-title">Card with stretched
link</h5>
    <p class="card-text">Some quick example text to
build on the card title and make up the bulk of the
card's
    content.</p>
    <a href="#" class="btn btn-primary stretched-
link">Go somewhere</a>
  </div>
</div>
```

- text-truncate

```
<!-- .text-truncate class requires display:
inline-block; or display: block; -->
<!-- Block level -->
<div class="row">
  <div class="col-2 text-truncate">
   Lorem ipsum dolor sit consectetur adipisicing
elit. Voluptate nisi, animi odit repellendus eos unde.
  </div>
</div>
<!-- Inline level -->
<span class="d-inline-block text-truncate"
style="max-width: 150px;">
 Lorem ipsum dolor sit consectetur adipisicing elit.
Voluptate nisi, animi odit repellendus eos unde.
</span>
```

- vstack

```
<div class="vstack gap-3">
  <div class="bg-light border">First item</div>
  <div class="bg-light border">Second item</div>
  <div class="bg-light border">Third item</div>
</div>
```

- hstack

```
<div class="hstack gap-3">
  <div class="bg-light border">First item</div>
  <div class="bg-light border">Second item</div>
  <div class="bg-light border">Third item</div>
</div>
```

- vr

```
<div class="hstack gap-3">
  <span>Second item</span>
  <div class="vr"></div>
  <span>Third item</span>
</div>
```

## CHAPTER SUMMARY

In this last chapter, we revised every concept of Bootstrap. In this cheat sheet, we went through every component of Bootstrap. We started by talking about what Bootstrap is and its features. Then we learned how we could set up Bootstrap in our system. We then learned about screen sizing, the grid system, typography, utility classes, and finally, we learned about all the key components.

# Bibliography

@MDBootstrap. (n.d.a). *Angular Radio with Bootstrap – Examples & Tutorial.* MDB – Material Design for Bootstrap; mdbootstrap.com. Retrieved July 11, 2022, from https://mdbootstrap.com/docs/b5/angular/forms/radio/

@MDBootstrap. (n.d.b). *Bootstrap 4 Breadcrumb – Examples & Tutorial.* MDB – Material Design for Bootstrap; mdbootstrap.com. Retrieved July 11, 2022, from https://mdbootstrap.com/docs/b4/jquery/navigation/breadcrumb/

@MDBootstrap. (n.d.c). *Bootstrap 4 Navs – Examples & Tutorial.* MDB – Material Design for Bootstrap; mdbootstrap.com. Retrieved July 11, 2022, from https://mdbootstrap.com/docs/b4/jquery/navigation/navs/

@MDBootstrap. (n.d.d). *Bootstrap 4 Pagination – Examples & Tutorial.* MDB – Material Design for Bootstrap; mdbootstrap.com. Retrieved July 11, 2022, from https://mdbootstrap.com/docs/b4/jquery/components/pagination/

@MDBootstrap. (n.d.e). *Bootstrap 4 Panels – Examples & Tutorial.* MDB – Material Design for Bootstrap; mdbootstrap.com. Retrieved July 11, 2022, from https://mdbootstrap.com/docs/b4/jquery/components/panels/

@MDBootstrap. (n.d.f). *Bootstrap Alerts – Examples & Tutorial.* MDB – Material Design for Bootstrap; mdbootstrap.com. Retrieved July 11, 2022, from https://mdbootstrap.com/docs/standard/components/alerts/

@MDBootstrap. (n.d.g). *Bootstrap Breakpoints – Examples & Tutorial.* MDB – Material Design for Bootstrap; v1.mdbootstrap.com. Retrieved July 11, 2022, from https://v1.mdbootstrap.com/docs/standard/layout/breakpoints/

@MDBootstrap. (n.d.h). *Bootstrap Cards – Examples & Tutorial.* MDB – Material Design for Bootstrap; mdbootstrap.com. Retrieved July 11, 2022, from https://mdbootstrap.com/docs/standard/components/cards/

@MDBootstrap. (n.d.i). *Bootstrap Carousel – Examples & Tutorial.* MDB – Material Design for Bootstrap; mdbootstrap.com. Retrieved July 11, 2022, from https://mdbootstrap.com/docs/b4/jquery/javascript/carousel/

@MDBootstrap. (n.d.j). *Bootstrap Collapse – Examples & Tutorial.* MDB – Material Design for Bootstrap; mdbootstrap.com. Retrieved July 11, 2022, from https://mdbootstrap.com/docs/standard/components/collapse/

@MDBootstrap. (n.d.k). *Bootstrap Dropdowns – Examples & Tutorial.* MDB – Material Design for Bootstrap; mdbootstrap.com. Retrieved July 11, 2022, from https://mdbootstrap.com/docs/standard/components/dropdowns/

@MDBootstrap. (n.d.l). *Bootstrap List Group – Examples & Tutorial.* MDB – Material Design for Bootstrap; mdbootstrap.com. Retrieved July 11, 2022, from https://mdbootstrap.com/docs/standard/components/list-group/

@MDBootstrap. (n.d.m). *Bootstrap Modal – Examples & Tutorial.* MDB – Material Design for Bootstrap; mdbootstrap.com. Retrieved July 11, 2022, from https://mdbootstrap.com/docs/standard/components/modal/

@MDBootstrap. (n.d.n). *React Buttons with Bootstrap – Examples & Tutorial.* MDB – Material Design for Bootstrap; mdbootstrap.com. Retrieved July 11, 2022, from https://mdbootstrap.com/docs/b5/react/components/ buttons/

@MDBootstrap. (n.d.o). *Tailwind CSS Accordion – Free Examples & Tutorial.* Tailwind Elements; tailwind-elements.com. Retrieved July 11, 2022, from https://tailwind-elements.com/docs/standard/components/accordion/

@MDBootstrap. (n.d.p). *Vue Background – Examples & Tutorial. Bootstrap & Material Design.* MDB – Material Design for Bootstrap; mdbootstrap.com. Retrieved July 11, 2022, from https://mdbootstrap.com/docs/vue/utilities/ background/

@MDBootstrap. (n.d.q). *Vue Bootstrap Accordion – Examples & Tutorial.* MDB – Material Design for Bootstrap; mdbootstrap.com. Retrieved July 11, 2022, from https://mdbootstrap.com/docs/vue/components/accordion/

3 Tips for Speeding Up Your Bootstrap Website – SitePoint. (n.d.). *3 Tips for Speeding Up Your Bootstrap Website – SitePoint*; www.sitepoint.com. Retrieved July 11, 2022, from https://www.sitepoint.com/3-tips-to-speed -up-your-bootstrap-website/

Alerts | Dash Ui – Bootstrap 5 Admin Dashboard Template. (n.d.). *Alerts | Dash Ui – Bootstrap 5 Admin Dashboard Template*; codescandy.com. Retrieved July 11, 2022, from https://codescandy.com/dashui/docs/alerts.html

Andrzej Kopanski, L. H. (n.d.a). *Bootstrap Alerts CoreUI*; coreui.io. Retrieved July 11, 2022, from https://coreui.io/docs/components/alerts/

Andrzej Kopanski, L. H. (n.d.b). *Bootstrap Card CoreUI*; coreui.io. Retrieved July 11, 2022, from https://coreui.io/docs/components/card/

Andrzej Kopanski, L. H. (n.d.c). *Bootstrap Collapse CoreUI*; coreui.io. Retrieved July 11, 2022, from https://coreui.io/docs/components/collapse/

Andrzej Kopanski, L. H. (n.d.d). *Bootstrap Scrollspy CoreUI*; coreui.io. Retrieved July 11, 2022, from https://coreui.io/docs/components/scrollspy/

Andrzej Kopanski, L. H. (n.d.e). *Images CoreUI*; coreui.io. Retrieved July 11, 2022, from https://coreui.io/docs/content/images/

Aprenzel. (2021, January 6). *Using Bootstrap Components with Custom JavaScript – LogRocket Blog.* LogRocket Blog; blog.logrocket.com. https://blog .logrocket.com/using-bootstrap-components-with-custom-javascript/

Best Bootstrap Development Company in Noida, Delhi, India. (n.d.). *Escale Solutions*; www.escalesolutions.com. Retrieved July 11, 2022, from https:// www.escalesolutions.com/services/bootstrap.php

Blazorise Component Library. (n.d.). Blazorise Component Library; blazorise.co m. Retrieved July 11, 2022, from https://blazorise.com/docs/helpers/utili- ties/position

Boosted Contributors, O. and. (n.d.a). *Accordion Boosted v5.0*; boosted.orange .com. Retrieved July 11, 2022, from https://boosted.orange.com/docs/5.0/ components/accordion/

Boosted Contributors, O. and. (n.d.b). *Breadcrumb Boosted v5.1*; boosted.orange .com. Retrieved July 11, 2022, from https://boosted.orange.com/docs/5.1/ components/breadcrumb/

Boosted Contributors, O. and. (n.d.c). *Collapse Boosted v5.0*; boosted.orange.c om. Retrieved July 11, 2022, from https://boosted.orange.com/docs/5.0/ components/collapse/

Boosted Contributors, O. and. (n.d.d). *RTL Boosted v5.1*; boosted.orange.com. Retrieved July 11, 2022, from https://boosted.orange.com/docs/5.1/getting -started/rtl/

Bootstrap – Columns Tutorials. (n.d.). *Bootstrap – Columns Tutorials*; www. techiematrix.com. Retrieved July 11, 2022, from http://www.techiematrix .com/Bootstrap-Columns.html

Bootstrap 4 not Working with Angular 2 App – Stack Overflow. (2017, December 29). *Stack Overflow*; stackoverflow.com. https://stackoverflow.com/questions/48028505/bootstrap-4-not-working-with-angular-2-app

Bootstrap 5 Breadcrumb – AdminKit. (n.d.). *Bootstrap 5 Breadcrumb – AdminKit*; adminkit.io. Retrieved July 11, 2022, from https://adminkit.io/docs/navigation/breadcrumb/

Bootstrap 5 Button Group – AdminKit. (n.d.). *Bootstrap 5 Button Group – AdminKit*; adminkit.io. Retrieved July 11, 2022, from https://adminkit.io/ docs/components/button-group/

Bootstrap 5 Buttons – AdminKit. (n.d.). *Bootstrap 5 Buttons – AdminKit*; adminkit.io. Retrieved July 11, 2022, from https://adminkit.io/docs/components/ buttons/

Bootstrap 5 Colors. (n.d.). Bootstrap 5 Colors; www.w3schools.com. Retrieved July 11, 2022, from https://www.w3schools.com/bootstrap5/bootstrap_colors.php

Bootstrap 5 Colors – DEV Community. (2021, March 29). *DEV Community*; dev .to. https://dev.to/mdbootstrap/bootstrap-5-colors-18ip

Bootstrap 5 Dropdowns – AdminKit. (n.d.). *Bootstrap 5 Dropdowns – AdminKit*; adminkit.io. Retrieved July 11, 2022, from https://adminkit.io/docs/components/dropdowns/

Bootstrap 5 Forms – AdminKit. (n.d.). *Bootstrap 5 Forms – AdminKit*; adminkit .io. Retrieved July 11, 2022, from https://adminkit.io/docs/forms/overview/

Bootstrap 5 List group – AdminKit. (n.d.). *Bootstrap 5 List Group – AdminKit*; adminkit.io. Retrieved July 11, 2022, from https://adminkit.io/docs/components/list-group/

Bootstrap 5 Modal – AdminKit. (n.d.). *Bootstrap 5 Modal – AdminKit*; adminkit.i o. Retrieved July 11, 2022, from https://adminkit.io/docs/components/modal/

Bootstrap 5 Modal – GeeksforGeeks. (2020, September 10). *GeeksforGeeks*; www .geeksforgeeks.org. https://www.geeksforgeeks.org/bootstrap-5-modal/

Bootstrap 5 Scrollspy – AdminKit. (n.d.). *Bootstrap 5 Scrollspy – AdminKit*; adminkit.io. Retrieved July 11, 2022, from https://adminkit.io/docs/navigation/scrollspy/

Bootstrap 5 Spinners – AdminKit. (n.d.). *Bootstrap 5 Spinners – AdminKit*; adminkit.io. Retrieved July 11, 2022, from https://adminkit.io/docs/components/spinners/

Bootstrap 5 Toggle Button. (n.d.). *Bootstrap 5 Toggle Button*; leonardoclarosmd.com. Retrieved July 11, 2022, from https://leonardoclarosmd.com/boe/bootstrap-5-toggle-button

Bootstrap Accordion – Tutorials with Advanced Examples | Torus Kit. (n.d.). *Torus Kit*; toruskit.com. Retrieved July 11, 2022, from https://toruskit.com/docs/components/accordion/

Bootstrap Alerts – Tutorials with Advanced Examples | Torus Kit. (n.d.). *Torus Kit*; toruskit.com. Retrieved July 11, 2022, from https://toruskit.com/docs/components/alerts/

Bootstrap Button group – Tutorials with advanced examples | Torus Kit. (n.d.). *Torus Kit*; toruskit.com. Retrieved July 11, 2022, from https://toruskit.com/docs/components/button-group/

Bootstrap Card – Tutorials with Advanced Examples | Torus Kit. (n.d.). *Torus Kit*; toruskit.com. Retrieved July 11, 2022, from https://toruskit.com/docs/components/card/

Bootstrap Carousel – Tutorials with advanced examples | Torus Kit. (n.d.). *Torus Kit*; toruskit.com. Retrieved July 11, 2022, from https://toruskit.com/docs/components/carousel/

Bootstrap Checks & Radios – Tutorials with Advanced Examples | Torus Kit. (n.d.). *Torus Kit*; toruskit.com. Retrieved July 11, 2022, from https://toruskit.com/docs/forms/checks-and-radios/

Bootstrap Collapse – Tutorials with advanced examples | Torus Kit. (n.d.). *Torus Kit*; toruskit.com. Retrieved July 11, 2022, from https://toruskit.com/docs/components/collapse/

Bootstrap Float – Tutorials with Advanced Examples | Torus Kit. (n.d.). *Torus Kit*; toruskit.com. Retrieved July 11, 2022, from https://toruskit.com/docs/utilities/float/

Bootstrap Form Control – Tutorials with Advanced Examples | Torus Kit. (n.d.). *Torus Kit*; toruskit.com. Retrieved July 11, 2022, from https://toruskit.com/docs/forms/form-control/

Bootstrap Forms Overview – Tutorials with Advanced Examples | Torus Kit. (n.d.). *Torus Kit*; toruskit.com. Retrieved July 11, 2022, from https://toruskit.com/docs/forms/overview/

Bootstrap Modal – Tutorials with Advanced Examples | Torus Kit. (n.d.). *Torus Kit*; toruskit.com. Retrieved July 11, 2022, from https://toruskit.com/docs/components/modal/

Bootstrap Position – Tutorials with Advanced Examples | Torus Kit. (n.d.). *Torus Kit*; toruskit.com. Retrieved July 11, 2022, from https://toruskit.com/docs/utilities/position/

Bootstrap Quick Guide Tutorials. (n.d.). *Bootstrap Quick Guide Tutorials*; www.techiematrix.com. Retrieved July 11, 2022, from http://www.techiematrix.com/Bootstrap-Quick-Guide.html

Bootstrap Scrollspy – Tutorials with Advanced Examples | Torus Kit. (n.d.). *Torus Kit*; toruskit.com. Retrieved July 11, 2022, from https://toruskit.com/docs/components/scrollspy/

Bootstrap Text – Studytonight. (n.d.). *Bootstrap Text – Studytonight*; www.studytonight.com. Retrieved July 11, 2022, from https://www.studytonight.com/bootstrap/bootstrap-text

Breadcrumb – Bootstrap 5 – W3cubDocs. (n.d.). *Breadcrumb – Bootstrap 5 – W3cubDocs*; docs.w3cub.com. Retrieved July 11, 2022, from https://docs.w3cub.com/bootstrap~5/components/breadcrumb/index

Browsers and Devices. (n.d.). *Material Design for WordPress*; mdwp.io. Retrieved July 11, 2022, from https://mdwp.io/browsers-and-devices/

Buttons – Bootstrap 5 – W3cubDocs. (n.d.). *Buttons – Bootstrap 5 – W3cubDocs*; docs.w3cub.com. Retrieved July 11, 2022, from https://docs.w3cub.com/bootstrap~5/components/buttons/index

Cards – Muze Documentation | Muze – Responsive Website Template. (n.d.). *Cards – Muze Documentation | Muze – Responsive Website Template*; fabrx.co. Retrieved July 11, 2022, from https://fabrx.co/muze-dashboards/documentation/cards.html

Clearfix | Trimble Modus Bootstrap Developer Guide. (2022, July 5). *Modus Bootstrap Developer Guide*; modus-bootstrap.trimble.com. https://modus-bootstrap.trimble.com/utilities/clearfix/

Close Icon | Trimble Modus React Bootstrap Developer Guide. (n.d.). *Close Icon | Trimble Modus React Bootstrap Developer Guide*; modus-react-bootstrap.trimble.com. Retrieved July 11, 2022, from https://modus-react-bootstrap.trimble.com/utilities/close-icon/

Codescandy. (n.d.). *Spinners – Bootstrap Spinner Examples*; codescandy.com. Retrieved July 11, 2022, from https://codescandy.com/coach/bootstrap-5/docs/spinners.html

Colors – Muse Documentation | Muse – Responsive Website Template. (n.d.). *Colors – Muse Documentation | Muse – Responsive Website Template*; fabrx.co. Retrieved July 11, 2022, from https://fabrx.co/muze/documentation/colors.html

Components – Collapse – 《Bootstrap v5.1 Documentation》 – 书栈网 · BookStack. (2021, August 9). *Components – Collapse – 《Bootstrap v5.1 Documentation》 – 书栈网 · BookStack*; www.bookstack.cn. https://www.bookstack.cn/read/bootstrap-5.1-en/d2a5284911761e87.md

Contributors, A. D. (n.d.a). *Browsers and Devices Arizona Bootstrap*; digital.arizona.edu. Retrieved July 11, 2022, from https://digital.arizona.edu/arizona-bootstrap/docs/2.0/getting-started/browsers-devices/

Contributors, A. D. (n.d.b). *Cards Arizona Bootstrap*; digital.arizona.edu. Retrieved July 11, 2022, from https://digital.arizona.edu/arizona-bootstrap/docs/2.0/components/card/

Contributors, A. D. (n.d.c). *Pagination Arizona Bootstrap*; digital.arizona.edu. Retrieved July 11, 2022, from https://digital.arizona.edu/arizona-bootstrap/docs/2.0/components/pagination/

CSS Features. (n.d.). *CSS Features*; cloges4.github.io. Retrieved July 11, 2022, from https://cloges4.github.io/FCC-Tech-Doc/

CSS Variables – The var() function. (n.d.). *CSS Variables – The Var() Function*; www.w3schools.com. Retrieved July 11, 2022, from https://www.w3schools .com/CSS//css3_variables.asp

Developers, P. (2021, November 19). *How To Speed Up Your Bootstrap Development Process 2022*. Custom Website Design and Development and SEO; pixelkraft.net. https://pixelkraft.net/how-to-speed-up-your-bootstrap-development-process/

Dropdowns – Get Docs. (n.d.). *Dropdowns – Get Docs*; getdocs.org. Retrieved July 11, 2022, from https://getdocs.org/Bootstrap/docs/5/components/dropdowns/index

Falcon | Dashboard & Web App Template. (n.d.). *Falcon | Dashboard & Web App Template*; prium.github.io. Retrieved July 11, 2022, from https://prium .github.io/falcon/v3.4.0/modules/forms/basic/range.html

Flex &middot; Material. (n.d.). *Flex &middot; Material*; daemonite.github.io. Retrieved July 11, 2022, from http://daemonite.github.io/material/docs/4.1 /utilities/flex/

Grid Column | Quasar Framework. (n.d.). *Quasar Framework*; quasar.dev. Retrieved July 11, 2022, from https://quasar.dev/layout/grid/column

Grid Row | Quasar Framework. (n.d.). *Quasar Framework*; v1.quasar.dev. Retrieved July 11, 2022, from https://v1.quasar.dev/layout/grid/row

Helen Reid, L. G. (n.d.). *Nigerian Oil Firm Lekoil Loses Board Fight with Top Shareholder*. Reuters. U.S.; www.reuters.com. Retrieved July 11, 2022, from https://www.reuters.com/article/uk-lekoil-shareholders-idUSKBN29E08V

Holeczek, Ł. (n.d.). *Bootstrap Carousel – Examples & Tutorials. Learn How to Use Bootstrap Carousel CoreUI*; coreui.io. Retrieved July 11, 2022, from https:// coreui.io/docs/2.1/components/carousel/

Hope–Ui | Responsive Bootstrap 5 Admin doc Template. (n.d.). *Hope–Ui | Responsive Bootstrap 5 Admin Doc Template*; templates.iqonic.design. Retrieved July 11, 2022, from https://templates.iqonic.design/hope-ui/documentation/laravel/dist/components/listgroup.html

How To Create Bootstrap 5 Sidebar Menu Collapse. (n.d.). *How To Create Bootstrap 5 Sidebar Menu Collapse*; shapeyourpath.com. Retrieved July 11, 2022, from https://shapeyourpath.com/tutorial/bootstrap5/bootstrap -collapse

https://data-flair.training/blogs/django-bootstrap/

https://htmlstream.com/space/documentation/accordion.html

https://htmlstream.com/space/documentation/borders.html

https://htmlstream.com/unify/documentation/backgrounds.html

https://htmlstream.com/unify/documentation/offcanvas.html

https://www.codegrepper.com/code-examples/html/bootstrap+5+line+height

Inc., C. (n.d.). *Grid System | CAST Figuration (v4.0). Grid System | CAST Figuration (v4.0)*; figuration.org. Retrieved July 11, 2022, from https://figuration.org/4 .0/layout/grid/

Iniodu, S. (2022, April 21). "Pagination." *Pagination*. Retrieved July 11, 2022, from https://www.linkedin.com/pulse/pagination-solomon-iniodu

Input Groups – Bootstrap. (n.d.). *Input Groups – Bootstrap – University of Houston*; uh.edu. Retrieved July 11, 2022, from https://uh.edu/marcom/resources/bootstrap/components/input-groups/

Interactions – WeCodeArt Documentation. (2022, April 8). *WeCodeArt Documentation*; support.wecodeart.com. https://support.wecodeart.com/documents/wecodeart-framework/getting-started/utilities/interactions/

Jump Start Bootstrap. (n.d.). *O'Reilly Online Learning*; www.oreilly.com. Retrieved July 11, 2022, from https://www.oreilly.com/library/view/jump-start-bootstrap/9781457174346/ch06.html

Kaliannan, S. (2014, June 20). *Bootstrap Button Groups*. JavaBeat; javabeat.net. https://javabeat.net/bootstrap-button-groups/

Metronic | Dropdown. (n.d.). *Metronic | Dropdown*; preview.keenthemes.com. Retrieved July 11, 2022, from https://preview.keenthemes.com/metronic-v6/preview/demo1/components/base/dropdown.html

Modal – Before Getting Started with Bootstrap's Modal Component, be Sure to Read the Following. (n.d.). *Modal – Before Getting Started with Bootstrap's Modal Component, Be Sure to Read the Following*; runebook.dev. Retrieved July 11, 2022, from https://runebook.dev/en/docs/bootstrap/components/modal/index

Modal – Components – Docs – Grayshift. (n.d.). *Modal – Components – Docs – Grayshift*; grayshift.io. Retrieved July 11, 2022, from https://grayshift.io/docs/components/modal/

Modal – Onekit Documentation. (n.d.). *Modal – Onekit Documentation*; onekit .madethemes.com. Retrieved July 11, 2022, from https://onekit.madethemes.com/docs/components/modal.html

Navbar – Muze Documentation | Muze – Responsive Website Template. (n.d.). *Navbar – Muze Documentation | Muze – Responsive Website Template*; fabrx.co. Retrieved July 11, 2022, from https://fabrx.co/preview/muse-dashboard/documentation/navbar.html

NobleUI. (n.d.). *NobleUI – HTML Bootstrap 5 Admin Dashboard Template*; www .nobleui.com. Retrieved July 11, 2022, from https://www.nobleui.com/html/template/demo1/pages/ui-components/badges.html

Not Familiar with CSS Variables, Here Are 5 Examples to See! – SegmentFault 思否. (n.d.). *Not Familiar with CSS Variables, Here Are 5 Examples to See! – SegmentFault 思否*; segmentfault.com. Retrieved July 11, 2022, from https://segmentfault.com/a/1190000040735569/en

Offcanvas | Dash Ui – Bootstrap 5 Admin Dashboard Template. (n.d.). *Offcanvas | Dash Ui – Bootstrap 5 Admin Dashboard Template*; codescandy.com. Retrieved July 11, 2022, from https://codescandy.com/dashui/docs/offcanvas.html

Pagination Component for React Bootstrap 5. (n.d.). *Devwares*; www.devwares .com. Retrieved July 11, 2022, from https://www.devwares.com/docs/contrast/react/navigation/pagination/

Position – Helpers – Docs – Grayshift. (n.d.). *Position – Helpers – Docs – Grayshift*; grayshift.io. Retrieved July 11, 2022, from https://grayshift.io/docs/helpers /position/

React List Group Component – CoreUI. (n.d.). *React List Group Component – CoreUI*; coreui.io. Retrieved July 11, 2022, from https://coreui.io/react/docs /components/list-group/

React Placeholder Component – CoreUI. (n.d.). *React Placeholder Component – CoreUI*; coreui.io. Retrieved July 11, 2022, from https://coreui.io/react/docs /components/placeholder/

React–Bootstrap. (n.d.a). *React–Bootstrap Documentation*; react-bootstrap .github.io. Retrieved July 11, 2022, from https://react-bootstrap.github.io/ components/alerts/

React–Bootstrap. (n.d.b). *React–Bootstrap React–Bootstrap Documentation*; react -bootstrap-v5.netlify.app. Retrieved July 11, 2022, from https://react-boot-strap-v5.netlify.app/components/forms/

RTL – Muze Documentation | Muze – Responsive Website Template. (n.d.). *RTL – Muze Documentation | Muze – Responsive Website Template*; fabrx.co. Retrieved July 11, 2022, from https://fabrx.co/preview/muse-dashboard/ documentation/rtl.html

RuangAdmin – Progress Bars. (n.d.). *RuangAdmin – Progress Bars*; indrijunanda .github.io. Retrieved July 11, 2022, from https://indrijunanda.github.io/ RuangAdmin/progress-bar.html

Rupesh. (2021, December 25). *Grid Declaration – CODE ONE*. CODE ONE; codeone.in. https://codeone.in/grid-declaration/

Sass–Bootstrap中文网. (n.d.). *Sass–Bootstrap中文网*; www.bootstrap.cn. Retrieved July 11, 2022, from https://www.bootstrap.cn/doc/read/13.html

Scott, Trevor Satterfield, & the Measured team, J. M. (n.d.a). *Checks and Radios Measured Style Guide v5.0*; styleguide.measured.com. Retrieved July 11, 2022, from https://styleguide.measured.com/docs/5.0/forms/checks-radios/

Scott, Trevor Satterfield, & the Measured Team, J. M. (n.d.b). *RTL · Measured Style Guide v5.0*; styleguide.measured.com. Retrieved July 11, 2022, from https://styleguide.measured.com/docs/5.0/getting-started/rtl/

Spinners – Documentation – HomeID. (n.d.). *Spinners – Documentation – HomeID*; templates.g5plus.net. Retrieved July 11, 2022, from https://tem-plates.g5plus.net/homeid/docs/components/spinners.html

ThemeSelect. (n.d.). *Bootstrap Cards – Chameleon Admin – Modern Bootstrap 4 WebApp & Dashboard HTML Template + UI Kit*; technext.github.io. Retrieved July 11, 2022, from https://technext.github.io/chameleon-admin/ cards.html

Thornton, J. and Bootstrap Contributors, M. O. (n.d.a). *Alerts Bootstrap v5.0*; get-bootstrap.com. Retrieved July 11, 2022, from https://getbootstrap.com/docs /5.0/components/alerts/

Thornton, J. and Bootstrap Contributors, M. O. (n.d.b). *Alerts Bootstrap*; brand .ncsu.edu. Retrieved July 11, 2022, from https://brand.ncsu.edu/bootstrap/ v4/docs/4.1/components/alerts/

Thornton, J. and Bootstrap Contributors, M. O. (n.d.c). *Breakpoints Bootstrap v5.0*; getbootstrap.com. Retrieved July 11, 2022, from https://getbootstrap .com/docs/5.0/layout/breakpoints/

Thornton, J. and Bootstrap Contributors, M. O. (n.d.d). *Browsers and Devices Boosted*; boosted.orange.com. Retrieved July 11, 2022, from https://boosted .orange.com/docs/4.0/getting-started/browsers-devices/

Thornton, J. and Bootstrap Contributors, M. O. (n.d.e). *Browsers and Devices Bootstrap v4.5*; getbootstrap.com. Retrieved July 11, 2022, from https://get-bootstrap.com/docs/4.5/getting-started/browsers-devices/

Thornton, J. and Bootstrap Contributors, M. O. (n.d.f). *Buttons Bootstrap v5.2*; getbootstrap.com. Retrieved July 11, 2022, from https://getbootstrap.com/docs/5.2/components/buttons/

Thornton, J. and Bootstrap Contributors, M. O. (n.d.g). *Cards Bootstrap*; brand .ncsu.edu. Retrieved July 11, 2022, from https://brand.ncsu.edu/bootstrap/v4/docs/4.1/components/card/

Thornton, J. and Bootstrap Contributors, M. O. (n.d.h). *Carousel Bootstrap*; brand .ncsu.edu. Retrieved July 11, 2022, from https://brand.ncsu.edu/bootstrap/v4/docs/4.1/components/carousel/

Thornton, J. and Bootstrap Contributors, M. O. (n.d.i). *Carousel Bootstrap v5.1*; getbootstrap.com. Retrieved July 11, 2022, from https://getbootstrap.com/docs/5.1/components/carousel/

Thornton, J. and Bootstrap Contributors, M. O. (n.d.j). *Carousel Bootstrap*; brand .ncsu.edu. Retrieved July 11, 2022, from https://brand.ncsu.edu/bootstrap/v4/docs/4.1/components/carousel/

Thornton, J. and Bootstrap Contributors, M. O. (n.d.k). *Collapse Bootstrap*; brand .ncsu.edu. Retrieved July 11, 2022, from https://brand.ncsu.edu/bootstrap/v4/docs/4.1/components/collapse/

Thornton, J. and Bootstrap Contributors, M. O. (n.d.l). *Dropdowns Bootstrap*; brand.ncsu.edu. Retrieved July 11, 2022, from https://brand.ncsu.edu/boot-strap/v4/docs/4.1/components/dropdowns/

Thornton, J. and Bootstrap Contributors, M. O. (n.d.m). *Floating Labels Bootstrap v5.2*; getbootstrap.com. Retrieved July 11, 2022, from https://getbootstrap .com/docs/5.2/forms/floating-labels/

Thornton, J. and Bootstrap Contributors, M. O. (n.d.n). *Getting Started &mid-dot; Bootstrap 3.3.4 Documentation – BootstrapDocs*; bootstrapdocs.com. Retrieved July 11, 2022, from https://bootstrapdocs.com/v3.3.4/docs/get-ting-started/

Thornton, J. and Bootstrap Contributors, M. O. (n.d.o). *Grid System Bootstrap v5.0*; getbootstrap.com. Retrieved July 11, 2022, from https://getbootstrap .com/docs/5.0/layout/grid/

Thornton, J. and Bootstrap Contributors, M. O. (n.d.p). *Images Bootstrap*; brand .ncsu.edu. Retrieved July 11, 2022, from https://brand.ncsu.edu/bootstrap/v4/docs/4.1/content/images/

Thornton, J. and Bootstrap Contributors, M. O. (n.d.q). *Input Group Bootstrap*; brand.ncsu.edu. Retrieved July 11, 2022, from https://brand.ncsu.edu/boot-strap/v4/docs/4.1/components/input-group/

Thornton, J. and Bootstrap Contributors, M. O. (n.d.r). *List Group Bootstrap*; brand.ncsu.edu. Retrieved July 11, 2022, from https://brand.ncsu.edu/bootstrap/v4/docs/4.1/components/list-group/

Thornton, J. and Bootstrap Contributors, M. O. (n.d.s). *Navbar Bootstrap v5.2*; getbootstrap.com. Retrieved July 11, 2022, from https://getbootstrap.com/docs/5.2/components/navbar/

Thornton, J. and Bootstrap Contributors, M. O. (n.d.t). *Navbar Bootstrap*; brand.ncsu.edu. Retrieved July 11, 2022, from https://brand.ncsu.edu/bootstrap/v4/docs/4.1/components/navbar/

Thornton, J. and Bootstrap Contributors, M. O. (n.d.u). *Placeholders Bootstrap v5.1*; getbootstrap.com. Retrieved July 11, 2022, from https://getbootstrap.com/docs/5.1/components/placeholders/

Thornton, J. and Bootstrap Contributors, M. O. (n.d.v). *Theming Bootstrap Bootstrap v4.5*; getbootstrap.com. Retrieved July 11, 2022, from https://getbootstrap.com/docs/4.5/getting-started/theming/

Thornton, J. and Bootstrap Contributors, M. O. (n.d.w). *Toasts Bootstrap v5.2*; getbootstrap.com. Retrieved July 11, 2022, from https://getbootstrap.com/docs/5.2/components/toasts/

twbs. (2022, June 9). *bootstrap/sass.md at Main twbs/bootstrap*. GitHub; github.com. https://github.com/twbs/bootstrap/blob/main/site/content/docs/5.2/customize/sass.md

Unit 5: Logarithms – Centennial Math Department. (2021, October 2). *Unit 5: Logarithms – Centennial Math Department*; mycentennial.sd43.bc.ca. https://mycentennial.sd43.bc.ca/mathdept/category/unit-5-logarithms/

Using CSS Custom Properties – CSS – W3cubDocs. (n.d.). *Using CSS Custom Properties – CSS – W3cubDocs*; docs.w3cub.com. Retrieved July 11, 2022, from https://docs.w3cub.com/css/using_css_custom_properties.html

Using CSS Custom Properties (Variables) – CSS: Cascading Style Sheets | MDN. (2022, July 10). *Using CSS Custom Properties (Variables) – CSS: Cascading Style Sheets | MDN*; developer.mozilla.org. https://developer.mozilla.org/en-US/docs/Web/CSS/Using_CSS_custom_properties

Utility API – Get docs. (n.d.). *Utility API – Get Docs*; getdocs.org. Retrieved July 11, 2022, from https://getdocs.org/Bootstrap/docs/5/utilities/api/index

Yoon, J.-Y. (2021, December 14). *Focal Adhesion | SpringerLink*. Focal Adhesion | SpringerLink; https://link.springer.com/chapter/10.1007/978-3-030-8369 6-2_7

# Index

## A

Abstract Syntax Tree (AST), 168
Adaptive design, 111
   advantages, 111–112
   disadvantages, 112
Admin panel
   add custom CSS, 118–119
   animated class, 125
   back-end frameworks
      Django, 130
      Express.js, 130
      Flask, 130
      Laravel, 130
      Ruby on Rails, 130
   back-end programming languages
      C++, 129
      Java, 129
      JavaScript, 130
      Node.js, 130
      PHP, 129
      Python, 130
   backend UI, 125–126
   Bootstrap icons, 114
   Bootstrap stylesheet, 114
   card header, 124
   CDN links, 131
   color codes, 125
   create, 113–114
   CSS properties, 149
   dashboard interface, 131
      breadcrumb, 137–145
      footer, 145–146
      navbar, 132–133
      sidebar, 133–137, 148–149
      stylesheet, 148

front-end development, 126
front-end frameworks
   AngularJS, 127
   Bootstrap, 128
   Flutter, 128
   jQuery, 128
   React.js, 127–128
   Sass, 128
generative *vs.* evaluation research, 155
horizontal navbar, 115–116
JavaScript file, 123
languages
   CSS, 127
   HTML, 126–127
   JavaScript, 127
main section, 119–122, 149–150
navbar, 115
Popper, 146–147
qualitative *vs.* quantitative research,
      153–155
striped class, 125
UI, 151–153
UX, 151–153
vertical navbar, 116–118
Alert, 173–175, 246–248
Application Programming Interface
      (API), 191–192
ASP.NET API, 200
ASP.NET Core, 200
ASP.NET file, 200–201
ASP.NET MVC, 200
ASP.NET web forms, 200
ASP.NET web pages, 200
Asynchronous I/O, 161
Atom, 14–15, 20
Attributes

affix, 173
alert messages, 172
buttons, 172
carousel, 173
collapse, 172
for dropdowns, 171
global, 169–170
global event, 170
for modals, 171
popovers, 172
scrollspy, 171
toggleable tabs, 171
tooltip, 171–172

B

Babylon, 164
Back-end frameworks
  Django, 130
  Express.js, 130
  Flask, 130
  Laravel, 130
  Ruby on Rails, 130
Back-end programming languages
  C++, 129
  Java, 129
  JavaScript, 130
  Node.js, 130
  PHP, 129
  Python, 130
Background color
  danger, 263
  dark, 264
  info, 264
  light, 264
  primary, 262
  secondary, 262
  success, 263
  warning, 263
Badges, 248–250
Basic Bootstrap pages, 28
Basic structure of, Bootstrap grid, 31–32
  code example, 33–34
  explanation, 32–33
  extra-large grid, code, 37–38
  extra-small grid, code, 34
  large grid, code, 36–37
  small grid, code, 34–35
    medium grid, 35

small and medium grid combined,
    35–36
Blocking I/O, 161
Bootstrap; *see also individual entries*
  accordion, 282–284
  accordion-flush, 284–286
  adding background color and borders,
    10
    example, 11
  adding padding and margin, 11
    example, 12
    property, 11
    sides, 11
    size, 11–12
  advantages, 8, 374
  background color
    danger, 263
    dark, 264
    info, 264
    light, 264
    primary, 262
    secondary, 262
    success, 263
    warning, 263
  border color
    danger, 266
    dark, 267
    info, 266–267
    light, 267
    primary, 265
    secondary, 265
    success, 265–266
    warning, 266
  carousel
    caption, 275–277
    controls, 274
    dark, 279–280
    fade, 277–278
    indicators, 274–275
    intervals, 278
    slides only, 273
  CDN package, 204–205
  collapse, 280–281
  colors, 10
  components
    alerts, 246–248
    badges, 248–250
    breadcrumb, 250–251
    button, 251–253

button group, 254–257
button plugin, 253–254
cards, 257–262
concepts, 9
containers, 9
  example, 10
  sizing, 9–10
  types, 9
definition, 203
disadvantages, 8–9, 374
download using a CDN, 17
download using package manager,
  15–16
  using composer, 16
  using NPM, 16
  using yarn, 16
dropdowns, 286–294
features, 204, 376
figures, 294
floating labels, 311–312
form layout, 312–314
forms, 308–311
form validation, 315–319
getting started, 15
  setting up, 14–15
grid system, 12, 13, 30–31, 206–211
  breakpoints, 12–13
  example, 13–14
history of, 2–3
horizontal collapse, 282
images, 294
input group, 305–308
list group, 319–325
modal, 326–330
multi-collapse, 281–282
navbar, 330–339
navs/tabs/pills, 339–345
NPM package, 205
overview, 1–2
prerequisites, 374–375
purpose, 8
screen sizing, 205
significance, 204
starter template, 17–18
synopsis, 18
tables, 294–304
text color
  danger, 268–269
  dark, 270–273

info, 268
light, 269–270
primary, 267–268
secondary, 268
success, 268
warning, 269
typography, 211–213
uses, 373–374
versions of
  Bootstrap 1, 3
  Bootstrap 2, 3
  Bootstrap 3, 3–4
  Bootstrap 4, 4–7
  Bootstrap 5, 7
Bootstrap badges, 61–62
Bootstrap buttons, 63
Bootstrap jumbotron, 62
Bootstrap template, 23–24
Border color
  danger, 266
  dark, 267
  info, 266–267
  light, 267
  primary, 265
  secondary, 265
  success, 265–266
  warning, 266
Border utility classes, 215–216
Breadcrumb navigation, 137–145,
  250–251
Bulma, 375
Bundler gems, 199


C

Carousel
  caption, 177–179, 275–277
  controls, 176, 274
  dark, 180–182, 279–280
  fade, 179, 277–278
  indicators, 176–177, 274–275
  intervals, 180, 278
  slides only, 175, 273
Cascading Style Sheets (CSS), 128, 375
Classic ASP, 200
Cocos2d, 164
Code movement, 187
Code optimization
  code movement, 187

common sub-expression elimination, 186–187
compile time evaluation, 186
dead code elimination, 187
definition, 183–184
goals, 185–186
strength reduction, 187
types, 186
Color class, 10
Color utility classes, 213–215
Common sub-expression elimination, 186–187
Compile time evaluation, 186
Components
alerts, 246–248
badges, 248–250
breadcrumb, 250–251
button, 251–253
button group, 254–257
button plugin, 253–254
cards, 257–262
Constant folding, 186
Constant propagation, 186
Containers, 9, 28–30
example, 10
size notation, 9
sizing, 9–10
types, 9
Content delivery/distribution network (CDN), 21
Bootstrap link and scripts, 21
CSS, 22
JavaScript, 22
Jquery Library, 22
Popper.js, 22
to use, 22–23
CreateServer() method, 161
Creating blog template
about section, 94
code, 94–96
blog post 1
code, 90–91
blog post 2
code, 91
blog post 3, 91
code, 91–94
blog section, 83
code, 83–90

code, 72–73
contact section
code, 96–98
footer, 98–99
home page, 78
code, 78–81
navbar, 73
code, 73–77
newsletter, 81
code, 81–83
Creating home page, Bootstrap
add HTML5 document type, 27
Bootstrap 3 is advanced, 27
Creating portfolio template, 99
about section, 102
code, 102–104
code, 99–100
contact section, 106
code, 106–109
home section, 101
code, 101–102
navbar, 100
code, 100–101
portfolio section, 104
code, 105–106
CSS FlexBox, 6

D

Dashboard interface, 131
breadcrumb, 137–145
footer, 145–146
navbar, 132–133
sidebar, 133–137, 148–149
stylesheet, 148
Dead code elimination, 187
Designing templates
creating blog template, 71–72
about section, 94–96
blog post 1, 90–91
blog post 2, 91
blog post 3, 91–94
blog section, 83–90
code, 72–73
contact section, 96–98
footer, 98–99
home page, 78–81
navbar, 73–77

newsletter, 81–83
creating portfolio template, 99
    about section, 102–104
    code, 99–100
    contact section, 106–109
    home section, 101–102
    navbar, 100–101
    portfolio section, 104–106
mobile-friendly design, 109–110
    types of, 110–112
synopsis, 112
Developing games
    Babylon, 164
    Cocos2d, 164
    Kiwi, 165
    Panda Engine, 165–166
    Phaser, 164
    Pixi, 166
    PlayCanvas, 165
    WebGL, 166–167
Display utility classes, 225–229
DNS, *see* Domain Name System
Document Object Model (DOM), 128
DOM, *see* Document Object Model
Domain Name System (DNS), 162
DOM API, 158–159
Download using CDN, 17, 21
Download using composer, 16
Download using NPM, 16, 20–21
    using cable, 21
    using composer, 21
Download using package manager,
    15–16, 20
Download using yarn, 16
Dropdowns, 66–67

**F**

Flexbox, 42–43
    flex-direction in Bootstrap, 45–46
        features, 46–47
    flex-flow, 48–49
    flex-wrap in Bootstrap, 47–48
    flex-wrap in CSS, 47
    properties in Bootstrap, 44
        flex-direction in CSS, 45
    properties in CSS, 43–44
Flex utility classes, 216–225

Floating labels, 311–312
Flutter, 128
Focus groups, 154
Form layout, 312–314
Form validation, 315–319
Foundation, 375
Framework
    active/disabled buttons, 64
    align items, 56–57
    align self, 55–56
    block-level buttons, 64
    Bootstrap badges, 61–62
    Bootstrap buttons, 63
    Bootstrap jumbotron, 62
    Bootstrap template, 23–24
    button sizes, 64
    button tags, 64–65
    CDN (*see* Content delivery/distribution
        network (CDN))
    colored spinners, 64
    components in Bootstrap
        alert links, 60–61
        Bootstrap alerts, 59–60
    downloading using CDN, 21
    downloading using NPM, 20–21
        using cable, 21
        using composer, 21
    download using package manager, 20
    Dropdowns, 66–67
    features, 26–27
    fill, 58
    Flexbox (*see* Flexbox)
    full-width jumbotron, 62–63
    getting started with bootstrap, 19–20
    grid works, 38–39
    grow and shrink, 57–58
    history, 24–25
        Bootstrap 2, 25
        Bootstrap 3, 25
        Bootstrap 4, 25
        Bootstrap 5, 25–26
    justify-content in Bootstrap, 54–55
    justify-content in CSS, 49
        positional alignment, 50–51
        syntax, 49–50
    navbar, 67
    order, 51–54
    outline buttons, 65–66

popper.js required for bootstrap 4, 24
responsive breakpoints, 58
   z-index, 59
responsive meta tag, 24
spinner buttons, 64
supported content, 68–69
synopsis, 69
three equal columns, 39
two unequal columns, 39–42
utilities, 69
Front-end development, 126
Front-end frameworks
   AngularJS, 127
   Bootstrap, 128
   Flutter, 128
   jQuery, 128
   React.js, 127–128
   Sass, 128

**G**

GET request, 190
Grid classes, 31

**H**

Helpers, 370–372
High-level optimizations, 185
Horizontal navbar, 115–116
Hypertext Transfer Protocol (HTTP), 189
   client, 191
   module, 161–162
   request, 190
   response, 190–191

**I**

In-depth interviews, 154
Input group, 305–308
Internet Protocol (IP), 162
IP, *see* Internet Protocol

**J**

JavaScript, 157
   adds interactivity to web, 159
   AST, 168
   back end, 163
   client requesting data, 163
   developing games
      Babylon, 164
      Cocos2d, 164
      Kiwi, 165
      Panda Engine, 165–166
      Phaser, 164
      Pixi, 166
      PlayCanvas, 165
      WebGL, 166–167
   HTTP module, 161–162
   HTTP request, 162
   I/O operations, 161–162
   machine code, 168–169
   mobile apps, 160
   Node.js, 161
   presentations, 167
   server applications, 162
   web applications, 160
   web development, 167
   web servers, 160–161
   zoom in and zoom out, 159–160
Jekyll, 198–199
Justify-content
   Bootstrap, 54–55
   CSS, 49
      positional alignment, 50–51
      syntax, 49–50

**K**

Kiwi, 165

**L**

Layout, 31
Liquid Templating system, 198
List group, 319–325
Low-level optimizations, 185

**M**

Machine code, 168–169
Material Design, 375
Material UI, 375
Miscellaneous utility classes, 229–232
Mobile apps, 160
Mobile-friendly design, 109–110
   adaptive design, 111–112
   responsive design, 110–111

Model View Controller (MVC), 200
MVC, *see* Model View Controller

## N

Navbar, 115, 330–339
Nonsequential I/O, 161
NPM packages, 199

## O

Offcanvas, 116–118
  start, 345–347
Order, 51–54

## P

Pagination, 348–351
Panda Engine, 165–166
Participant observation, 154
Phaser, 163–164
Pixi, 166
Placeholders, 347–348
PlayCanvas, 165
Popovers, 363–365
Popper, 146–147
Position utility classes, 232–234
POST request, 190
Progress bars, 361–363

## Q

Qualitative research, 153–154
Quantitative research, 154–155

## R

Responsive design
  advantages, 110–111
  disadvantages, 111
Ruby gem, 199

## S

Screen size, 27
Scrollspy, 351, 353–361
SDK, *see* Software development kit
Sizing notation, 6

Software development kit (SDK), 128
Space optimization, 186
Spacing utility classes, 234–241
Spinners, 367–368
Strength reduction, 187

## T

Tailwind CSS, 375
Text utility classes, 241–244
Time-based optimization, 185
Time optimization, 186
Toasts, 365–367
Tooltips, 368–370

## U

User Experience (UX), 151–153
User Interface (UI), 151–153
Utility API
  adding, 196
  changing, 196
  class, 194
  enable responsive, 197
  modify, 197
  options, 193
  print, 196
  remove, 198
  rename, 197
  responsive, 195
  RTL, 198
  states, 194
  variable, 193–194
Utility classes
  borders, 215–216
  color, 213–215
  display, 225–229
  flex, 216–225
  misc, 229–232
  opacity, 245–246
  position, 232–234
  spacing, 234–241
  text, 241–244

## V

Vertical navbar, 116–118
VS Code, 14, 19–20

W

Web applications, 160
Web browsers, 189
WebGL, 166–167

Web page notation, 6
Web servers, 160–161
WordPress plugins, 199
World Wide Web (WWW), 189

Printed in the United States
by Baker & Taylor Publisher Services

Printed in the United States
by Baker & Taylor Publisher Services